LETTERS TO HITLER

Baltic Sea

Ostland

Neman

Kovno

Königsberg

Danzig

East Prussia

Bialystok

Wartheland

Poznan

Zbaszyn

Vistula

Warsaw

SOVIET
UNION

Lodz

Bug

Lublin

Breslau

General Government

Vistula

Nisko

Krakow

Dniester

of
oravia

March

SLOVAKIA

ROMANIA

enna

Bratislava

HUNGARY

Germany in 1933

Germany in 1939

Germany in 1943

Sudetenland

er
ia

CROATIA

| 0 | 100 | 200 | 300 | 400 | 500 km |

| 0 | 50 | 100 | 150 | 200 | 250 | 300 miles |

LETTERS TO HITLER

EDITED BY HENRIK EBERLE

ENGLISH EDITION EDITED, AND WITH AN
INTRODUCTION, BY VICTORIA HARRIS

TRANSLATED BY STEVEN RENDALL

polity

First published in German as *Briefe an Hitler* (ed. by Henrik Eberle) © Verlagsgruppe Lüppe GmbH & Co. KG, 2007. All rights reserved.

This English edition © Polity Press, 2012

Polity Press
65 Bridge Street
Cambridge CB2 1UR, UK

Polity Press
350 Main Street
Malden, MA 02148, USA

ISBN-13: 978–0–7456–4873–6

A catalogue record for this book is available from the British Library.

Typeset in 10.75 on 14 pt Janson Text
by Servis Filmsetting Ltd, Stockport, Cheshire
Printed and bound in Great Britain by MPG Books Group Limited, Bodmin, Cornwall

The publisher has used its best endeavours to ensure that the URLs for external websites referred to in this book are correct and active at the time of going to press. However, the publisher has no responsibility for the websites and can make no guarantee that a site will remain live or that the content is or will remain appropriate.

Every effort has been made to trace all copyright holders, but if any have been inadvertently overlooked the publisher will be pleased to include any necessary credits in any subsequent reprint or edition.

For further information on Polity, visit our website: www.politybooks.com

Contents

Part III Crisis and War: 1938–1945

ACKNOWLEDGEMENTS

VICTORIA HARRIS (ENGLISH EDITOR)

I would like to thank Polity Press for commissioning me to do the English edition of this remarkable collection and for all their hard work throughout this process. In particular I would like to thank Sarah Lambert for her continued support throughout the process of putting the English edition together. I would also like to thank the translator Steven Rendall for his hard work and assistance, as well as his patience with what was often rather tricky German prose and poetry. Richard Evans kindly read various drafts, offering advice and corrections. So too did Peter Chetwynd. Finally, many thanks to David Wheeler for helping with the maps and for patiently discussing the project with me, often rather late at night.

HENRIK EBERLE (GERMAN EDITOR)

First of all, I would like to thank the staff of the former Special Archive in the Russian State Military Archive. Its deputy director, Vladimir Korotaiev, allowed me access to its holdings. But this book is also indebted to the support of the German Historical Institute in Moscow, whose support made it possible. Its staff, especially Andrei Doronin and Matthias Uhl, helped me overcome many problems.

Sebastian Pannwitz, the creator of the private Internet site www.sonderarchiv.de, willingly answered many questions.

The staff of the Federal Archives in Koblenz and Berlin also deserve thanks, not only for providing easy access to the archival materials collected there, but also for what people call 'service'. Above all, I owe thanks to their decades-long efforts to open up the National Socialist regime's files and thereby make clear the gaps in the German collections. I have received encouragement, support, and expert criticism from colleagues and alumni of my Alma Mater, Martin-Luther-Universität in Halle-Wittenberg. I mention in particular Dirk Wesenberg, Sabine Häseler, Stefan Schäfer, Jana Wüstenhagen, Dietmar Schulze and Thomas Pruschwitz. Financial questions were dealt with by Thomas Karlauf, with vigilance and understanding, as always.

Unfortunately, I do not know the names of the many members of the staff of the Lübbe Verlag who worked on this project. I thank Elmar Klupsch, Inge Leo and Christian Stüwe as their representatives.

Michael Eberle, Andreas Wittig and Michael W. Thiede must also be mentioned here. They know why. In particular, I would like to thank my mother, Sabine Ludewig. It is high time that I expressed my gratitude to her.

INTRODUCTION

Victoria Harris

Popularity, wrote Hitler in his political treatise *My Struggle* (Mein Kampf), is the first foundation for establishing authority. The second is force. It is force which we usually connect with totalitarian dictatorships such as Germany's Third Reich. To be sure, Hitler and his Nazi Party constantly utilized force – from removing their early rivals, to cementing their authority, to waging war on much of Europe. Against the violent dominance of the National Socialists, the opinions of individual Germans or Europeans might seem irrelevant. But as Hitler himself acknowledged in *My Struggle*, without the backing of the population, it was impossible to act forcefully. And the search for popularity was most certainly a two-way street. In establishing a successful dictatorship, Hitler needed his people. And needed to establish a dialogue with them. If he was to convince them that he had the answers for Germany, in return he had to listen to their problems, accept their advice, and respond to their concerns – or at least appear to. The secret to the Third Reich's success during its height in the 1930s and early 1940s was Germans' sense that they could engage in a conversation with their leader, and that he was in some way listening.

This book chronicles Hitler's relationship with his people and the rise and fall of his popularity, using a selection of the thousands of letters he received between 1925, when the Nazi Party began its rise to power, and 1945, when the regime collapsed at the end of the Second World War. Most of these letters, which were kept in the Chancellor's Office in Berlin during the Third Reich, were seized by the Soviet Armed Forces immediately after the war. The letters were found together with thousands of other documents used by the Allies to convict major Nazi perpetrators of war crimes during the Nuremberg Trials. But the vast majority of private letters were of no use for determining guilt, seemingly trivial as they were. As a result they sat uncategorized in the Moscow archives. Further letters sent to Hitler on his birthday in 1945, which never made it to Berlin, were eventually located in Germany's Federal Archive in Koblenz, where they had been deposited after being found by American soldiers.*

The true worth of these collections of letters was only recently recognized, when Henrik Eberle analysed and published them in a large collection, together with his commentary, in 2007. In bringing the letters to an English audience, Eberle's original collection has been abridged and further contextualizations have been added. The letters which appear here are emblematic of the thousands of letters that Hitler received each year, and a representative selection from each era of his political life have been included, covering the full range of themes about which Germans wrote to him. Some minor editorial changes have been made in order to make some of them more accessible. The modern day geographic locations of the many cities and towns in Hitler's expanding Reich have been inserted, and this, together with the map at the front of this book will help readers to visualize the widening influence Hitler enjoyed. While full biographies of significant individuals in the regime would have distracted from the flow of the text, relevant details about their lives are included to help give a flavour of the many types of people involved in writing and responding to these letters. Thanks to the Internet, further information about many of them is available online. At the end of the book there is a short selection of further reading which may be of interest to those readers who wish

---

* The letters can be found in the following archival files: Russian State Military Archive (RGWA) Record Groups: 519, 1235, 1355, 1413, 1525; Bundesarchiv (BA) Koblenz NS 6/106. Further information can be found in the original German edition of this text: Henrik Eberle (ed.), *Briefe an Hitler: Ein Volk Schreibt seinem Führer. Unbekannte Documente aus Moskauer Archiven – zum ersten Mal veröffentlicht* (Lubbe: 2007).

to learn more about these individuals, the Third Reich, and Germany's recent history.

The rich and varied tone of the correspondence has been masterfully captured by translator Steven Rendall. In certain cases, where the particularities of the German language have made a fully literal translation difficult, some editorial licence has been taken to approximate the sense of the German as closely as possible. The many poems and songs sent to Hitler each year presented a particular challenge. Ordinary Germans, obviously, were not great poetic talents, and preserving the rhyming schemes often made the poems either nonsensical in the English or involved making them 'better' than they might have been in the original. In these cases, they have been translated into free verse. German abbreviations have been translated into the full English words to help with the flow of the text.

Although English readers have become accustomed to dealing with some Nazi terminology, all German words have here been translated into English. These include the approximate English equivalents of the ranks of the armed forces. Terms which often appear untranslated in English, such as Führer (Leader), Heil (Hail) and Sieg Heil (Hail Victory), for example, have here been translated, in order to reveal fully what Germans understood themselves to be doing or saying when they used them. Only the word Reich, which has no precise English translation but means roughly 'nation' or 'empire', has been preserved in the German when letters refer to Hitler as the 'Reich Chancellor' or to the National Socialist dictatorship as the 'Third Reich'. In all but one case German acronyms have been translated into the full English term. Thus, the National Socialist Worker's Party, or NSDAP, is always referred to by its full name, or as the Nazi Party. The Nazi's paramilitary organization, the SA, is referred to as the Storm Battalion throughout. This is both for clarity, and because using the full name reveals the emotive nature of the term itself, something which Germans would themselves have understood. The idea of a 'Storm' Battalion staffed by 'Stormtroopers' is far more viscerally evocative than the abbreviated German equivalent. The SS is the only exception here. The paramilitary organization's full title, Protection Squadron, is rather chilling – the use of the word 'protection' in the title of armed forces responsible for rounding up millions of innocent 'enemies' of the Reich was euphemistic at best. However, given that most readers are familiar with the SS, and the corresponding symbol on its officer's uniforms, it would be confusing to refer to them differently here.

The book is divided into three parts, each containing several smaller chapters. The first part follows the Nazi Party from its emergence as a political force in 1925 to Hitler's seizure of power in 1933. The second chronicles the development of Hitler's popular dictatorship during the peace years of the Third Reich between 1933 and 1938. The final section traces Hitler and his followers' fortunes from the declaration of the Second World War in 1939 to the destruction of the Reich in 1945. Throughout this chronology attention has been given to a variety of themes including political, economic and foreign policy developments; the intricacies of Nazi Party ideology, including its views on religion, its social organization, and its anti-Semitism; the development of Hitler's charismatic leadership, which brought with it letters of veneration and idolatry; and, finally, conflict with and resistance to the Nazi Party.

By presenting these personal and often emotional letters within this narrative framework, it is possible to trace the Nazi Party's development from a small, radical fringe party to a mass movement revered by German speakers within and outside the borders of the German state. In other words we are presented with a history of the Third Reich which takes into account the views of its citizens, as opposed to just those of its leaders. The letters Hitler received show which aspects of his political programme were appealing, and also which were not. During the early years not all aspects of the Nazi ideology were clear to Germans, and they often wrote asking questions or requesting clarifications. Some also complained when they thought Hitler's plans were taking the wrong path; or suggested routes they thought were better.

Critical discourse and overt protest continued into the 1930s and did not stop even when the Nazi Party seized power and established a dictatorship in 1933. While Hitler may have used force to silence many of his political opponents, particularly Communists, during this period, he could not afford to alienate the core group of Germans whose prophet he felt himself to be. As a result, many criticisms went unchallenged and many self-serving requests were fulfilled. While Germans were prepared to accept Hitler as dictator, overwhelmingly they did not understand his rule to be unquestionable. Although few Germans openly opposed the more draconian of Hitler's plans, many seemingly chose to ignore those aspects with which they did not agree or those they found unpalatable. This is most striking in writers' persistent comments about Hitler's role in bringing peace to Germany, despite the government openly militarizing and even beginning to annex other sovereign areas. Despite the veneration and devotion Hitler attracted, the myth Hitler cultivated, of his role as the messianic Leader of a united, and uniformly 'Aryan' master race, willing to bow to his every whim, was just that – a myth.

There was nothing inevitable about Nazism. Ideas of racial superiority emerged in all imperial nations during the nineteenth century. Charles Darwin's ideas of natural selection were combined with emerging medical knowledge and enabled Europeans to connect their political superiority with their racial background. Thus, those individuals who did not enjoy this superiority, whether colonial subjects or Jews or the lower classes, could be interpreted as biologically and racially inferior. In order to protect and enhance racial superiority, it was crucial to prevent these less worthy individuals from breeding, and also to ensure that racially superior individuals did not reproduce with them. Much of this discourse about the need to protect the nation from degenerates was aimed at the lower classes. But this racially based prejudice, particularly anti-Semitism, also enabled lower-middle-class skilled labourers and artisans, who suffered during industrialization and during the economic downturn in the 1870s, to believe that there was a specific enemy responsible for their problems. It was much easier to believe that Jews, who were often themselves merchants, were responsible for their suffering, as opposed to complicated, increasingly global, market forces. Germany, France, Russia, Austria, and the United Kingdom all had problems with racial anti-Semitism during this period.

Other countries also had politicians, doctors, social workers, and other professionals who believed that it was scientifically the case that certain individuals were biologically 'less valuable' than others. Not all these believers in racial hygiene would have identified themselves as right wing; nor were all of them anti-Semitic. Few had any political influence. Lanz von Liebenfels, for example, an Austrian who is sometimes credited with influencing Hitler, advocated the development of a blond super-race and flew a flag with an ancient Indian symbol – the swastika – on it, was on the lunatic fringe of politics. But more moderate versions of these ideas were pervasive. Others used the swastika too. When combined with the emergence of extreme nationalistic feeling, such ideas became more politically consequential. By the eve of the First World War it was common for Europeans to believe that theirs was a race and nation superior to others, which both deserved more space for its population and also needed to purge itself of those social elements who weakened it.

Adolf Hitler, who was born in Austria in 1889, spending his younger years in Linz and Vienna, was only one of many individuals who were influenced by these ideas. He moved to Germany in 1913 and was living in Munich when the First World War broke out. He soon volunteered for service in the army, ready to serve a country and a people he, like many other Germans, felt to be militarily, morally and racially superior to its enemies. This Germany deserved more space – within and outside Europe – both to integrate the millions of 'ethnically' German individuals who remained outside the borders of the Empire, and to give these individuals space to dominate the world. A war of conquest would also enable Germany to embark on its mission to purify and consolidate itself internally, by providing an ideal situation for the weaker to be removed from it. Because of Germany's superiority, victory was considered inevitable.

Thus, its defeat in November 1918, after four years of a war fought, until Russia's defeat in 1917, on two fronts, was devastating. Hitler for one could not believe that his beloved Germany had surrendered – particularly not given that the German Army still occupied foreign territory. Politicians, some civilians, and Jews at home, he and many others decided, were responsible for 'stabbing' the German Army 'in the back'. The outbreak of revolutionary activity within Germany in the last days of the war had led to the proclamation of a Republic on 9 November 1918; the country signed an armistice two days later. The left-wing government which established the Republic was thus seen as responsible for the loss of the war and, worse, for the signing of the Versailles Treaty in 1919. The Treaty forced Germany to accept full responsibility for the war and pay the victors in both land and money.

Many upstanding Germans became politicized during the course of

Germany's military defeat and the subsequent revolution in the winter of 1918–19. Having fought for four years for the cause of Greater Germany, many Germans connected the loss of the war, the punitive stipulations of the peace treaty signed at Versailles, and the abdication of the Emperor with the creation of the democratic Weimar Republic. Many Germans saw its establishment as further endangering the ideal Germany they had fought for and seemingly lost. Families, colleagues, and friends discussed politics both at home and at taverns, some more fervently than others. At the same time, working-class Germans were given new opportunities to make their own political views known. While some spoke in favour of the social-democratic revolution, others joined the right-wing nationalistic cause.

In this messy, but highly participatory, political climate, a range of nationalistic groups emerged. Some were overtly anti-Semitic or anti-Communist; others more vaguely embraced the ethnic or racial (völkisch) movement, using myth and folklore to conceive of a German people united not by the geographic boundaries of the stripped down German state created by Versailles, but instead by a common language and blood. Fifteen nationalistic organizations emerged in Munich alone during the revolutionary period of 1918–19. One of them, the German Workers' Party, was founded by Anton Drexler, a thirty-three year-old locksmith and war veteran. Drexler's political ideology combined a radical and highly anti-Semitic nationalism with a desire for working-class political dominance. In Drexler's mind, socialism would emerge from the creation of an ethnic nationalist state, a development which would only be possible by purifying Germany – in other words by removing poisonous and non-German influences such as Jewish and other international capital, as well as anti-nationalistic Communist thought. Drexler termed his outlook 'National Socialist'.

The thirty-year-old Adolf Hitler first attended one of Drexler's meetings on 12 September 1919. He was a vocal participant and soon was a dominant force in the German Workers' Party, becoming the leader of the newly renamed National Socialist German Workers' Party (Nazi Party) by summer 1921. Hitler wanted to do more than simply discuss politics over a beer or two; he sought a political movement with a national focus. This movement would oversee the rebirth of the German nation, uniting working- and middle-class Germans into a true ethnic national community. Hitler's success was immediate – by 1922 the Nazi Party was the largest nationalist party in Bavaria. It had its own newspaper, the Racial Observer, a paramilitary organization called the Storm Battalion whose men were instantly recognizable in their brown uniform shirts, and a youth organization. Its meetings also began to fill auditoriums of up to 7,000 people.

By 1922, even national politicians and military leaders started to pay attention to this Bavarian fringe party. The young Republic was in crisis, already struggling to stabilize its currency after the expense of war and the reparations payments demanded by the Versailles Treaty. In June 1922 the value of the German mark fell sharply after the assassination of the Jewish Foreign Minister Walther Rathenau by right-wing paramilitaries. The runaway inflation which followed made it impossible for the German government to develop any stable economic policy. In an attempt to demonstrate its political strength and legitimacy, the centre-left national government banned many nationalist organizations, which served only to enflame the hatred of anti-Republican nationalists and many in the military. More embarrassing still was France's 1923 invasion of the Ruhr, a vital industrial district on the French–German border, which had been forcibly demilitarized as part of the Versailles Treaty. The German state's response to the occupation, which the French undertook in response to Germany's inability to pay its war reparations, was to encourage workers and civil servants to ignore the occupying army's orders, through passive resistance. This weak response enabled nationalists to garner increased support from the population; the termination of passive resistance later in 1923 by the new chancellor Gustav Stresemann only made the situation worse and central authority weakened further.

It led the leader of the state of Bavaria, Gustav Ritter von Kahr, to assume emergency powers. Kahr, together with some military, backed Hitler and the Nazi Party's attempt to take advantage of the Weimar Republic's weakness and unpopularity by launching a coup d'etat on 8 November 1923. The Nazis and their armed supporters stormed into Munich's Bürgerbraukeller, a popular beer hall, during a rousing speech by Kahr, and declared a national revolution. Erich Ludendorff, a German military officer and one of the leaders of Germany's First World War effort, who was in attendance and who had backed the Nazi

Party during conversations over the previous year, was identified as the new national dictator. But only 3,000 people attended the speech, and Hitler had exaggerated the strength and desire of his armed backers. This, combined with the national army and police's unpreparedness and lack of support, as well as the refusal of the Bavarian government to align with Hitler against the national government, meant that Hitler's putsch quickly fell apart. Fourteen Nazi Party members were killed, and the national government used the event to consolidate its power and exert its authority over the German federal states, including Bavaria. By the end of the year, the government had succeeded in renegotiating its debts to its First World War opponents using the Dawes Plan and, as a result, French and Belgian troops began to withdraw from the Ruhr. This, together with the success of a currency reform in ending the hyperinflation that had so destabilized the German Republic, put an end to the crisis. The Weimar Republic was safe, for the time being.

Part I

The 'Time of Struggle': 1924–1932

1

HITLER AND THE NAZI PARTY

The abject failure of Hitler's 1923 putsch demonstrated that neither he nor the Nazi Party enjoyed the level of mass popular support necessary for a successful revolutionary movement. While the Party had brown-shirted paramilitary volunteers called the Storm Battalion, headed by Ernst Röhm, and also counted many police as sympathizers, it would take more than limited military support to wage war against the Weimar Republic and the other perceived enemies of the Reich – both internal and external. To do so, Hitler needed widespread grassroots support. He and his fellow National Socialists needed to attract greater numbers of more moderate Germans by presenting themselves as a legitimate political force. In other words the Nazi Party would need to work within the political system it so despised.

It also needed to garner more publicity. It was in this regard that his putsch enjoyed some limited success. Hitler, Kahr and Ludendorff, as well as some other Nazi Party members, were tried for treason in 1924 as a result of their role in the Beer Hall Putsch. The widespread reporting of these events brought Hitler and the Nazi Party to the attention of the nation. More crucially, Hitler's demeanour at the trial transformed him into a believable leader. Until that time Ludendorff had been envisaged as the obvious leader of the national socialist revo-lution. But he sought to distance himself at the trial and seemed aloof and tense. Hitler was approachable and charismatic. He admitted and even embraced his role in the putsch, using his testimony as a platform to announce his desire to forcibly remove the Weimar system and reinvent Germany. In doing so, his words filled newspaper headlines throughout Germany and other German-speaking areas.

Hitler realized quickly the ramifications of this publicity. He also now understood that traditional German elites, including Ludendorff, were of only limited use in building his movement. After being sentenced to five years in prison on 1 April 1924, Hitler sought to use his time in Landsberg Jail in southwest Bavaria to focus on rebuilding the Nazi Party along these lines and preparing to mobilize it for its next phase.

Hitler also committed his political views to paper, through writing his treatise, *My Struggle* (Mein Kampf). Part autobiography, part rant, and part ideological exposition, Hitler's book was egotistical, unoriginal and often unreadable. But in it he mentioned two key elements of his future political programme. The first was a strident anti-Semitism. The second was Germany's need for increased living space (Lebensraum) for 'Aryan' German people in eastern Europe. For the first time too, Hitler referred to himself as Germany's Leader (Führer), the man who would reinvent the German nation and lead it to its destined glory.

Given all this, it is impossible to believe the comments of Rudolf Hess, Hitler's assistant, to an old Party member, written from his own cell in Landsberg, that for the time being Hitler didn't 'want to hear anything about current political questions'. More accurately, it would seem, Hitler was not yet ready to respond with his own analysis of them. Regardless, it was not until after Hitler's release, just one year into his five-year sentence, that he began to answer the growing number of letters addressed to him.

Hess, who revered Hitler, and to whom Hitler had dictated *My Struggle* while in Landsberg, became Hitler's personal secretary. He answered many of the letters addressed to Hitler. During this early period, this was not a particularly onerous task.

In 1925, Hitler received only about 300 letters, and he and Hess answered only fifty of them. The combination of the ban on the Nazi Party, Hitler's time in prison, and the stabilization of the economic and political scene, meant that the Nazi Party was not in a strong position. Nor was right-wing nationalism more generally. Other nationalistic parties tried to use the popularity Hitler garnered during his trial to help their own campaigns to enter the Reichstag, but they did not succeed. Nor did Ludendorff, whose attempt to run for President in 1925 was a disaster. Although the Nazi Party was decriminalized on 16 February 1925, Hitler was soon banned from public speaking in most German states, which did not help matters. As a result, despite having attracted national attention during Hitler's trial, National Socialism remained a very small movement and attracted consistent attention only from those on the radical fringe of politics. What is more notable, however, is that the total failure of other right-wing parties made Hitler's Party the only significant extreme right party in Germany. More importantly, whatever limited support the Nazis did enjoy was no longer limited to Bavaria, but came from across Germany.

Some of these political extremists wrote with words of support and advice; others offered contacts or even made demands. Still others simply added Hitler to the network of political radicals to whom they sent circulars and brochures. One such individual was the anti-Semitic philosopher Arnold Ruge. As well as writing a popular introduction to his field, he garnered popular appeal during the First World War through his patriotic speeches and an edited collection of war songs. Ruge was the grandson of the more famous philosopher of the same name. While Ruge the senior was a radical social democrat and friend of Karl Marx, Ruge the younger lost his authorization to teach in 1920 because of his hate speeches against Jews. On 11 July 1925, Ruge sent Hitler a circular in which he urged Germans to fight against a 'system that hands over all power and all values to organized Jewry and brings Bolshevist impoverishment nearer'.

Despite their shared anti-Semitism, Hitler did not seek to cultivate a close connection with Ruge. Feeling they had little in common, Ruge's circular was noted merely as having been 'dealt with', and it does not appear that a personal answer was sent. Ruge had closer ties with twenty-five year old Heinrich Himmler, who joined the paramilitary organization the Protection Division (the SS) that year and almost immediately became the Nazi Party's district leader in Bavaria.

Himmler and Ruge ran a propaganda publishing house together. And in the 1930s Ruge produced a series of historical reports for Himmler, in which he focused on the Catholic Church and its involvement in witch hunts. It was probably Ruge's friendship with Himmler that led the Nazi Party to appoint Ruge as an archivist in Karlsruhe in 1934.

About half the letters and postcards received in 1925 professed loyalty to Hitler or approved the Nazi Party's programme. On 8 June 1925 at 9.45 a.m. Hitler received the following telegram from Dresden in the state of Saxony, eastern Germany:

> national socialists who have come together from all districts in greater germany on the occasion of the fifth germanic agricultural college week greet their leader adolf hitler with unyielding loyalty and unshakeable faith
>
> > as representative, walter zickler.

Such messages were not answered by Hess, probably in part because he did not think an answer was expected. Nonetheless, in these early days, approval was gladly received and filed away.

More important were activists who could be useful to the Nazi Party, and, in the most extreme cases, were willing to sacrifice themselves. During this period Hitler chose to speak almost exclusively to small groups and was still seeking to gain a clearer idea of what the road to power might look like. In reorganizing the Nazi Party, and having learned from the unsuccessful use of Ludendorff in 1923, he carefully chose cadres who were personally devoted to him and had no political ambitions of their own. This paid off: these individuals appreciated Hitler's trust and thanked him for it. They included the Austrian-born mathematics professor Theodor Vahlen. Vahlen had joined the Nazi Party in 1922, and in 1924 became the first regional leader of Pomerania as well as a Nazi Party representative in the German parliament. The same year his employer, the University of Königsberg Albertina, placed him on leave after he incited a crowd to remove the flags of the Weimar Republic. His career would flourish after 1933, given that he had full support of the Nazis. He wrote to Hitler on 6 April 1925:

Highly esteemed Mr Hitler!

I thank you for confirming me as district leader for Pomerania, and hope to be able to assume my duties towards the end of this month . . .

You may be sure of my unconditional loyalty, and I hope soon to have an opportunity, during a meeting of national leaders, to strengthen this vow by shaking your hand.

Ludendorff's candidacy will also separate the wheat from the chaff in the camp of the freedom parties.

Hail!
Your true devotee
Vahlen

In his letter Vahlen used the greeting 'Hail!', which the Nazis had adopted from the ethnic nationalist movement, who had started to use it at the turn of the century. In 1926 the use of 'Hail' became compulsory when addressing the 'Leader' – Hitler. This term too was taken from the ethnic nationalist movement.

While trying to attract recruits from across the country, Hitler insisted on keeping Munich, the capital of Bavaria in southern Germany, as the headquarters of his movement. This irritated Fritz Vogel, who came from a village near Erfurt, the capital of the free-state of Thuringia in central Germany. Vogel wrote Hitler the following letter on 24 April 1925:

Esteemed Mr Hitler!

I am loath to bother you, but I think it necessary to inform you of the following.

In general, people are surprised that you are so insistent on the inhospitable and ungrateful Bavaria. If they won't let you speak there, which will remain a disgrace and a scandal for all time, it would be better that you hold meetings outside Bavaria, in order to make the movement large and strong. In our opinion, the next opportunity to do so would be at Oldenburg [in northwest Germany], where new elections are to take place on May 24. [Y]ou must speak there in all the larger towns, and in that way the movement will grow big and strong, gigantic. In the meantime, new elections will take place in other provinces, and you must go there too, and so on.

However, above all you should apply for German citizenship. [Hitler, remember, was Austrian.]

It is true that it is a great outrage that you are not simply recognized as a German, but can you expect more from the people who are now in power? But precisely for that reason you have to become a German citizen, and if you can't do that in Bavaria, then come to Thuringia and submit your application here. The people currently in power are only too glad that you have not yet applied for citizenship.

With the greatest respect,
Your entirely devoted
Fritz Vogel

Hitler probably thought he could do without such advice. In any case he did not reply to this message.

H. Ockel from Kiel also received no answer from Hitler, which is why he wrote to him again on 15 May 1925:

Dear Mr Hitler!

According to the return receipt, my registered letter of 3 April was given to you personally, but unfortunately you have not yet had the time or the opportunity to answer it or have it answered. I sincerely regret that, since I should have thought that a German man, who is neither an officer nor a graduate, but who has remained true to his leader through a difficult time and has been abused on account of it, would receive an answer to his heartfelt letter from precisely this leader of his.

In my letter I pointed out that the revival of Germany could never come from the Jesuit-contaminated Bavaria [this region of Germany was predominantly Catholic], and that it is therefore necessary that you, very esteemed Mr Hitler, shift the field of your activity away from Bavaria to northern Germany, where such a dark wind does not blow [in other words, where Catholicism is insignificant]. In addition,

I allowed myself to mention that to all appearances the National-Socialist movement is in a crisis and [to ask] whether it would be possible to renew our people with economic and nationalist goals alone. I referred to the spiritual and religious renewal for which the people itself longs. I only made these suggestions in the expectation that you would somehow, either agreeing or disagreeing or asking for more detailed explanations, write back to me. These problems are of such enormous profundity and grandeur that it would be well worth the time to write about them.

I remain, with a true German salute
your devoted
H. Ockel

Rudolf Hess replied on Hitler's behalf on 29 May 1925, clarifying what the true goals of the Nazi Party should be. Religious revival was not among them. Although the National Socialists distrusted religion, and sought to be a supra-denominational political movement – or even a replacement to religion – they did take religious questions seriously. Hitler made sure he was pictured attending church services, and Hess sometimes answered letters by cryptically referencing the Bible. But often the answers were evasive, or categorized Hitler's religious beliefs as personal questions.

Very esteemed Mr Ockel!

I confirm the receipt of your letter of 15 May. You seem to have no idea of the enormous number of letters that are constantly arriving with suggestions, criticisms, encouragements, etc., if you think Mr Hitler should or could reply personally to all of them. Were he to do so, he would have no time left for real work.

Whether you are an official or an academic or not is of no importance – I hope you yourself have not assumed that it was! Your continued fidelity is shared by thousands of others, which does not mean that Mr Hitler is not pleased about each individual.

So far as the area of activity is concerned, in the near future Mr Hitler's forthcoming book [*My Struggle*] will answer your questions

regarding the purely economic and national goals. Mr Hitler is focusing all his strengths on the political and spiritual renewal of our people.
He must leave work on religious renewal to someone else; he cannot
splinter himself.

With a German salute
[no signature]

Despite not answering either Vogel or Ockel, and being at odds with
Ockel's religious sensibilities, Hitler may have taken the idea of speaking outside Bavaria on board. At the very least, he began to see it as
necessary for capitalizing on his national profile. Given he was banned
from speaking within Bavaria, speaking elsewhere was clearly sensible.
In November 1925 Hitler spoke in Brunswick, northern Germany, one
of the few places in which he was not banned from speaking. So many
people wanted to attend that special trains were used to carry listeners
from the nearby towns of Hildesheim, Hanover and Halberstadt, all in
Prussia, where the Party was banned until 1928.

Few women wrote to Hitler during this period. The vast majority
of Nazi Party members were men – and young men. Two-thirds of
activists were under the age of forty. One of the few female activists
was thirty-five-year-old Elsbeth Zander, who founded the German
Women's Order in 1923. This Nazi women's organization was incor-
porated as a Party affiliate in 1928, and had 4,000 members by the end
of the 1920s. Paradoxically, it campaigned in public for the removal
of women from public life and service. It also ran soup kitchens,
engaged in propaganda campaigns, and offered nursing for wounded
Stormtroopers.

Zander wrote to Hitler on 19 May 1925, and reported on the formation of her organization and the political mood in northern Germany.
Like Vogel and Ockel, she also asked Hitler when he would be travelling outside Bavaria. The tone of her letter indicates that she had at
least conversed with Hitler before. Interestingly too, she clearly had
not herself internalized his new self-image as 'Leader', given the series
of rather demanding requests she made of him. Her letter bore a red
swastika on its first page.

Very esteemed Mr Hitler!

I am being bombarded from all sides with the question of when you are finally going to come to Berlin. People assure me that there is no longer any obstacle to your coming to Berlin. At the moment, everything in Berlin is at a standstill waiting for your arrival. As a matter of urgency, I would like to ask you to let me know very soon, so that I know what answer I should give. Haste is urgently necessary.

Additionally, I would like to ask on which day you could travel to Halberstadt, since things have to be prepared there; or would you like to go to Magdeburg afterward?

As agreed, I hereby remind you of the German Women's Order's national meeting in Magdeburg on 6 and 7 June. Could you perhaps let me know when you can be in Magdeburg? We might also arrange for you to speak with the leaders of the Harz area [in northern Germany]. Mr and Mrs Kricheldorff, from Derenburg (who are financially powerful), are sure to be there, and I believe many of the Nazi Party leaders from the Harz and nearby areas are coming. Mrs Bechstein also promised me that she would come to Magdeburg. Princess Luise von Altenburg and Miss Lenz have also accepted. I would now like to urgently request that you write me to tell me on what day we may expect you. His Excellency Ludendorff is coming to the German Day meeting on Sunday 7 June. I would like it if you were already in Magdeburg in order to take part in the meeting itself.

I would also like to remind you once again of the contribution to the commemorative publication. It is now high time that we sent it to the printers. I would be grateful if you could send the manuscript directly to Mrs Emma Wittchen ... no later than Friday 22 May. I will be in Magdeburg on Sunday and we want to put the newspaper together then. And please, dear Mr Hitler, for God's sake don't tell me you can't come. We have done what we could to bring together everything that is valuable for you.

In Breslau, where I was last Friday, our affairs are advancing splendidly. There everything is moving in the direction of the Nazi Party, and the Freedom Party [another far-right party], with all its lies, has fallen behind. There too people really want you to come because they know that then our cause will really take off. The same is the case in Liegnitz as well.

The leadership in Liegnitz is very good, as it is in Breslau. [Both of these towns are in Silesia. Both were in Prussia and became part of the German Reich in 1871. They are now located in southwest Poland.] I hear that there is to be a German Day in Breslau on 21 June, and it is generally hoped that you will also take part in it. Indeed, people will only see it as a complete success if you do so. I consider it very important that this vital location be 'taken'. It opens up all of Silesia to you. All your friends are paralysed, in a way, because they are waiting for you and hoping you will arrive.

Dear Mr Hitler, don't make us here in Berlin wait too long – come as soon as you possibly can.

I was told that you would speak here on 24 May, but yesterday I learned that nothing had yet been heard from you. Could some letter have been lost, or are there compelling reasons why you have not yet been able to come here? In any case, here we need to be informed so that we know how to answer questions.

In the hope of a prompt answer, especially with regard to the contribution to the commemorative publication, I remain,

with a German Hail salute
your
Elsbeth Zander

On behalf of Hitler, Rudolf Hess replied to the German Women's Order on 22 May 1925:

In reply to your letter of 19 May, Mr Hitler asks me to tell you that he will come to Magdeburg on 6 June and probably depart the same evening. In no case will he speak in public. He would also prefer that his presence there not be known.

However, he asks you to see to it that on Saturday he is able to speak with the persons you have brought there. However, they should be limited to a small group of important people.

Mr Hitler will probably already be in Berlin and travel from there to Magdeburg. For the time being, he will not go to Halberstadt [although, as we have seen, he would do later that year]. The branch office has been informed that the German Women's Order meeting will take place. The local groups will be notified from there. Unfortunately, Mr Hitler is currently not in a position to send a contribution to the commemorative publication.

With a German salute
R. Hess

P.S. I regret that I must respond negatively to you on several points. But the main thing is that Mr Hitler is coming at all. Mr Hitler never promised to speak in Berlin on 24 May. When they asked, the gentlemen were told that Hitler wanted to assess the situation there himself before he spoke.

Best wishes,
Your
R. Hess

Zander ultimately did not turn out to be the kind of organizer who was wanted by the Nazi Party. In 1931 the German Women's Order fell apart, after being embroiled in a number of accusations including corruption, and being so seriously in debt that Zander herself was on the verge of bankruptcy. She was soon squeezed out of the leadership and authority was transferred to the rival National Socialist Women's League, which was founded in October 1931 and comprised several formerly independent nationalist women's associations. In 1934 Gertrud Scholtz-Klink became the National Women's Leader and head of the Women's League, a post that she retained until 1945. Ironically, given her position of extreme importance, Klink was a staunch opponent of women's participation in political life. Despite serving time in a Soviet Prisoner of War Camp in 1945, and then being sentenced to 48 months in prison by the Allies, she remained a convinced Nazi until her death.

Alfred Barg, a metalworker, wrote to Hitler from Kohlfurt in Lower Silesia on 25 May 1925. He decorated his letter with swastikas. Barg had already surveyed the jungle of right-wing parties and chosen the Nazi Party. Barg was also well-informed about the anti-Jewish right wing and was in general highly politicized. He hoped Hitler could tell him which labour union he should now join.

First a people's salute!

Before I come to the real reason I am writing to you, I would like to tell you a little something about me. I was born in Kohlfurt-Dorf, Görlitz district [in eastern Germany], on 23 December 1907, the son of the railway worker Reinhold Barg and his wife Selma. I attended the Protestant primary school there until I was fourteen. Then I worked as a farm labourer for a short time. Since 15 May in the year 1922 I have been training to be a metalworker. I work at the 'Kosmos' machine works in Görlitz, proprietor Rudolf Pawlikowski. For this purpose I travel every day from Kohlfurt-Dorf to Görlitz. This doesn't cost me anything, because my father works for the railway, and I have a free pass. Since 11 July 1922 I have been a . . . teetotaller. In addition, as a Protestant I am a member of the Evangelical Association. I also belong to the German Youth Movement in Kohlfurt-Dorf.

Two years ago, that is, in the summer of '23, one of my co-workers, the metalworker Rudolf Scholz, who is a member of Kunze's party, told me about the people's movement. [Richard Kunze's party was the German Social Party, an early north German rival to the Nazi Party. Richard 'Truncheon' Kunze joined the Nazi Party in 1930 and was elected to the Reichstag in 1933.] Since then I have been wearing the swastika with conviction, and I have paid careful attention to everything that is happening in the movement. The attempt to save the country in 1923 (which unfortunately failed) [he is referring to Hitler's Beer Hall Putsch], . . . the trial of Hitler, the period when he was in prison, Kunze's speeches in the Reichstag, . . . [and] the nomination of Ludendorff for the presidency of the Reich (which I could only applaud). In addition, I have read Richard Ungewitter's book Nakedness and Ascent [a treatise on nudism and the future of the German people], with which I agree. I have kept close tabs on all the parties, from the Communists and the Free Economy proponents to the German Nationalists. From all this I have recognized where I belong as a German worker: in the camp of the Nationalists, and more particularly in the Nazi Party. I know about its goals or goal through the Greater Germany, the National Socialist, and the Observer [newspapers] that I sometimes buy. This feeling is shared by four co-workers. Most of them are Social Democrats. In Kohlfurt-Dorf I have already been seen as a 'Swastiker.' But many enemies, much honour! Swastika and black-white-red are displayed.

I come now to the subject itself.

(1) Since, as He [Hitler] himself also says (*My Struggle*), I say that there must be labour unions, as a metalworker I would like to join a union (just not a 'free', Liberal, or Christian one). Thus I ask you to tell me to which nationalist union I can turn in this matter.

(2) What is His stand on the alcohol question?

(3) Is the Nazi Party (if there ever is a nationalist Greater Germany) for the black-white-red colours with the swastika? How does it see this question being resolved now?

I hope He understands me, and will write me his answer as soon as he has time.

With a nationalist Hail salute
Alfred Barg
(Return postage enclosed)

Rudolf Hess replied on 4 June 1925 'on behalf of the Leader':

Very esteemed Mr Barg!

Mr Hitler gives you many thanks for your letter. Here are the answers to your questions:

On 1: Unfortunately, we do not yet have any labour unions. However, at present we are engaged in negotiations and discussions regarding the foundation of one. A great deal of money is involved, and the movement doesn't have it. In any case, don't join 'yellow' unions. Instead, stay in the Marxist ones and try to win over enough like-minded comrades so that you acquire influence in the company council elections and in time the existing unions can in this way be National Socialistically infiltrated and won for us. That is what happened in Czechoslovakia.

On 2: Mr Hitler does not drink alcohol, except perhaps a few drops on very exceptional occasions. He does not smoke at all.

I · 30/5 ·   — 21 —

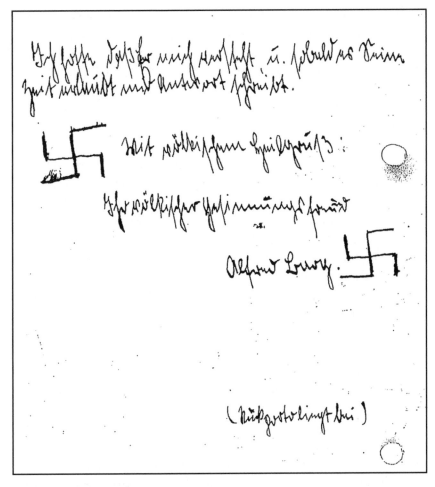

In May 1925 the metalworker Alfred Barg asked Hitler which labour union he should join. On Hitler's behalf Rudolf Hess, the Führer's private secretary, recommended a strategy of infiltration: Barg should pursue National Socialist goals as a member of a social-democratic or communist employees' organization. As a 'friend in nationalist spirit,' Barg decorated his letter with swastikas – in 1925 this was still unusual, but later became extremely common.

Source: RGWA (Moscow)

On 3: As to how we stand on the black–white–red colours, as on the swastika, you probably already know that we never deny them. Besides, the main thing is the spirit that is connected with the colours and the signs. We are going to change the spirit, and the flag will follow!

With a German salute
R. Hess

Since Hess provided this information very carefully under Hitler's letterhead, we can assume that his statements actually reflect Hitler's opinion. Given that, it is interesting that Hess suggests to Barg that he should stay in a Marxist union and try to infiltrate it. The Nazi Party's attitude towards the 'Liberal labour associations', that is, the 'yellow' unions that were favourable to the employers, was still highly controversial in the Party.

Hitler also received requests that, on the surface, seem rather politically insignificant. On 9 July 1925 Dr R. Niedermayer, an attorney, wrote to 'Mr Adolf Hitler':

As executor of the estate of the deceased director's widow, Mrs Margarete Meindl, in Munich, I have the honour of informing you of the following:

Before her death the deceased, who was a great admirer of your political efforts, expressed the wish that a large palm tree that she had in her apartment should be given to you after her death. The heirs would like to carry out this bequest, and for that reason I permit myself to direct to you the question whether you would be interested in taking delivery of this object. Should that be the case, I request that you inform me as soon as possible, so that I can convey it to you, at what point in time you could have the palm tree picked up.

With the greatest respect,
Niedermayer
Attorney at Law

While on one level the bequest of a palm tree was politically insignificant, the very fact that individuals such as Mrs Meindl were thinking of

Hitler in their wills was significant indeed. Rudolf Hess replied on 14 July 1925:

In response to your letter of 9 July, concerning Mrs Meindl's estate, I inform you that Mr Hitler would be glad to receive the palm tree. I look forward to hearing from you regarding its delivery.

With the greatest respect,
R. Hess

Whether or not Hitler wanted the palm tree, it would have been short-sighted not to accept it. He did not feel the same about all gifts, however. Hess returned three handkerchiefs a lady from Berlin had sent, and informed her:

Very esteemed Mrs Tröltzsch!

On behalf of Mr Hitler I am enclosing the handkerchiefs you and Miss Zander embroidered, together with your letter of 28 May. So far as the handkerchiefs with a picture are concerned, Mr Hitler does not give permission for handkerchiefs with his picture to be made.

With a German salute
R. Hess

The tone of this reply was quite cold. Perhaps Elsbeth Zander and her German Women's Movement were already out of favour. However, in general, Hitler did not like devotional items. He was later to prohibit other such presents, including, for example, so-called Hitler cakes.

2

VENERATION AND ADVICE

Hitler's period of consolidation paid off. In 1926 the Nazi Party gained 23,000 members, and did the same in 1927, before adding another 35,000 a year later. By the time of the parliamentary elections in 1928, the Party boasted 110,000 members from across Germany. This was more than several of the more mainstream liberal parties. The Nazi Party also succeeded better than many other political parties in developing local Party branches, giving it the wide organizational base that it had been lacking in 1923. Thus, while the Weimar Republic may on the surface have seemed much more stable than it had done in the first half of the decade, under the surface extremist groups like the Nazi Party were slowly gaining steam, bolstered by nationalist victories including the election of Paul von Hindenburg, the chief of the general staff in the First World War, as President in 1925. The Social Democrats, who had negotiated the peace settlement and established the Republic, and had been the ruling party since 1919, were now out of power. The Liberals all but collapsed.

Despite all this, in the parliamentary elections of 1928, the Nazi Party received only 2.6 per cent of the votes. But the numerous letters that Hitler had begun to receive already foreshadowed his future success. By this point, the Party had become masters of manipulating local interests for their own gain. They infiltrated patriotic networks and organized public protests against the Republic, leaving German nationalist politicians to complain that the Nazis were better liked than them by even their own children. At the same time, they gained support among many middle-class voters, who viewed them as more trustworthy than the mainstream parties that they felt had betrayed their interests during the inflation and subsequent deflationary policies employed to stabilize the economy. This feeling increased dramatically as the Depression started to bite in 1929. Their socialist aspects appealed to working-class voters and, more strangely given the anti-Catholic aspects of their ideology, they started to perform better among Catholics than any other party besides the Catholic Centre Party. And, finally, with their focus on technology, scientific racism, and anti-communism, they could present themselves as a modern party that offered a radical departure from the past, while still honouring all that had once made Germany great. As a result of this masterful movement building, the economic catastrophe ensured that in the next national elections in September 1930 the Nazi Party polled 18.3 per cent.

The Nazi Party was now part of the political mainstream. This meant that Hitler began to receive far greater numbers of letters, and from a far wider range of people. Germans who previously may not have dreamed of supporting an extremist right-wing party or expressing their own racist views out loud were emboldened. Mrs von Ponief, for example, who wrote to Hitler from Peenemünde in northeastern Germany on 28 February 1930, gave him advice that makes her own political attitude clear:

Dear Mr Hitler!

As a member of the Nazi Party the following matter is very important to me! In order to do completely Jew-free work, we must require our members to agree not to buy from Jews, in this way we can gradually succeed in driving Jews out of retailing and thus put the middle class back in the saddle. It will not be so easy to drive them out of wholesaling, since in ready-made clothing and footwear for the most part only Jewish capital is probably at work. But locally our movement would be greatly advanced by these radical measures.

Among most people it is simply thoughtlessness, and the Jew quietly rejoices in the stupid German buyers!! He himself always buys only from his co-religionists.

> *With a true German*
> *Hail to the Struggle!*
> *Your devoted*
> *Mrs von Ponief*

Hitler's office replied on 6 March 1930:

Dear gracious lady,

Mr Hitler thanks you for your letter of 28 February and for the encouragement it contains. In any case it is our intention in future to see to it, through a corresponding command in our publications, that our Party members buy only from other members, so far as possible.

Unfortunately, a command not to buy from Jews is considered impairment of business, and is punishable by law, at least so far as Jews are mentioned as such.

> *With a German salute*
> *Your very devoted*

The carbon copy bears no signature, but it can be assumed that Rudolf Hess signed the letter. Despite their increased electoral support as well as their overt anti-Semitism and anti-Republicanism, this letter demonstrates that the Nazi Party were not yet ready to endanger their political legitimacy. Once they took power in 1933, the Nazis began to boycott Jewish businesses. But in 1930, because they did not yet make the laws, this was illegal, and so the Party leadership would not countenance it.

Important individuals such as the Munich consul general F. F. Pflüger also felt ready to lend their support to the Nazi Party. He also had some advice about making the Party as broadly appealing as possible. Unlike Mrs von Ponief, he thought the Nazis should adopt a more conciliatory line towards the Jews. On 3 September 1930 he wrote to Hitler:

Dear Mr Hitler!

I know about you and thus also have a fair idea of your goals. You will know less about me. I am a friend of Mr Major Siry, who is also quite close to you.

As an old soldier and an industrialist, I have for years been helping to rebuild our Fatherland; in particular, I have been concerned with the physical and psychological fitness of our youth and educating our workers so that they understand national and social questions. You can best see a little of this in the enclosed copies of my letters to privy councillor Dr Duisberg on 14 June and to Mr Wittke on 16 July.

In the coming weeks the number of your supporters will sharply increase – as a result of large groups' justified dissatisfaction with everything that is happening or not happening in our Fatherland.

However, your following would develop more strongly and more quickly – in numbers and in conviction – if you were able to make the two following lines of thought your own.

The swastika is too strongly emphasized and an obstacle to many Germans from good circles joining in your efforts. England and other countries appropriate the abilities, connections, etc. of apparently well-suited, good Jewish groups in order to carry out national, economic, and political tasks, often of the most difficult kind.

And the other line of thought!

You have been able to win over broad sections of the labour force and ally them to yourself. No doubt – without the labour force Germany cannot exist. But this allegiance has implied to a wide range of concerned German groups the (easily refutable!) idea that your supporters are 'hostile to property'. It must be in the interest of your movement to refute these strongly held views, and to eliminate them so far as possible. Your declaration on 13 April 1928 (see Frankfurt Gazette no. 611 of 18 August 1930!) may not be enough to achieve this. [On 13 April Hitler published a clarification of Section 17 of the Nazi Party programme, emphasizing that the Party fundamentally believed in private property. Although Section 17 called for the expropriation of land, Hitler clarified that this was only to be used for seizing land held illegally or not in accordance with national welfare, in other words for seizing land held by Jewish companies who were accused of land speculation.]

See to it that it is repeatedly emphasized in the speeches of all Nazi leaders that management, capital accumulation, and private property [are] necessary – naturally in certain healthy forms and within certain boundaries. Then large groups of Germans that still keep their distance somewhat warily, will go over to you with their physical, intellectual, and economic means. This is also the sense of the two previously mentioned letters of mine to Mr Duisberg and Mr Wittke. Making no concession to the middle, and still less to the left, can now more than ever be your especially characteristic principle.

I would be glad to provide further details etc.

With my special regards
your devoted
Pflüger
Maj. (off duty)

For Christmas 1930, thirty-two-year-old Elsa Walter, from Karlsruhe in Baden, southwest Germany, sent Hitler a book. She had written and illustrated this clothbound book by hand. She had joined the Party on 1 November and was member number 358,061. Elsa Walter was unmarried, her family belonged to the lower middle class and had lost its savings during the period of extreme inflation in the early 1920s. Walter had attended a grammar school for girls, was interested in politics, and apparently had extensive experience in housekeeping. In this eighty-page text entitled 'The German Woman', she sought to tell Hitler what motivated her. At the same time she assumed that many women thought the way she did. Her letter is written in fluent and clear handwriting, and points to an energetic woman with strong feelings. Sometimes the depth of these feelings clearly interfered with her punctuation. In the interest of clarity some of these grammatical mistakes have been corrected in the following extracts.

Walter began her text abruptly:

What ails our dear Fatherland? In particular its women, and a woman is the soul of the house and of the country. That is why our people's soul is hurting, since the greater part of the German women's world has abandoned its divinely ordained place. Woman is man's complement, his relaxation, in whose nature he can refresh and elevate his heart and mind after the struggles and efforts of everyday life, with innermost love and respect.

Woman should lean on man as her strong protector and guardian in the hard battle of life, [and should be] full of devotion as his spouse and the mother of his children. That is the divinely ordained calling of woman, and deviating from this path results in her forfeiting her most essential purpose. Countless women of 'today' regard their most essential task as out of date and cast it away with a negligent wave of the hand and a deprecating smile, and compete with men in all areas, blind to the fact that it is precisely the tender, vulnerable, gracious woman who is attractive to man. Most women and girls of 'today' hustle and bustle about in blind madness, nervous and overexcited, instead of being a place of repose for the man who fights. The modern athletic girl must not remain the German model for women, woman's strength must reside in the soul not in the muscles!

Walter then goes on to explain that the First World War gave birth to these modern women, because it forced women to work. Worse it awakened women's 'unhealthy ambition' to have equal status. Here, Walter had clearly internalized right-wing attacks on the so-called 'new woman' and also the Weimar Republic's granting of legal equality under the law and voting rights. Walter considered these developments repulsive:

Now why, in order to prove our intelligence in relation to man, to shunt him aside, should we impress on him the idea that he is superfluous? No matter what the motive, that is a mistake. Woman's greatness lies not in her brain, but in her heart, not in the power of her will but rather in the power of her soul. And therein also lies all her real ability, from these sources also springs her true activity. As soon as we German women once again fully realize this inalterable truth, the blindness of our eyes will be relieved in the grace of divine love, [and] we shall certainly make the greatest contribution to healing our beloved Fatherland.

Walter thought there was 'a wide field of noble female occupations that would correspond to women's nature'. But women should not be 'forced into service'. The fact that 'private and governmental offices' were now 'almost all' filled with 'young girls, a large number of them from good backgrounds' meant that there was a 'great army of unemployed businessman, officials, and employees who were going about desperate and with nothing to eat. First they risked their lives for us on the battlefield and now they are sitting in the street starving. Poor blind Germany, is that the way to thank the courageous men, have you so quickly forgotten the heroes and their deeds?' asked Walter.

For Walter, that was the wrong path; the only way to go back was to follow the principle: 'man at the plough, woman at the stove'. It was women at the plough who were causing Germany's men to starve through unemployment. Walter, like many other conservatives, was also firmly against the existence of 'double earners', in other words, couples in which both partners worked. An increasing number of Germans, including Walter, had begun to argue that because of the rampant unemployment during the Great Depression, two-worker households should be actively prohibited.

In any case, she thought, in the area of love 'the masculinized woman' had probably won less respect from men. In short, what was most important was the woman's role as mother, if only in order to 'shape the life of a child's soul'. Modern education, which encouraged women to pursue higher education, was partially responsible for this masculinization of women and also their annexation of men's jobs.

Walter demanded 'the quickest possible end to these contradictions in the education of girls'. For her, 'the eight-year elementary school for girls' was entirely sufficient to make us into 'serviceable creatures'. While languages, crafts and religion should be taught in the girls' schools, most important was homemaking, so that German girls would be well prepared for marriage. Unmarried women should devote themselves to crafts. It was their responsibility to sell clothing and customs in the 'German style'.

The combination of an absence of these traditional clothes and poverty had made it impossible for girls to dress in accord with their social status. Worse, many girls wrongly wished to wear 'silk stockings', 'elegant little shoes', and 'tight-fitting dresses'. Walter thought these fashions were as 'superfluous for healthy bodies as hair put in a bob or cut like a man's'. 'German woman', she lamented, 'you are not a sophisticated coquettish Frenchwoman, not a moody spoiled American whose conception of life makes fixing up necessary; in your case it is the personality, not the dress, that matters.'

Modern popular culture was in part to blame. Walter laments that 'dear old farmers, who dance to the splendid sound of German waltzes with mothers still wearing becoming traditional clothing' were forced to watch their 'children contort[ing] themselves to the jazz music of the Negroes'. 'Today', Walter continued, 'Wagner, Beethoven, and other God-given musical geniuses are played with one and the same instrument as Negro music, jazz music, in full knowledge of the dreadful difference.' Walter's personal musical favourites were the 'splendid wise men from Vienna'. In waltzes, 'eyes shine, the heart laughs for pure joy, not even grandma was too proud to dance. But jazz and all that other foreign trash, we will gladly leave to other countries with high cultures. German art must emerge anew; it must not die out on us, God forbid! Hail!'

Films were also a problem. Productions such as 'The Blue Angel and countless others' were 'entirely unsuited for educating German youth'. It's not difficult to see why *The Blue Angel* bothered Walter. It was a 1930 film directed by Josef von Sternberg, based on Heinrich Mann's novel *Professor Unrat*, and starring Marlene Dietrich. It was the first significant German film with sound and made Dietrich a world superstar. The film was banned by the Nazi Party in 1933, but apparently Hitler watched it multiple times in his private cinema. It chronicles the fall of teacher Immanuel Rath, who pursues several of his students into a cabaret club, The Blue Angel, and there falls for the star, Lola. After resigning his position at the school, Lola and Rath have a brief interlude of happiness, before financial pressures force Rath to start working as a clown in the cabaret club. Rath becomes increasingly consumed by jealousy for Lola's other love interests and this, combined with his humiliation in his hometown, causes him to go mad. He later dies in his old classroom.

About fifteen pages before concluding her letter to Hitler, Walter emphasized that she was now coming to the end, but still had a few things to say. She proceeded to give her opinions on a variety of social issues, including the minimum wage, retirement funds, and the effects of optimization in commerce and industry, that is, of department stores and assembly-line systems in production ('the American system'):

Now in concluding these pages I would like to highlight the deficiencies in the nation as seen by a German woman. I will not go into exhaustive detail, because fighting is a man's affair, while love and care are a woman's. But we may let men know how we see things. Today we hear a great deal about salary questions, and therefore it would be good to make it clear what a poor country can do in this regard. I believe a minimum wage and a maximum wage could be established that would correspond to current conditions, for example between 300 and 900 marks for a married government official, and half that for an unmarried official, this was possible in earlier times, in better and also more modest times, why not today, when the people is in need!

Pensions require major reforms, a book could be written about the errors that have been made in the German Fatherland in this regard. I believe great sums could be saved without acting unjustly. I am delighted that one of the main points of the National Socialist Workers Party is opposing the department stores and consumer cooperatives. When their situation is healthy, the so often mocked and scorned petty bourgeois and middle-class people who are the butt of the Social Democrats' bad jokes are the basis for a country's prosperity. The good, industrious savers are to be found among them, and they are good and efficient in work as well. During the period of inflation, the funds they had earned and taken pains to save were stolen from them overnight, and now that they are seeking with bitter diligence to create a new life to feed their families, loving, caring Social Democracy sets its program before these people. Death to the middle class, long live consumer cooperatives, department stores, and also the newspaper full of the meanest-spirited jokes about the dying middle class. And yet this party of the internationalists is surprised to find the Nazis so strongly supported by the middle class!

In the future, citizens' gainful activities must be protected by high taxes on department stores, and each person must be allowed to run only one business, that is, no branches. Basic food cooperatives, consumer cooperatives must be done away with, they are absolutely the ruin of the small businessman.

Now, about factories. As we are told by old, experienced foremen and workers, the introduction of the American system is one of the greatest evils. Working on an assembly line governed by the theoretician's stopwatch; that is work without a soul, harried work without quality. Let's eliminate the American system from our factories and do German quality work with soul, industriousness, joy – and do it with precision –, for again we are German and are producing wares that are presentable. It is good to use technology to help humanity, but it must not rule over them, or deprive many people, very many people, of bread, for then technology is no longer a blessing. It is in fact soulless. Therefore craftwork above all, German quality work. Let that be the reputation of German work throughout the world. So far as concerns the poverty of the labour force today, it consists of precisely this excessive power of technology and the need of the unemployed, but Social Democracy, which calls itself first of all a working man's party, has in twelve years found no solution to this problem of widespread unemployment. Out with the American system, then a year of work service for the young, prohibit people from holding two jobs, give men priority for jobs, retirement at the age of sixty for workers or government officials, and then we'll see how many unemployed people still remain.

Worse was that the department stores of the American system were often run by Jews.'Now, what is a German woman's attitude towards the Jewish question?', asked Walter.

Precisely in accord with her predisposition, down deep she does not feel hatred in the sense of the word battle, no. But she does have a pride that protects her from making a mistake of falling for the blandishments and flatteries addressed by a Jew to a Christian woman. For example, I never felt hatred for Jews, but so far as love was concerned, even before the swastika existed, Jews never had any luck with me, though I was not crudely insulting, but once, to tell the truth, since there was no other way, I told one exactly what I thought of him. But if you were to ask me, Adolf Hitler, what my position with regard to the Jewish question is, I would tell you unhesitatingly, in a genuinely womanly way: I pity the Jews, who are undeservedly abused in moral and spiritual ways. But I would always be in favour of the growth of the Christian's feeling of pride in being a Christian, with all honours. Not slaves to the Jews, not *handmaids* to the Jews, but simply Christians, proud of Christianity, and a sincere battle against the Jew's predilection for Mammon in accord with his predisposition, by setting limits to it, to moderate it. Craftwork and not only commerce. Or emigration for anyone who does not want to earn his bread with his hands. But as soon as their homeland, their old homeland, can be opened up for the Jews, then they, those without a homeland, can simply move there. We will rejoice with them because in their whole conception of life they do not fit into our country.

To every Christian girl and woman, however, I would like to say, stay away from this foreign race, because it desires from you hardly anything more than your body, not and never your foreign soul, because you are a Christian. And these Jews are so good at bewitching women, as if they had a poison that they try to instil into our blood. They are effusive in their love for women and their otherwise money-grubbing race spends huge amounts of money on its love and inclination for women. However the only women who fall victim to this drug are those who are no more than body! I am not disgusted by Jews, but I wouldn't let one kiss me – my race and my natural feeling refuses to accept that.

But one other thing, before Jewish men leave German districts for once and for all, I have a request to make of German men: just look at their reverence for woman, their spouses, their parents, and the very old, because you can still learn something from them in this regard. A Jew really cares for his own, he cares that things go well for them. Of course he considers every means permissible, there is no question about that, but how beautiful it is to be loved and completely cared for as a woman.

From these tirades of hate Walter immediately turned to her own experience in the dairy business. She deplored the existence of large dairy farms and bureaucratic over-regulation in this area, because 'earlier' 'a dairyman bought his milk directly from the countryside', and we absolutely 'prospered in that way, and so did our purses'. She then recommended that imports from abroad be prohibited if they are not absolutely indispensable: 'first of all people should feed themselves on the bread of their own land'. But, despite wanting Germany to be totally self sufficient, Walter did not want Germans to 'forget all the

German brothers and sisters abroad' who are 'fighting for their right and their freedom'. It is a disgrace that 'no help was found for German distress in Poland!' Although German women 'fundamentally love peace, one must have a will and a word that have value and effect, so that the world does not trample on a country and a land that is called upon in itself and in its essence to be the healing of the world!'

Next followed a rant against the Social Democrats and modern views of contraception and medical health:

As a German woman, I would like to say one more thing about social democracy. Shouldn't they be ashamed to lecture us in such a shameless way about marriage and birth, to write newspaper articles that cause a decent woman to blush when she reads or hears such things. Recently a doctor, who might have deserved another good German name, delivered on behalf of the [Social Democratic] Party a completely shameless lecture on topics whose names I don't even want to write down. He said, after venting his opinions in the most vulgar detail, that anyone who was embarrassed should leave the lecture hall. And the newspaper boasted that no one had left, and it's true that in an assembly of the despised Nazis such a speaker would certainly not have discussed such a subject, and if he had, a storm of indignation would have prompted him to leave the hall. It is not enough that we have been driven financially into the ground, now they are trying to destroy us intellectually and morally as well. Our women used to be healthier than they are today, without instruction in such matters. Little children and happiness and bliss in a family. See to it that Germany's men have bread and work again, then Germany will need no contraceptive measures for births. Indicting false thinking on this problem are the *countless* women who today fill the waiting rooms of gynaecologists. In these ideas as well a true, honourable German woman cannot possibly adhere to Social Democracy. Marriage, love and motherhood are things that one feels and about which one hardly ever speaks, or at least only in such a way as to keep these things sacred for oneself. My grandmother had fourteen children and has up to now never needed a gynaecologist.

Germany, woman must go back to the hearth, man must go back to work to earn a living, and motherhood must become sacred! Hail!

The following pages, which were actually the last ones, explained once again Walter's deeply felt wishes – and the occasion and form of her letter:

I have written these pages for you, Adolf Hitler, in order to inform you about the feelings and thoughts of a German woman, and also to say, let woman take part in your work, her part. The Social Democrats accuse the Nazi Party of wanting to exclude women completely from their work. That should not and must not be true. We used to have a National Mother who as a mother took care of the Fatherland in matters that concern only women, only the maternal. Woman can no more be excluded from the national economy than from the home. But precisely the fact that the Social Democratic leadership found no substitute for this National Mother and her care, has in recent years brought hardships, both mental and moral, to all of us. Leader Adolf Hitler, do not forget that, because an army of women with an inner love of the Fatherland and energy stands behind you. Allow them to take part in your work for a new Fatherland!

I still have a great Christmas request in mind, look at the Cross on the roof. It is the order of the Knights Hospitaller, composed of two swastikas. Deep, deep meaning lies in this sign and its influence. It always appears in times of the greatest need. Give this sign of collaboration to German women as a New Year's gift. For men, the battle, the swastika. For women the Cross, the sign of love and care. I once read in one of your speeches, Adolf Hitler, your answer to the question why you gave the swastika sign to the movement. We are not yet worthy, you said, of bearing the Christian Cross as a symbol. These words made a deep impression on me. What you said was only too right, but give German women the Cross nonetheless, this Cross composed of the two swastikas of battle. We want to put our all into love and care, in order to become worthy of this Cross. Hail!

However, I want to pray, because I believe our prayers are heard, that God, who has called you to lead a people out of the night into the light, might grant you strength, health, and wisdom in order to complete your work. Hail!

And now, Adolf Hitler, leader of the German freedom movement, if you are missing a woman in a place of action and care, you must call on me, I am ready. What do father, mother, the parents' house matter when the Fatherland calls. I would have achieved my highest life goal and innermost wish if I were allowed to serve the so beloved Fatherland. Hail! Adolf Hitler Hail!

Your Elsa Walter
born in Karlsruhe in Baden
6 September 1898
Christmas 1930

What kind of work Elsa Walter did during the first phase of the Nazi regime we do not know. In 1940 she became a high Party official in the Baden district. A little later she was recorded as working in Colmar in Alsace, an area annexed from France. Her last recorded employment is indicated on her Nazi Party file card as a staff member of the district NS Women's League in Posen, in the Wartheland district, which had been annexed to the German Reich from Poland.

Beyond demonstrating a clear internalization among supporters of the National Socialists' views on issues including women's emancipation, unemployment, and the Jewish question, Elsa Walter's letter reveals Hitler's developing role as both confidant and saviour. She believed in him, and saw him as called by God. But she also wanted to help him better understand women's feelings. The degree to which Walter was representative of the 'average woman' is up for debate, but certainly her wishes and hopes for a brighter future, as well as her fears of the moral decline of the Republic and the destruction of the middle classes by the Jews, were shared by increasing numbers of Germans.

3

WISHES FOR THE NEW YEAR

As the Depression worsened in 1931, support for the Nazi Party and the popularity of Hitler personally grew. For Christmas 1931 Hitler received numerous cards wishing him the best; they came from individuals and whole groups of government employees and members of the Stormtroopers. Several of these showed a winter landscape with the rising sun, only the artist had put a swastika in the place of the sun.

The Christmas greetings sent by a women's group from Vollmerhausen in the Rhineland are typical:

The Women's League of the Dieringhausen-Vollmerhausen local group offer the Leader of our wonderful movement their sincere greetings for Christmas, the festival in commemoration of the German family. We German women faithfully follow the banner of the swastika. It will lead us – out of the dark onward and upward and through.

Hail!
On behalf of the women's league
of the Dieringhausen-Vollmerhausen local group
the leader
Mrs Elisabeth Kritzler

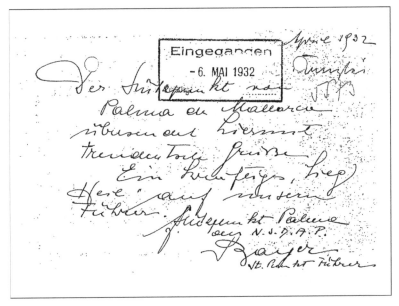

The Nazi Party's base on Mallorca congratulated Hitler on his birthday in 1932 with an energetic 'Sieg Heil!' Postcards showing landscapes or cities with a rising swastika-sun were common. Obviously the local Party organizations used them as propaganda.

Source: RGWA (Moscow)

High-ranking Party officials often sent two telegrams, one on Christmas Eve, the other on New Year's Eve. One such telegram was sent by Joseph Goebbels, one of Hitler's closest associates, who had joined the Party in 1924 and was a fervent anti-Semite. After the Nazi seizure of power Goebbels would become the Minister of Propaganda, but at this time he was the District Leader (*Gauleiter*) of Berlin. He sent the following telegram on 31 December 1931 at 10:45 a.m.:

To our beloved and revered Leader for the decisive year 1932 we wish you health energy insight and strong warm heart and cool head and luck and iron nerves in all storms and dangers victory will be ours

GREATER BERLIN DISTRICT
YOURS, GOEBBELS

Goebbels was not the only one who predicted that 1932 would be the year of victory for the Nazi Party. From Quezaltenango in Guatemala came the following greetings card:

A very happy and victorious '1932' is wished to you and your movement by a German anti-Semite living abroad.

Josef Dietz, Jr

Anna Fröhlich of Rostock in northeastern Germany sent a postcard with a poem by Friedrich Schreiber called 'to the Leader', which included the line 'we love you and your brown locks'. On it she had written:

Very esteemed Mr Hitler!

We elderly retirees are all supporters of the swastika and stand resolutely behind you. We sincerely ask you to take care of us; things are not going well for us.

We heartily wish you good luck and victory all down the line in the coming year!

With the greatest respect
Mrs Anna Fröhlich

Karl Reiff, the leader of the Nazi Party local group of Letschin in Brandenburg [today on the German-Polish border], put his New Year's wish in the form of a poem that he sent to his 'beloved Leader Adolf Hitler' on 27 December 1931:

My wish!

A new year stands again before the gates.
A new year rises up out of the future.
Will Germany finally be reborn?
Will all Germany finally wake up?
We have endured endless hardship,
Unbearably hard, such as no people ever has.
What we suffered in days gone by,
Brought us desperately close to death.
But let us bravely put our hopes in the future,
For God does not abandon true Germans.
Heaven remains always open to the brave,
The light of victory winks to the bold.
They have laughed at us and mocked us.
Many thousands have they killed and wounded,
banded together in strong superior force.
They have oppressed us with deception and lies.
But the sun of victory is already beginning to shine
on the horizon to dispel the dark.
The storm is still growing but the joy of freedom
is already moving into our hearts in anticipation.
The time is near for Germany to be free again.
And so is the day that binds people together,
And puts an end to Red jugglery.
Roaring, rising through all German lands
A single mighty cry of longing!
Help us, Hitler, escape all hostile bonds!
Help us, and make us free again!

A local group in Greiffenberg, a town in Pomerania in what is now far eastern Germany, declared its loyalty unto the death and at the same time its confidence in victory.

To the national leadership

The Greiffenberg . . . local group takes the liberty of expressing to the national leadership of the Nazi Party its most sincere good wishes for the new year. A year of battle lies behind us, and even if the new year brings more hard struggles, we will go into battle with fresh spirit and unshaken confidence in victory, fearing neither death nor wounds.

We hereby renew our pledge of inalterable fidelity and devotion unto the death to our leader Adolf Hitler. May the new year bring us the final victory!

> *In unchanging loyalty*
> *Hail to our Leader*
> *Local group leader*
> *Hans Borrhart*
> *Secretary*
> *Erich Hammermanns*
> *Business manager*
> *Kohlhepp*

On 29 December 1931, the Stormtrooper Lorenz Kircheis from Brand-Erbisdorf, in the Ore Mountains on the German-Czech border, offered new year wishes to a man he considered the 'supreme Leader' and 'saviour' not only of 'our German nation', but 'of the whole world'.

A group of girls from western Germany also lauded Hitler. On their behalf, Marga P. wrote:

To you, the greatest leader of the greatest German freedom movement of all time, the German girls of the Rhineland send their greetings. In the firm belief in you and the awakening national feeling of the whole German people, we believe in the liberation year 1932. To our great liberating leader a German salute and an energetic 'Hail!'

> *Marga P.*

Forty Nazi Party workers at the financial office in Stettin sent greetings by anonymous telegram, and the writer Heliodor Harald Löschnigg, author of *The Decline of the West or German Cultural Renewal*, sent the brief wish: 'Hail Victory 1932'. A further telegram came on 1 January 1932 from Diessen am Ammersee, in Bavaria:

TO OUR LEADER A PLEDGE OF LOYALTY UNTO DEATH AND SINCEREST HAIL GREETINGS FOR 1932.

DOERFFLER

A few days later, greetings came in from Hitler's favourite hotel in Thuringia:

A happy and healthy new year is wished you by

The Elephant
in Weimar

4

RAGE AND HOPE

Despite the good wishes of Party members, 1932 was not yet the expected year of victory. But the Nazi Party did continue to make electoral gains. In the elections held on 24 April 1932, the Nazi Party was the strongest or second strongest party in several of Germany's federal states. In Anhalt it was entrusted with forming the government. In Bavaria, the parties associated with religious denominations won a small majority. In Prussia, the largest of the German states, the elections resulted in a draw. From Lauban in Silesia, on 25 April 1932, came congratulatory greetings from a government official who began his letter with the motto 'Hail Victory':

Dear Mr Hitler!

A National Socialist and his family send you, esteemed Leader, heartiest congratulations on yesterday's election victory. When years ago I chose Simbach am Inn as my residence, I was able to say that from Braunau on the Inn had come a man to whom the German people had entrusted themselves. [Simbach on the Inn is a town on the Inn River in Bavaria. The town of Braunau on the Inn lies on the opposite side of the river, in Austria, and was the town in which Hitler was born in 1889]. Your achievements tower over those of Hindenburg! In fact Mr

Hitler, we have fought and suffered so much, we have done it willingly, with love, warm love for you, our Leader, our popularly developed Saviour from this slavery. *But*, Mr Hitler, we have not bled and given our lives for a National Socialist leadership that wants to collaborate again with our former enemy. That is not why Horst Wessel and others lie in their graves!!! [Horst Wessel was an early Nazi activist who became a hero and martyr to the movement after he was shot in the face and killed – supposedly by communists – in 1930.] We want you to free us completely from those who have up to now brought us into hardship and poverty. We don't want to hear anything more about the government, we want only

ADOLF HITLER

as our leader, as the sole strong hand, as dictator.

We want Adolf Hitler, who promised to remove these bigwigs from their positions, to immediately get rid of the priests who practise politics. We want Adolf Hitler, who never surrenders and who never makes concessions or engages in negotiations with former enemies who cast dirt and aspersions on our beloved Leader. We want to see the rise and liberation of Germany soon, and not years from now. We give our lives for this goal and for our Leader! We will never leave Adolf Hitler in the lurch, because otherwise it won't be possible to win. We do not yet have the power for our Leader. Mussolini is strong, Hitler should be still stronger and more rigorous. We fighters wish that and want to be freed from Jewish business. We shall have won only when we have achieved that.

We are ready and willing to march for our Leader Adolf Hitler and his idea! We have waited for our saviour for thirteen years [since the defeat of Germany in the First World War and the signing of the Versailles Treaty], and that is long enough. We have to move forward. We want Adolf Hitler as dictator and not Hindenburg, who stood against the revolt. We do not want an insurrection, which is sensationalistic to many people. We want to win our freedom with a bold surprise attack.

We National Socialists want a prohibition on all the newspapers that have spewed poison against our Leader, the expulsion of all Jews, the removal from office of all community representatives who have persecuted village residents and committed outrageous injustices. We want a prohibition of multiple parties. Punishment for inflation criminals, no salaries, pensions, etc. for deposed ministers.

Adolf Hitler, for whom we give our blood: take the recalcitrant in an iron grip and a strong hand, and fulfil the program with dictatorial will. No negotiating, just action! We trust our Leader, and give him our hearts with every pulse beat!

Hail Hitler!
Save us from enslavement to the internal enemy!
P.F. Beck

On 27 April 1932, Ernst Buchwald, the owner of a market gardening operation, who ran his own tree and rose nurseries as well as a factory for 'unfermented fruit processing' in Cottbus, southeast of Berlin, sent Hitler a crate of fruit juice and an accompanying letter:

I take the liberty of offering my heartiest congratulations to the much revered Leader on such a splendid election success. From the fine book *The Unknown Hitler* [a best seller by Hitler's personal photographer Heinrich Hoffmann, which was published in 1932], I have learned that you lead a vegetarian way of life, and to strengthen you after the hard election campaign, today I have taken the liberty of sending a crate of my factory's fruit juice to your esteemed address, and ask you to accept it.

I hope that Leader will lift a glass in commemoration of Germany's ascent [presumably of juice, given that Hitler did not drink], and sign

With a German salute!
Ernst Buchwald

The letter of thanks from Hitler's private office dates from 20 May 1932 and was written by Albert Bormann. Albert was the brother of the more famous Martin Bormann, who was Reich Leader. Albert had been head of the Hitler Youth in Thuringia from 1929 to 1931, before moving to a job in Hitler's private office. Bormann wrote:

Dear Mr Buchwald,

Mr Hitler thanks you very much for your letter and for the crate of fruit juice you sent. He was very glad to receive it. However, because he is extraordinarily busy it is not possible for him to answer you personally.

With a German salute
Albert Bormann

An openly expressed wish that Hitler would become dictator sent with a crate of fruit juice for the private man and quasi-vegetarian. Both Beck's and Buchwald's letters illustrate the mood that made the success of the Nazi Party possible during this period. The writers were radically belligerent on the one hand, but moderate, polite and middle class, on the other. For them, mainstream politics offered them no solution comparable to that of Nazism.

Now that the Party was more developed and enjoying electoral success, Hitler's office clearly felt it could stop responding to critical questions regarding the Party's programme. Nor did it continue to explain aspects of its program to writers. Ruth Dellmann from Berlin received no answer, because with her apparently naive questions she had put her finger on a point on which the Nazi Party was vulnerable. On 31 May 1932 she wrote:

Dear Mr Hitler,
I take the liberty of asking you a few questions that are important for me and for those around me. We are welfare students and seminarians in a seminar for youth leaders and adhere to National Socialism. Naturally, many well-intentioned attempts are made to get us to abandon this worldview. Although we are able to refute some of the criticisms incorrectly directed against the Party, there are two points on which we ourselves have strong doubts. We would therefore politely ask you for specific information.

Point 1. Population policy in National Socialism: it is said that Nazism seeks an increase in birth rates in the Third Reich.

Question: where are these people later to find a way of earning a living, when today there is unemployment in all large countries with the exception of Russia?

Point 2. The status of woman in the Third Reich: the other side is constantly referring to the disparagement of women's dignity through methods such as Darré describes in his book *New Nobility from Blood and Soil*. [Walter Darré, who was born in Argentina to German parents, and moved to Germany just before the First World War, was an upper group leader in the SS. He was also one of the leading proponents of the blood and soil ideology, which focused on ethnicity as defined by descent (blood) and homeland (soil). The movement championed the connection of individuals to land, and encouraged rural living as the most virtuous way of life.]

However, we also find quite repellent the idea that the females are to be divided up and *into classes* and married on breeding farms, and that Germany's progeny will no longer have its natural origin in the family, but will be raised instead on breeding farms.

If you, very esteemed Mr Hitler, could have information on these two questions sent to us, [both] the great cause and we would thereby be greatly served.

Hail!
Ruth Dellmann

Ironically, in her support for National Socialism, Ruth Dellmann was helping to sabotage her own career goals. It's conceivable that after the Nazis came to power, she would have been forced either to interrupt her training as a social worker, or would have been removed from her position if she had already started work. From 1933 on, under Nazi Party pressure, the number of female students was radically reduced, in line with the Party's belief in traditional gender roles. Her interpretation of the Nazi Party's programme, and especially of the book by the later Reich Minister of Food and Agriculture Walter Darré, was not at all incorrect. It was absolutely the SS's intention to divide women into different classes, and an officer was to be allowed to marry only if Himmler (the Squadron's head) or Hitler gave his permission.

On 7 June 1932, a woman from Wiesbaden in southwest Germany

asked for an explanation of Nazi economic policy, based on her fears of another inflation like that suffered by Germany during the early 1920s:

Dear Mr Hitler!

I became a National Socialist through my three sons. I have already begun to work for the coming election campaign. Today I would like to tell you why many women do not go over to the Nazi Party. [They say:] We cannot vote for Hitler because he is bringing on another period of inflation. It has taken me years to lay away some savings again, and if it should now be lost again, what then? This and similar arguments are made against me. Another woman told me that she had saved a few hundred marks for her sick son, and has to vote for the man who will try to preserve the savings of widows and orphans. I would advise you to see to it that in all electoral speeches it is said that people with small savings will not lose what they have put by when you take office.

Then our work will be easier, because what the public fears in the coming time is inflation.

With a 'Hail Hitler'
Mrs Luise Cramer

The official who read Kramer's letter wrote on it with a green pencil: 'lie about inflation'. She received a letter from Albert Bormann:

Dear Mrs Cramer!

Your letter of the 7 June was received by Mr Hitler. The lie that the Nazi Party intends to produce inflation or that the latter would result from its taking power, was already systematically spread during the last election campaign by its opponents, and in fact precisely by the parties that are themselves partly to blame for the last inflation.

I am enclosing a small brochure stating our position regarding this lie.

With a German salute
Albert Bormann

Something entirely different moved the writer Otto Siegfried Diehl, who on 25 April 1932 entrusted his latest play to Hitler. He had published his first volume of poetry in 1910, and worked primarily as a healer.

Most estimable Mr Hitler!

A German writer takes the liberty of sending you with the deepest respect on the latest great day of victory for the German movement, his recently published play *The Apocalyptic Dragon* as a powerful weapon in the battle against Bolshevism as it was described by still right-thinking men.

The play was performed in several major German theatres, but the slavish turn of mind, the lack of courage of convictions, has at this point not only repressed but also silenced it, because it seeks to arouse misled and dormant minds. And yet this would serve freedom, the liberation of our people from the disgrace of subjection, for which purpose I wrote it.

It would spur me on to see in your recognition a confirmation that the right path has been followed. Regarding me personally, Party Member Dr Frank, attorney-at-law who has known me for years, may be best able to provide information.

With a genuine salute of agreement
with the deepest esteem
Party Member O. Diehl
Writer

Diehl received a reply on 13 May 1932:

Dear Mr Diehl!

Mr Hitler has asked me to express his gratitude to you for sending your play *The Apocalyptic Dragon*. Because he is extraordinarily busy, it is unfortunately not possible for him to answer you personally.

With the German salute
Albert Bormann

Diehl's play was not performed after the Nazis took power, either. Between 1933 and 1945 Diehl published just one book, presumably because his works were insufficiently 'future-directed'. After the Second World War he had more success, publishing primarily esoteric or apocalyptic writings.

The combination of Hitler's growing popularity and his self-styled image as saviour, and the worsening economic situation as a result of the Great Depression, meant that Hitler began to receive an ever-increasing number of requests for loans.

Without exception, these were filed away without being answered. Sometimes the word 'loan' was written on the letters, but for the most part only a red mark signals that the letter was filed without reply. On 23 May 1932, for example, August Dick wrote from Altenglan in the Palatinate, a region in southwest Germany:

Dear Mr Hitler!

Living in need and great hardship, I have decided to turn to you with an urgent request. I was born in Bossenbach [in the Palatinate], and after completing my schooling trained as a tinsmith and plumber, and opened my first shop here in Altenglan in 1923, where I made a good start until, after two years' work, I began to have serious problems. My left knee became inflamed, I underwent six operations in the Kaiserslautern Hospital, and was released after sixteen weeks of treatment and without any income. Naturally the leg remained stiff. In 1927 I had an operation in Homburg [a city in the Saarland, southwest Germany] for an inflamed appendix, and in the autumn of the same year I had an accident during the potato harvest and needed medical treatment again, because my right leg was shattered.

I had no health insurance, and had to bear all the costs myself, for that reason I was forced to borrow 800 marks from the bank. And now since there is no more work and often no money for food, I can no longer go on living this way. When in February of this year the local Nazi Party group was established here, I regained hope that better times were coming and despite my stiff leg I joined the Stormtroopers. Since most of my customers belong to opposition parties, my income has become still smaller, because most of them avoid my shop. Thus I know of no other solution than to turn to you with a request for support.

In the hope that you will respond to my request,
signed most devotedly with
Hail and Victory!
August Dick and spouse and child

[P.S.] The typewriter on which I wrote this letter has been pawned. I was in Kreuznach when you spoke there, and on that day I travelled 120 km by bicycle because I had no money for the train.

The desperate situation of women and the growth of the number of electoral votes for communists also inspired Emmy Hoffmann from a petty-bourgeois neighbourhood in Dresden to write her letter to Hitler. She also wished to inform her Leader of popular opinion. She wrote to the Party office on 2 August 1932:

Dear Mr Hitler!

I send you my heartiest congratulations on the electoral success of the National Socialist movement, which I have joined.

The growing number of Communist votes has its cause in the recent deductions from the support payments to the unemployed; I would like to tell you about an experience that a friend of mine, a wet nurse, had shortly before the election. As she crossed the street in her nurse's uniform one morning, an elderly, poor woman approached her, accompanied by three children. The woman asked for help. She was a widow, her husband having died of lung cancer. She had a welfare payment of 9.60 marks per week to live on and said that after paying her rent on Sunday the money was already spent. Then she went door-to-door with her children to beg at least the most necessary nourishment. She had already tried to commit suicide once, by lying down with the children and turning on the gas cap. But the little girl stood up again and said: 'but mother, I still want to grow up!' Then she lost the courage to carry out her plan. She concluded: 'in Russia it is still possible for poor people to live, only in Germany no one takes care of us!' – Such people vote Communist.

I know from my own experience that widows and orphans in wealthy, pre-war Germany were not better off than they are today. My father was a Prussian official, and was station assistant when he died in 1894, and up until the period of inflation my mother received a monthly widow's payment of 18 marks, from which rent and all other living costs had to be wrung. There is no need to describe the circumstances under which we two children grew up with much hunger and deprivation, although my mother did everything she could to earn some money herself by working at home, renting out rooms, and so forth.

The state is going under because it allows mothers to go under, and the men who are governing today are no more capable than those of the pre-war period. From you, dear Mr Hitler, German women expect a better future.

Ask God's help, that you might succeed in justifying the trust of millions, and through the grace of the Almighty you will be granted a complete victory.

> *With the heartiest good wishes for your work you are greeted by*
> *Emmy Hoffmann*

Emmy Hoffmann received no reply.

Unlike poor August Dick and Emmy Hoffmann's unfortunate friend, Hitler was enjoying financial success. As the publisher Franz Eher and sons in Munich reported to him on 24 May 1932, his growing popularity had transformed his once obscure political treatise *My Struggle* into a bestseller:

Dear Mr Hitler!

Between the beginning of this year and 21 May we have been able to sell a total of 29,385 copies of your work. Therefore we are crediting you with a payment of 21,157.20 marks in accord with the enclosed honorarium statement.

> *With a German salute*
> *your most devoted*
> *Amann*

By the end of the year, 124,000 copies had been sold, meaning that Hitler earned more than 4,000 marks per month. A skilled industrial worker during this time was lucky to earn 200 marks per month. Many such workers were unable to find work at this time, as a result of the Great Depression.

Hitler could have made still more money if he had followed the recommendation of the owner of a printing office in Neustadt in Saxony. On 27 May 1932 he made Hitler the following offer:

Dear Mr Hitler,

As an old, loyal, and long-time supporter, I hope I may make a request to the future father of our country. I would like to put a *Hitler cigarette* and a *Hitler cigar* on the German market, and to that end I would like to politely ask Mr Hitler for exclusive permission or the *exclusive right* to do so. I would then apply to have these cigarettes and cigars *legally protected* under this name. In the expectation that Mr Hitler will graciously grant my wish I remain, awaiting a cherished reply, and with special esteem

Fritz Dittrich
Printing office owner

The reply sent on 2 June 1932 was negative.

Dear Mr Dittrich,

Your letter of 27 May was received by Mr Hitler. However, the permission you ask for can unfortunately not be granted, because in principle the Leader does not wish his name to be used in commercial propaganda. I regret that I cannot give you a more positive reply.

With a German salute!
Albert Bormann

Hitler's personal distaste for smoking may have also played a role here. In a further letter from 10 June 1932 Dittrich said that he was 'very' sorry that 'Mr Hitler has refused' his 'request', and mentioned that in England 'Prince of Wales' and 'Lord so-and-so' were very successful brands of cigarettes. 'Despite this great disappointment, nothing will prevent me from continuing to be an avid supporter of our Mr Hitler who is respected everywhere . . .'

With the increasing number of members and the increased popularity of *My Struggle*, the foundational myths of the Nazi Party also became public property. In *My Struggle*, Hitler had written that the number on his provisional Nazi Party membership card was 7. This was untrue. Hitler was the 55th member, and his number was 555, because membership numbers began at 500. But Hitler's rewriting of his own personal history became the accepted truth. Some Party members from Vienna referred in their letter of 20 June 1932 to the magic number:

Esteemed Leader!
7
This remarkable number, which already has so often played an important role in the development of the Nazi Party – this number has now become significant as well for the employees of Kathreiner's Malt Coffee Factory, Vienna.

Until recently there was only one registered Party member among the employees. Today there are already seven. These seven have today decided to wage a battle, with all the passion and the glowing, fanatical zeal that pulses through our whole movement, against Marxist tendencies among the employees and for deliberate action on behalf of a German, and even for a National Socialist German view.

They promise to wage the battle with resolution and unconditional consistency; they promise that they will never for a moment forget the Leader's example, and they promise that they will not rest for an instant until they are able to report to you that there are seventy National Socialists among Kathreiner's employees.

> *With this in mind we greet you with our*
> *heartiest salute*
> *[7 signatures follow]*

The number '7' also featured in a poem of homage sent in the summer
of 1932 by thirteen-year-old Armin H. from Neuenhagen near Berlin.
His poem reads:

Germany's Brown Freedom Movement

About twelve years ago
There were once seven men.
They had understood that
Germany could not exist,
If bigwigs and Jews
took turns in office,
So they fought hard and stubbornly.
They didn't want to lose freedom and Prussia.
With Adolf Hitler, the first guard,
The National Socialist Party began.
Out of love for the Fatherland and sacred zeal
a movement was born,
that, undeterred by great dangers,
Strove forward, to move the German spirit.
In the swastika they sought new courage,
to fight on for the Fatherland.
And after years there were
already millions
who for the Fatherland's freedom
come together in the brown unity.
From the very start one saw discipline,
that had never been seen in the system parties.
But soon the brown shirt
was no longer foreign to the bigwigs.
They often had the power to prohibit the SA.
But these trivialities could not stop Hitler;
and in a short time
he will be ready.
Then comes the last judgement
for the Jews and the rabble.
Then the system will be toppled,

salaries cut no more.
The slave parties will flee.
Hail Hitler!!!
You will win!
To the great Leader of the brown army!
To you, you great fighter, dedicated
by the Hitler youth

Other members of the Hitler Youth, a paramilitary organization estab-lished in 1926 for individuals between the ages of ten and eighteen, sent Hitler a different form of homage, in the form of birthday letters. From the re-foundation of the Nazi Party in 1925 onwards, Hitler's birthday had been celebrated within the context of the glorification of Hitler as charismatic Leader. As Hitler's popularity grew, the number of personal birthday cards and presents he received increased. On 16 April 1932, for example, Hitler received birthday greetings and a small gift from some members of the female branch of the Hitler Youth, the League of German Girls, in Salzwedel, northern Germany:

Councillor Adolf Hitler,

We send our esteemed, beloved Leader Adolf Hitler our heartiest wishes for success and happiness. As a sign of our gratitude and rever-ence we are sending a small sample of Salzwedel layer cake. We the undersigned girls of the Hitler Youth would be very happy to receive a picture of our Leader with his signature.

With heartiest greetings, Hail!
Sophie Beyreiss
Hilde D.
Henni K.
Martha T.
Anneliese Sch.
Martha R.
Hilde H.

Albert Bormann replied on 4 May 1932.

Dear Miss Beyreiss!

Mr Hitler has taken great pleasure in the good wishes and the Salzwedel layer cake the Hitler Girls sent him, and desires to express his warmest thanks.

Unfortunately, your wish for a picture of the Leader with his hand-written signature cannot be granted. Because he receives many hundreds of such requests, the Leader now gives his picture only to very old, venerable fighters for the movement. I am sorry not to be able to give you a different answer. Perhaps it will be possible to fulfil your wish at some later, calmer point in time.

With a German salute
Albert Bormann

Hitler also began to receive letters expressing concern for his safety. One such letter came from Ruth Hübner, who lived in Nieder-Petersdorf in the Giant Mountains (in German, the Riesengebirge and in Polish the Krkonoše), which are located on the border between what is now the Czech Republic and Poland. In the summer of 1932, she wrote:

A Salute in Greeting!
Dear very esteemed Mr Hitler!

Please do not be surprised that you are receiving a letter from a person unknown to you. But my fear and concern about your life are increasing daily.

Please, please be careful.

Make all your trips by air, so that the murderous rabble cannot get their hands on you. They intend to try to drive you into exile between 12 and 14 August. In my opinion, it is not the communists, but could be those who arranged for Schiller's death. You probably already know the story.

Whom I mean by that, you will best be able yourself to determine. In any case keep yourself safe, and don't go anywhere without your guards. Although I know that *God* is with you and has up to this point guided you wonderfully, my dear Mr Hitler. For wherever God Almighty holds his hand over someone, the murderous rabble can do you no harm. The savage hordes are struck blind. Just think, here they put up posters before the election that said: Hail [heal] Hitler of madness. It is not really possible, as a result, to clean out the government gently. The best way would be to put a cage in front of the doors with tigers, lions; but they must not have been fed for three days so that they will attack hungrily. Because if the animals are not hungry enough, they will forego their prey; as I can hardly believe that even a healthy beast's stomach would be able to digest such poisonous flesh.

Thus my good, noble Mr Hitler – finally rush in with thunder and lightning.

Putting your life in the hands of the Almighty with the prayer that he guide you, our true Leader, I will now close.

Your true supporter
Ruth Hübner

Hail! Hail! Hail!
Now once again it is in God's hands.

If people thought that a 'cleaning out' of the government required its members to be thrown to tigers and lions, that suggests in retrospect and astonishing radicalization of some of the population. In the Reichstag elections to which Ruth Hübner refers, which were held on 31 July 1932, the Nazi Party achieved an astonishingly good result. It received 37 per cent of the vote. The Social Democrats got only 21.6 per cent, and the communists 14.4 per cent. The middle-class parties in the centre were nearly wiped out. Their voters had gone over to the Nazi Party.

Many people voted for Hitler because they hoped, like Ruth Hübner, that he would radically change the government, and rescue Germany from its economic, political, and international crises. For many people, the new national departure they longed for was obviously identified with Hitler personally.

But for others, a vote for the Nazi Party seems either to have been one of protest or one from which they quickly recoiled because

„Heil zum Gruß!" — 204 —

Sehr geehrter lieber Herr Hitler!

Bitte wundern Sie sich nicht, wenn
Sie von einer Ihnen unbekannten
Person einen Brief erhalten.
Aber die Angst und Unruhe um
Ihr Leben steigern sich von Tag
zu Tag immer mehr in mir.
Bitte, bitte, sind Sie vorsichtig.
Machen Sie alle Fahrten im
Flugzeug damit Sie für das
rote Mordgesindel nicht zu packen
sind. Man hat vor Sie zwischen
dem 12–14 August in eine Ver-
bannung zu schleppen. Meines
Erachtens nach kämen nicht
nur Kommunisten in Frage,
sondern bin ich der Meinung,
dass es diese sein können, die
für Schillers Heimgang besorgt
haben. Die Geschichte dürfte

In the summer of 1932 a Silesian woman supporter of Hitler warned against being
carried off into 'exile'. She meant that the Freemasons, who had already murdered
Schiller, might be involved. The line drawn in coloured pencil across the upper left
corner means 'file away', without further comment.

Source: RGWA (Moscow)

of the violence that they realized was inherent in the Party. Albert Bormann noted in a survey of public opinion taken later that year that the Stormtroopers' terrorism was 'confusing middle-class groups'. Whatever the reason behind it, the Nazis were unable to maintain their momentum, and in a second round of parliamentary elections in November 1932, their share of the vote declined to 33 per cent. In early December, local elections in Thuringia saw the Party slip even further. These later elections had much lower turnout, and many who had voted for the Nazis in the summer returned to voting for the more mainstream German Nationalists. Whether this electoral decline would have continued is of course impossible to determine.

Regardless, what the Nazi success in the summer of 1932 demonstrated was the failure of mainstream parties to offer solutions to Germany's economic woes, as well as the radicalization of the German population more generally, with voters moving to the extremes on both the left and the right of the political spectrum. At the end of the year the Nazi Party had reconciled itself to the fact that 1932 had not been the expected year of victory. What mattered most to them was winning middle-of-the-road voters for the Nazi Party or else entering into some kind of coalition government without new elections.

Part II

Worship, Protest and Consent: 1933–1938

5

RECOGNITION, GRATITUDE AND
VENERATION

After the July 1932 elections, the Nazi Party had 203 seats in the Reichstag, more than any other party. Despite this, they did not hold enough to have a majority. Thus, the Reichstag faced a political impasse. The calling of another election in November 1932 provided the same result, although, as we have seen, the percentage of the vote won by the Nazis dropped. President Hindenburg, who had only run for re-election in 1932 because he was seen to be the only person who could prevent Hitler from winning, did not want to grant Hitler any real executive power. But the 84-year-old was out-manoeuvred by chancellor Franz von Papen, his successor Kurt von Schleicher, and press magnate Alfred Hugenberg, who together convinced him that he should name Hitler Reich Chancellor. In giving Hitler a cabinet with only a minority of Nazi Party ministers, and by serving as Vice Chancellor himself, Papen thought that Hitler could be controlled. He thought wrong.

Hitler's supporters viewed Hitler's appointment as Chancellor of the Reich on 30 January 1933 as the victory they had been waiting for. The Stormtroopers organized a torchlight parade and celebrated. Although they were 'surrounded' by conservative ministers in the cabinet, it was now 'their' Leader who determined Germany's political course.

The flood of mail from the population now rose so fast that Hitler's office had to hire four additional employees. Every improvement in the social situation, no matter how small, was honoured with effusive letters of thanks and small gifts. In the first weeks of his chancellorship, Hitler was already being inundated with saints' pictures, embroidered handkerchiefs, ties, and stockings. While one German sent him hand-sown Edelweiss flowers, another offered to find him a good watchdog.

While he was enjoying the flood of well-wishes, Hitler began to tear apart the political system that the Weimar Republic had put into place fourteen years earlier. Incredibly, Hindenburg made this possible, by granting a succession of Presidential Decrees. On 4 February, the new government gained the authority to imprison citizens for up to three months if they were accused of breaching the peace. On 28 February, after an arson attack on the Reichstag building the previous evening by ex-communist Marinus van der Lubbe, Hitler was granted vast emergency powers. The Order of the Reich President for the Protection of People and State invoked Article 48 of the Weimar Constitution, an emergency decree which allowed the President to take any necessary steps to maintain public safety. It enabled the suspension of most civil liberties, including the freedoms of the person, expression, and the press, as well as the right of free assembly and the secrecy of post and telephone.

It also granted the Nazis the power to arrest virtually anyone who could be considered a political opponent and detain them without trial. The Nazi Party used the spectre of a potential Communist takeover to arrest around 10,000 people, most of them Communists. This was the decisive action that many Nazi supporters had been waiting for. In gigantic staged rallies Hitler announced a programme to increase employment and promised a 'new national departure'. In the parliamentary elections held on 5 March 1933, his party received 17.28 million votes, that is, 43.9 per cent.

Just one day later, on 6 March 1933, Ernst Keppler from Schönaich in Baden-Württemberg, southern Germany, sent Hitler two poems (which unfortunately did not translate well), with the hope that they 'would give' him 'a little joy in' his 'so difficult and so demanding office!'

With the deepest reverence
Ernst Keppler

The next day Hitler, who was now also a member of parliament, received a congratulatory letter from its director:

Dear Mr Chancellor,

According to the reports in the newspapers, you have been elected a member of the German Parliament, and therefore in accord with Paragraph 1 of the law of 15 December 1930 regarding the compensation of members of the Parliament, during your membership in the Parliament you have the right to travel free of charge on all German railways. A similar perquisite is provided by the National Postal Service on all post-bus lines. To prepare tickets, two photographs (passport size) are required, and I respectfully request that you send them promptly to the Parliament office. The tickets will then be sent to you directly from here. In addition, please send a photograph, which may be returned to you if you wish, for the official Parliament handbook, along with a few personal details on the enclosed form. I enclose an envelope and a few biographical details from earlier handbooks to guide you. I take the further liberty of noting that for the handbook we would prefer a good photograph on glossy paper (celluloid paper), not larger than 10 x 15 cm and if possible without a hat. Good reproductions cannot be produced from pictures on matte paper, especially since only a little time remains to make the handbook available.

I attach a copy of the rules of order for the Parliament and a guide to the Parliament building. With exceptional respect, I have the honour of being

your devoted
Galle

These instructions were soon irrelevant. Three weeks later, on 24 March 1933, Hindenburg signed the Enabling Act, which granted Hitler the power to make laws without needing parliamentary approval. In other words, it made him dictator – in just under two months from his appointment as Chancellor.

Unsurprisingly, the Nazis successful seizure of power during the first months of 1933 meant that Hitler's birthday in April 1933 was celebrated on a much larger scale than ever before.

Fritz Wiedemann, who had first met Hitler during the First World War, and who was serving temporarily as Hitler's adjutant before falling out with Hitler in 1938, recalled the great hall in the Chancellor's Office, in which the birthday gifts were displayed, as a 'huge department store'. Everything was there, Wiedemann said, 'from a valuable oil painting that some industrialist had sent him to a pair of stockings that some old lady had given'. Wiedemann remembered chocolate cakes with 'Hail Our Leader' written on them in white frosting and a home-made model of a naval cruiser flying flags with swastikas. According to him, there were always about a thousand gifts, a 'moving expression of the veneration and love felt by the broad mass of the people for this man'.

To be sure, some of this gift-giving was an expression of people's naive veneration. But it was also specifically encouraged by the Nazi leadership, who worked hard to present Hitler as the saviour of the nation and to foster the population's total trust in the person and institution of the Leader. The well-known pictures of endless parades and happily smiling children presenting flowers did not just happen but were instead set up by experienced directors, cameramen, and photographers.

In developing Hitler's birthday as a national event, the Nazi propagandists built on the tradition of the Kaiser's birthday, which since 1914 had been celebrated with parades and popular celebrations. If Hitler's splendour were to outshine that of the Kaiser – if only in order to discredit monarchist tendencies as old-fashioned and superseded – then the celebrations had to be just as public and even more lavish.

As head of Hitler's private office, Albert Bormann wrote to all those who had sent their congratulations thanking them on behalf of Hitler 'for the veneration that you have shown for the Leader'. Hitler himself signed a few of these letters, but only if the correspondent was considered 'important'.

The playwright Hanns Johst, who had joined the Nazi Party in 1932, was one of the individuals who received a personal reply from Hitler. On 8 April 1933 he sent Hitler his birthday gift, the printed version of his play *Schlageter*. In it he dramatized the life of Albert Leo Schlageter, who had been a member of the German Free Corps, a right-wing volunteer paramilitary group, and worked to sabotage the French occupying forces in the Ruhr, before being arrested and executed by the French in 1923. Right-wing nationalists used his death and status as a martyr to promote their interests, using it as an example of French brutality and the incompetence of the central government. Schlageter achieved hero status during the Third Reich. In the play Schlageter's last words were as follows:

Germany!
A last word! A wish! Command!
Germany!!!
Awaken! Catch fire!
Flare up! Burn tremendously!

(Pointing to the French soldiers:)

And them . . . Fire!

In the accompanying letter, Johst wrote:

Esteemed Mr Chancellor,

I take the liberty of sending you today in book form the work that I have dedicated to our beloved Leader. The consummation of this gift would be achieved if you, esteemed Mr Chancellor, were to attend the first performance, which will take place on your birthday. I sign with the expression of unalterable devotion

Hanns Johst

Hitler replied on 25 April 1933:

Dear Mr Johst!

I send you my belated thanks for the gift of the handsome volume with your Schlageter play, which you dedicated to me.

Unfortunately, it was not possible for me to attend the first performance of this play. However, I am delighted that, as was reported to me, the performance was a great success for you.

With a German salute!
Adolf Hitler

For Johst, the leading figure in the National Socialist 'hero-worship theatre', involvement with the Nazi Party paid off. He became president of the German Academy for Poetry and the president of the German Writers' Union, and also a senator and state councillor. He regularly received highly endowed prizes and was almost overwhelmed with honours. Henceforth he put his creativity exclusively in the service of the Nazi Party and produced dozens of texts 'full of songs of praise and love for his homeland'. In 1945 he was imprisoned in Bavaria and in 1949 de-Nazified as a 'fellow traveller', an individual who sympathized or cooperated with the Nazi regime, without being heavily involved in it.

Johst was more than a fellow traveller. As an SS brigade leader he accompanied Heinrich Himmler on trips through Eastern Europe and then wrote tendentious reports on their journeys. In 1938 he travelled with Hitler to Austria and thanked him 'with all his heart' for this 'exhilarating' experience. When Johst appealed against his categorization as fellow traveller and his fine of 500 marks, the appeals court categorized him as the more serious 'Major Offender', and sentenced him to three and half years in a labour camp. He was also prevented from publishing his writings for ten years.

Most birthday offerings were rather more simple than Johst's. One of these more mundane expressions of good will came from from four deaconesses in Wuppertal in western Germany on 11 April 1933:

Dear esteemed, beloved Mr Reich Chancellor!

With true German hearts we would like to greet you on your birthday and wish you with all our hearts God's blessing, much energy, joy, and wisdom.

We know that you bear a great deal of work and care on your

shoulders, but we also know that you are pursuing your work self-lessly and for everyone in our beloved Fatherland with a solid German thoroughness.

Therefore we are eager to thank you very sincerely, dear Mr Reich Chancellor, your loyal ministers and aides, and we pray that God may keep you energetic and happy for a long time, so that our poor people become once again a noble German people.

> *With a true German salute*
> *we commemorate you,*
> *your grateful*
> *Augusta Obergössel, Deaconess*
> *Friede Haede, Deaconess*
> *Wilhelmine Burggraf, Deaconess*
> *Martha Schmidt, Deaconess*

Similar good wishes were sent by the nurses and Party members of Roth bei Nürnberg hospital in Bavaria. They congratulated Hitler 'from the bottom of' their 'hearts' on the day 'on which God brought' him 'into being'. A wood sculpture entitled 'Hunter' was sent by J. Helmensdorfer from Munich. He had seen Hitler in Munich on 19 April and in his letter he extolled his 'inexpressible happiness on being able to see my Leader up close for the first time'. For the rest of his life, this moment would be 'unforgettable'. Someone wrote in the margin of the letter, 'very nice'. Perhaps this is why he received a personal letter of thanks from Hitler on 10 May 1933:

Dear Mr Helmensdorfer!

I should not like to fail to give you and your family, even belatedly, my heartfelt thanks for the wonderful wood carving that you sent me for my birthday.

You have given me a very special pleasure.

> *With a German salute*
> *Adolf Hitler*

Birthday greetings were also received from politicians as well as from members of the armed forces. Admiral Eric Raeder had not been a supporter of the Nazi Party, but he endorsed Hitler's plan to rebuild Germany's navy. As an anti-Republican he also supported the Party's abolition of the traditional Republican black-red-and-gold flag as the state symbol. On 19 April 1933 he wrote:

Dear Mr Reich Chancellor!

On the occasion of your birthday I take the liberty of expressing, on behalf of the German Navy and myself, our heartiest good wishes. The navy, together with myself, hope with all our hearts that your work for the rebuilding of our Fatherland will also be crowned in the coming year with the best success.

The navy is sincerely grateful to you that we are once again allowed to sail under the glorious old colours and that you, esteemed Mr Reich Chancellor, are showing such a warm, understanding interest in German sea power. It is prepared to support all your work for Germany with self-sacrificing, enthusiastic devotion.

In this vein I remain, highly esteemed Mr Reich Chancellor,

> *Your sincerely devoted*
> *Raeder*
> *Admiral, Honorary Doctor*

Hitler replied on 10 May 1933:

Dear Mr Admiral!

Among the thousands of letters of good wishes that were received for my birthday, unfortunately yours was not presented to me before today. The good wishes that you sent me personally and on behalf of the German Navy gave me special pleasure. I express to you belatedly my warmest thanks for them.

> *With a German salute*
> *Adolf Hitler*

It is probable that Raeder felt obliged to write to Hitler on his birth-day, using it to demonstrate his loyalty. However, the letter was not in any way official. He used private stationery and wrote by hand, and his letter was filed together with non-official post.

Some private citizens even sent gifts of significant monetary value. When this occurred, the sender received a personally signed letter of thanks, as did a professor from Eisenach in Thuringia, who congratu-lated Hitler on 1 May 1933:

Dear Mr Reich Chancellor!

The iron 'patriot's ring' from 18 October 1813 is still revered by my family. [Presumably it was received in commemoration of fighting against Napoleon in 1812.] I beg you to accept it from me. Today no one else has such a right to own this symbol.

May the radiant sun that shines over the date signify that we are once again moving upwards in successful battle under your leadership!

Prof. Dr Helferich

He was thanked on 3 August:

Dear Mr Professor!

With your gift of the valuable iron patriot's ring from 18 October 1813 you have given me very special joy.

I offer you my warm if belated thanks for it.

With a German salute
Adolf Hitler

Others could not afford to give so freely. Peter Kissel from Gernsheim, a town situated on the Rhine in western Germany, wrote to Hitler on 26 June 1933:

Dear Mr Reich Chancellor!

I am enclosing, Mr Reich Chancellor, a framed picture for you. I intended to send it to you for your birthday, but that was not possible because I designed and produced it myself as an amateur. I am 22 years old and the son of an ordinary railway worker. Including myself we are a family of five, of whom I am the eldest and receive no welfare support, since the threshold set by the labour office is 18 marks [per week], and my father earns 20.50 marks per week. Given my financial difficulties it was not easy for me to make this picture. But for your sake Mr Reich Chancellor, I have saved every penny in order to give you a pleasure, and sign with the most devoted esteem

Peter Kissel
Hail Victory!

An employee at Hitler's office wrote by hand on Kissel's letter: 'thank, send 20 marks'. The reply read:

Dear esteemed Mr Kissel!

The Leader received your letter of 26 June and wishes me to convey his sincere thanks for the picture you sent.

With a German salute
Brückner

The excitement surrounding Hitler after the Nazis' seizure of power was so great that gifts and messages of veneration and support continued to pour in, well after Hitler's birthday.

Mrs C. Klose from Wiesbaden, southwest Germany, offered as a gift a poem she had written, which she wanted to place in newspapers in Berlin, Munich and Wiesbaden:

Adolf Hitler 1933

Everyone claims you,
you give hope, joy, and peace!
Ô, you our salvation!
Burdens and troubles have you many!
But keep your eye on the goal!

Adolf Hitler Hail!
'Hitler exalted!' the whole world calls,
in every heart you are a hero!
We remain loyal to you!
Let his praise ring out here!
More will be achieved,
cheer 'Hitler exalted!' and fight.

The German original, reproduced on the next page, is an acrostic: the first letters of each line spell out ADOLF HITLER.

Hitler's adjutant, Brückner, replied on 19 June 1933:

Dear Mrs Klose!

The Leader sends you his warmest thanks for your letter. However, permission to print your poem can unfortunately not be granted, because the Leader declines on principle the glorification of his person.

This reply is perhaps surprising given the cult of personality that the Nazis sought to cultivate around Hitler. But it is precisely this issue of control that led Hitler to deny the population the opportunity to mythologize their leader. In order to make his persona most effective propaganda-wise, Hitler needed to control its presentation and perception completely. A poem like the one written by Mrs Klose was therefore neither useful nor helpful. She was supposed to receive the Leader myth, not try to help create it.

   That a cult of personality was developing around Hitler is also clear from the many enquiries his office received as to whether he would agree to be godfather to the correspondents' children. Thus Werner M. from Oranienburg near Berlin wrote to Hitler on 10 November 1933:

My Leader!

While yesterday, 9 November, was a day of mourning, it was also a day of spiritual edification, especially because of the influence of your

A d o l f   H i t l e r   1 9 3 3 .

A lle Menschen jubeln Dir zu,

D u gibst Hoffnung, Freud' und Ruh !

O Du unser Heil !

L ast und Mühe hast Du viel !

F est im Auge doch das Ziel !

    Adolf Hitler Heil !

H och Hitler ! Ruft die ganze Welt,

I n allen Herzen bist Du Held !

Treu zu Dir, halten wir !

L asst sein Lob erklingen hier !

E s wird mehr gelingen ,

R uft " Hitler hoch " im Ringen .

When Hitler took power, the stream of enthusiastic letters increased so greatly that the chancelleries could no longer reply to them. Permission to print this eulogy was not granted. Official eulogies were reserved for professional writers registered with the chambers of culture.

Source: RGWA (Moscow)

great speech in Munich [on the tenth anniversary of the Hitler putsch]. On this day, my first child, a strong boy and future Stormtrooper, was born to me, a Stormtrooper and fighter since 1927 and a guard in the Oranienburg concentration camp. [Oranienburg was one of the first camps established by the Nazis after their takeover. It was in the town centre of Oranienburg, just outside Berlin, and was a disused factory. It was later replaced by the Sachsenhausen camp.]

In commemoration of this very important day for us National Socialists, may I ask you, my Leader, to be godfather [to my son] on the day of his baptism, which is still to be determined?

Your feeling of comradeship, my Leader, is already so great that I believe my request is not inappropriate.

Assuring you of my constant love, loyalty, and obedience, I sign with all the highest esteem and a Hail Hitler!

Werner M.

Head adjutant Brückner replied on 20 November 1933 with a form of letter that had by that point become routine.

Dear Party member!

I thank you and confirm the reception of your letter to the Leader of the 10th inst. requesting that the Leader be godfather to your first child.

As much as the Leader is pleased by the honour and adherence that are expressed with requests to serve as godfather, in view of the large number of such requests he is not able to comply with all of them. He has therefore decided to agree to be godfather only in very exceptional cases, that is, in the case of at least the seventh son or the ninth living child. Since these conditions are not met in your case, the Leader begs you to refrain from entering his name as godfather.

He wishes your child the best in his future life.

With a German salute
Brückner

On 22 November 1933, sixteen-year-old Anny M. from Frankfurt am Main expressed her adoration for Hitler in a different way:

Dear Mr Reich Chancellor!

Overleaf I take the liberty of sending you, dear revered Mr Reich Chancellor, a drawing I have made. As I reached my 16th year of life in July of this year, and despite many efforts I have not yet succeeded in finding a position in an office or in sales, I would be very grateful to you, dear revered Mr Reich Chancellor, if you could employ me in a Party office, especially since my father is the sole support for five people. I can make available good recommendations.

With a German salute
Anny M.

Albert Bormann replied on 18 December 1933:

Dear esteemed Miss M.!

I confirm the reception of your letter of 22 November to the Leader. Unfortunately I must inform you that no position in the Party office is available.

With a German salute
Albert Bormann

Teachers certainly helped schoolgirls like Anny M. develop their love of Hitler. A nun, Fridolina Fehringer, a teacher in a Bavarian convent school, was apparently much taken with National Socialism and wanted to educate her pupils about it. She wrote to Hitler in December 1933:

Dear Mr Reich Chancellor!

Perhaps I am the first 'sister' who has dared to knock on your generous heart with a humble request. Your book *My Struggle* led me to do so! I would so much like to have a copy of it and would have hoped to receive it for Christmas, if I didn't know that our income is not enough to live on.

Then the dear Christ-child gave me a somewhat bold idea: try the source itself! And so here I am asking you, Mr Reich Chancellor, in the steadfast hope that I might receive the book from your constantly open hand: as a teacher, I want then in gratitude to educate the big girls entrusted to me in a very national way, and pray daily for rich blessings on the successful realization of your difficult but uniquely beautiful task. With a heartfelt 'Hail Victory' I close, trusting in your generosity,

M. Fridolina Fehringer, O. S. F.
Convent School teacher

The letter from the naive teacher was not deemed worthy of an answer.

Another teacher, Wilhelm Becker from Horbach, located in the Odenwald Mountains of western Germany, was more persistent about his request to Hitler. On 18 December 1933 he wrote to Angela Raubal, Hitler's half-sister, who was working as Hitler's housekeeper at his Bavarian retreat:

Dear gracious lady!

My schoolchildren have taken extraordinary pains to give our beloved Leader and Reich Chancellor a little joy on Christmas, and have written and illustrated their Christmas letters with great devotion and care.

In both form and content they are entirely the intellectual production of each individual child, and from the fineness of the composition you will be able to see the feeling of happiness that has inspired each individual child. The portfolio was sent to you yesterday. I beg you to receive it.

Your brother will certainly take a few days off from the exertions of political life and seek rest and relaxation in the stillness of your mountain landscape.

We know how much he loves children; so many delightful pictures show us that.

I would like to ask you most cordially in the name of my school-children to lay the portfolio before him during some leisure hour. Perhaps the tender little work of the Odenwald village children will become a Christmas radiance for him.

With German Christmas greetings!
For the Hornbach Elementary School
Wilh. Becket

Becker's letter was forwarded to Berlin along with other mail. Hitler's private office replied on 27 February 1934.

Dear Mr Becker!

Mrs Raubal forwarded your letter of 18 December of this year to us for reply. The Leader received the portfolio and took great pleasure in it. He sends you and the children his heartfelt thanks.

He would like to write each of the children personally, but he is extremely busy and unfortunately cannot do so.

With a German salute

But by 23 January 1934, Becker had already written a follow-up letter to Angela Raubal:

Dear gracious lady!

Every day since classes have begun again, my children look at me with big questioning eyes, and some of them have even slipped up to me and shyly asked: 'has he written yet?'

You won't hold it against me, if as the intellectual custodian for 47 little people, I ask you today whether our Christmas portfolio for the Mr Reich Chancellor, which we put in the mail on 20 December 1933, reached you on time and whether it was possible for you to present it to your brother over the holidays. That he had an exceptional number of things to do at the turn of the year we can very easily imagine. But it would be very painful for my children if the gift that they created with all their hearts and with the devotion of all their inner energies was not able to perform the task that they had set themselves: to give our Leader five minutes of joy.

My children are not impatient, but I still feel so strongly how their little hearts quivered in response to the echo to which their gift gave rise in our Leader. Several of them have already come to tell me with delight that they had dreamed of him; one of the little ones had already done so three times. And they are constantly seeing the Chancellor coming up the village street!

This feeling of togetherness was particularly strong when a friend recently read to us a splendid little book [Frances Hodgson Burnett's *The Secret Garden*]. It could be seen in every eye and it sprang from every heart that the royal son who thus frees his people and makes it happy is none other than Adolph Hitler.

I hasten now to send you the delightful little book.

Do with it whatever you wish.

My children would be overjoyed to hear what happened to the portfolio and perhaps also the book.

With a German salute!
Wilh. Becker

On 10 April 1934 Becker's letter was received in Berlin. On the same day Albert Bormann, the head of Hitler's private office, replied:

Dear Mr Becker!

Your letter of 23 January of this year to the Leader's sister, Mrs Raubal, was received here.

Because of the quantity of incoming mail, Mrs Raubal cannot reply to it herself, and from time to time she sends the letters in large packets to be dealt with here.

In the meantime the letter of 27 February should have reached you. The Leader conveys his warmest thanks as well for the little book enclosed with your last letter.

With a German salute
Albert Bormann

Becker's insistence on receiving a response from Hitler was the product of Nazi propaganda itself. Numerous staged photos of Hitler with
children were intended to show teachers like Becker how much Hitler
loves children. It was implied that teachers would then urge their
pupils to write or send gifts to Hitler. Whether the children (or even
the teachers) were necessarily keen to do so is impossible to determine.
But it is unlikely that a single child in a small city would have refused
to do so, without facing social exclusion, or worse, running the risk
that his or her parents would be denounced or attacked. The same was
true for individual teachers working within those schools that undertook veneration projects. This social pressure was deliberate; precisely
at Christmas and on his birthday Hitler received hundreds of such
portfolios.

The physician Erich Feld, from Düsseldorf in western Germany,
sent Hitler a choral composition during the Christmas period 1933.
Like the teacher Wilhelm Becker, Feld felt it was no problem to follow
up his gift when an answer was not immediately forthcoming.

With great gratitude I received yesterday your letter indicated
above. Unfortunately, however, it does not make clear whether
my musical composition, which I dedicated to the Leader before
Christmas, was actually presented to him and whether he accepted
my dedication.

Since I am now sending the choral work 'Leader to the Holy Grail'
and would like to publish it, I request a prompt reply regarding the
two questions above, since according to the information made available to me the dedication to the Leader can be printed on the score
only if express permission to do so has been granted. I hope to receive
this permission, since I have received very positive assessments of this
composition, and several National Socialist conductors (Gillessen of
the Düsseldorf Opera and Dr Pauling of the Dortmund Opera, as well
as music reviewers in the local newspapers) have described my song as
'a born mass chorus' and as 'what we have long been seeking as a festival chorus for Fatherland events', and I have already been promised
performances in several places.

Given these assessments I hope I may be allowed to request that the
work for a male chorus, 'Leader to the Holy Grail' will not disappear

into oblivion, but rather be presented to the Leader in person, and that it will move him to accept my dedication.

On 12 March 1934 Feld received an answer from Hitler's office:

Dear Dr Feld!

Your letter from the second of this month was received.

After further reflection I must unfortunately tell you, that the Leader cannot accept the dedication. As you undoubtedly know from various publications in the press, the Leader does not desire any glorification of his person. In addition, I fail to understand why you wanted to dedicate your work to the Leader again, since the content of the composition already constitutes a dedication to the Leader. I inform you once again that the Leader took great pleasure in the honour done him by the composition. However, on the grounds mentioned I ask you to refrain from a personal dedication.

> *With a German salute*
> *A. Bormann*

Particularly large numbers of gifts were received on the anniversary of Hitler's accession to power. For example Friedrich Fischer from Magdeburg wrote to Hitler on 26 January 1934:

My supreme Leader,

On the first anniversary of your being called to the Reich chancellorship and the Third Reich's first year of existence we send our sincerest congratulations as well as a picture of my last German Shepherd, which I had trained as a guard-, police-, and watch-dog.

The picture was my first embroidery, which I, as a trained locksmith, made during my 5½ years of unemployment. Now that I have work again, it is a pleasure for me to send this picture to my supreme Leader as a token of my thanks, which is also meant to be in memory of your poisoned dog.

My supreme Leader, our only wish is now to see my supreme Leader in person.

In devoted loyalty
Stormtrooper
Friedrich Fischer and wife

Embroidered pictures of dogs were complemented by many pictures of German children, sent by their proud parents.

Ida Fiebig from Haynau in Silesia sent pictures of her family on 2 February, together with the following letter:

Dear esteemed Mr Reich Chancellor!

As a German mother, I sit here in silent meditation on my dear Leader ADOLF HITLER! And praise destiny and pray every day to the Almighty, that he might keep you healthy.

It is also my heart's need to thank you that we who have many children are considered valuable again.

And so I combine all in one.

Accept my sincere thanks, worthy Mr Reich Chancellor. And you be assured that I shall raise my nine children in your way and for our cherished Fatherland.

By way of thanks I enclose a small picture. It is the littlest [child].

When he hears: 'the flag high, the ranks tightly closed' [lyrics from the Horst-Wessel song], he holds up his hand.

I would be delighted if I could receive any little thing written by my dear Leader.

HAIL VICTORY!
Mrs Ida Fiebig

The Fessler family from Mannheim in southwestern Germany followed suit on 1 March 1934:

Our esteemed Leader!

Our little Rita would like to greet the Leader with a Hail Hitler! Therefore we are taking the liberty of sending you a picture of her, in which she is raising her little hand in the German salute.

She is ten months old and the youngest of five children. If she is shown a picture of uncle Hitler she immediately salutes.

If it is not inappropriate or asking too much, may we ask for a word of reply? We would very much like to know if you have received the little picture and whether it pleases you. In all the greatest esteem, ever German with a German salute

Hail Hitler!
Karl Fessler Family

Other love gifts to Hitler included four-leafed clovers through Persian carpets to a roll of alligator skin sent him by an admirer from Namibia, the former German colony in southwest Africa. When Hitler shouted himself hoarse in a radio speech, the next day several dozen packages with home remedies were received by his office.

Mrs von Heyden-Plötz from Pomerania in northeast Germany sent Hitler a large container of honey and also instructions for 'caring for' this food product. She was delighted that her gift actually arrived, as her thank-you letter of 5 March 1934 proves.

My Leader,

I was very happy to learn that my gift of honey actually reached you personally, which I had hardly dared hope, but certainly assume on the basis of the personally signed thank-you note. It would make me even happier if you would allow me to make a small contribution to your breakfast table and now and then send you a little honey – but I would not want to put you to any personal trouble by doing so. A simple confirmation of the delivery by your secretary would suffice.

May the enjoyment of this original, unadulterated natural product of

Pomeranian soil help a little to compensate the enormous energy used by the mind and body.

With esteem and love
your
M. von Heyden-Plötz
née von Zitzewitz

Albert Bormann replied on 18 April 1934:

Dear gracious lady!

The Leader conveys his belated thanks for your letter of the 5th April and especially for the latest delivery of the exceptional honey.

With a German salute
Albert Bormann

Children sent Hitler handmade things and pictures they had painted themselves, along with sweets that they themselves had been given. On 11 April 1934 Evamarie B. from Albig in the Rhineland enclosed a small card with her package:

A hearty Easter greeting to our Leader from our Easter nest of the four-leafed clover in the Albig rectory.

Evamarie B.

To my Leader a triple 'Hail Victory!'

Reinhard B.
Gerlind B.
Ursula B.

On the card, an employee in Hitler's private office noted: 'Easter bunny, Easter eggs, sweets; thank nicely.'

Dear Evamarie!

The Leader received your lovely Easter greeting and warmly thanks you and your brothers and sisters for it. You have really given him pleasure with it.

With a German salute
Albert Bormann

While in some cases these children's gifts may well have been spontaneous, it is probable that many of them were suggested, or at least encouraged, by their parents.

A letter from Heinz H. on 22 April 1934 from Rottweil am Neckar in Baden-Württemberg, displays quite obvious parental interference:

Dear Aunt Raubal!

I too would like to give Uncle Hitler something on his birthday, but I have nothing but my little picture, & that was completed just today. Be so good, dear Aunt, as to give it to him & say that I pray for him every evening: Dear God, help Germany out of its great distress; give Uncle Hitler power so he can make a new Germany. Protect and look after him on all his paths, and give him your blessing.

Hail Hitler!
Heinz H.
Rottweil a. N.

P.S. Mama had to write for me, because I am just four years old.

It can probably be assumed that the parents prayed with their son and encouraged him to paint a picture for Hitler. Had Heinz felt compelled to do so himself, he may well have finished the picture on time.

Karl H. from Fellbach bei Stuttgart wrote on behalf of his daughter Doris to Hitler's sister Angela Raubal, whom he mistakenly addressed as Miss:

Dear Miss Hitler!

Our little Doris, the sunshine of her parents, would like to send her birthday comrade, our treasured Mr Reich Chancellor, a little picture for his birthday. She is devoted to 'her Adolf Hitler' with all her heart. For example, when flags are run up on any occasion, her first question is: 'Papa or Mama – is today my and my Adolf Hitler's birthday?' Every day when she says her prayers with her siblings, who are two and one year older, respectively, she closes with the request that God might make her mother healthy and keep her Adolf Hitler healthy. It is often moving to be able to experience these moments. We parents gladly share in these wishes proceeding from pure children's hearts and would be thankful for the delivery of this commemoration of your Mr brother's birthday from a dear little Schwäbisch girl. Trusting that you will not be offended by the liberty we have taken, I close with the best German greetings.

K.H.
Mayor, ret.

These birthday greetings from 1934 were among around 10,000 such letters received by Hitler, more than ever before – and more than he would receive ever again. This birthday was another good excuse for the people to express their boundless veneration.

On a simple scrap of paper, though free of wood pulp, a priest from Düsseldorf in western Germany congratulated Hitler on 20 April 1934:

My Leader!

After I was ordained a priest on 15 April 1934, it was my sincere desire to offer my first mass as well as today's to God with a prayer for his richest blessing on your noble work. This for you, my Leader, on your birthday today!

Hail!
Albert Spelter
Priest of the Free Catholic Church in Germany

One greeting included the printed visiting card of a woman who could also afford to travel by train to Berlin. By contrast the Seeger family, who came from a small city in Anhalt in what is now eastern Germany, wrote on a sheet torn from a common writing tablet and sent their greetings on this cheap, pulpy paper on 20 April 1934. It contained the following text:

To our People's Chancellor Adolf Hitler on the occasion of his forty-fifth year heartfelt wishes for happiness and blessing for 'today' and all times.
May God give health.

Hail Hitler!
A messenger-woman at the Völkisch Observer
Mrs Gertrud Seeger

On the reverse side we read:

Mr Reich Chancellor Adolf Hitler!

We express our very sincere thanks that through our movement I have finally received, after four years, a position as a messenger-woman. My husband has already been unemployed for 4½ years, but it will sometime be his turn, too. At least we can now eat our fill.

Full of respect we look up to our Leader
Hail Hitler!
The Seeger Family

Another individual sent Hitler a model train:

Mr Reich Chancellor Adolf Hitler!

The undersigned requests your permission, Mr Reich Chancellor, to send you by railway express the model, called 'Presence' produced by my own work in all allegiance for your 45th birthday. The undersigned asks you to accept this gift as a sign of the greatest humble respect by someone who works at the Hamburg harbour, who at the same time takes the liberty of expressing to you, Mr Reich Chancellor, the most obedient blessings on the occasion of your new year of life.

Hail!
Chr. Jacobsen

The entry stamp bears the date 20 June 1934, which suggests that the letter was initially lost in the flood of good wishes.

On 6 June, Jacobsen followed up, and the stamp shows 20 July as the entry date.

Mr Reich Chancellor!

The undersigned enquires whether the model, a steamer in a glass case named Presence, that was sent to you from Hamburg by railway express for your 45th birthday, arrived in good condition.

With the greatest respect
and with a German salute
Hail!
Chr. Jacobsen

The letters probably crossed in the mail, since Hitler's private office had already answered on 21 June 1934. Hitler personally signed the letter of reply.

Dear Mr Jacobsen!

The beautiful homemade model ship you sent me for my birthday gave me special pleasure.
    Belatedly, I send you my sincerest thanks for it.

With a German salute
Adolf Hitler

Gerhard H. from Berlin also congratulated Hitler on his birthday on 19 April 1934 and added a very special wish.

Dear Mr Reich Chancellor Adolf Hitler,

We German boys and girls do not want to fail to offer you our best wishes on your day of honour. We wish with all our hearts that God might still keep you many years so that we grow, under your rule, to become true, brave Germans and enjoy the fruits of your labours in the newly awakened Germany under the radiant sun of your splendid victory.

We have heard that you will be godfather to the seventh child. Since that seems to us too long to wait, and since not all of us have already been baptized and would love to be your godchildren, we ask you to give our feeling for God the proper consecration and become godfather to us all. We have no one else who would do it, because we are so many children. Would you grant this wish of ours? Please, please!

Your youngest well-wishers, who revere you above all
Gerhard 11 years old (Hitler Youth), Horst 8 years old, Evi 5 years old,
Dietrich 3 years old, Sigfrid 2 years old

The processing note on this letter reads: 'not possible'. The answer to Gerhard H. was accordingly negative.

Dear Gerhard!

Your letter to the Leader of the 19th of last month was received here.

I regret that I must tell you that in view of the excessively large number of requests arriving every day the Leader cannot accept any belated sponsorships.

The Leader wishes you and your siblings the best for your future lives.

With a German salute!
Albert Bormann

Hugo Hertwig from Gräfenroda in Thuringia was also not able to have his request to Hitler on his Leader's birthday fulfilled. He sent a play that was intended as a tribute, and combined this present with the wish for the financial means to print the work. Around the salutation 'My Leader!' he had drawn a kind of bow.

My Leader!

I herewith send you the sincerest good wishes for your birthday today!

As a gift I have written for my Leader a little work entitled: The Blood Brothers.

If I had money, the gift would have looked better. I worked for almost seven years at the Labour Office, but fell victim to the reactionary intelligentsia and now I've been sitting around the house for five weeks without any income.

My Leader!

It is not possible for me to finance the enclosed little work. Please help. The local Hitler Youth is waiting for its publication and the right to mount the first performance!

My four brothers, who in gratitude also wear the Leader's uniform, join me in sending our best wishes.

In the hope that I have not done anything objectionable, I salute with

Hail Hitler!
Hugo Hertwig

Hertwig had written a fourteen-page *Tragedy in 4 Parts*, the subtitle of which was *First Blood and Tears Must Flow*. The content of Hertwig's play recounts the basic myth of the rise of the Third Reich, and chronicles the story through five distinct time periods: The Decline of the German People, Under Foreign Domination, A Leader is Born, The Battle for the German Man, and Victory and Hail to the Leader and the German People.

Hertwig's own life had been a tragedy as well. His father, a postman, died of an incurable disease during the First World War. His eldest brother was seriously wounded in the war, so that his mother and the six other children were dependent on state support. Hertwig worked as a bookkeeper but lost his job in 1927. In the same year he found a position in municipal administration. Later he worked in the Labour Office, where he learned, as he put it, 'the hard side of life'. As a result of his experiences there, he became a supporter of National Socialism: 'We weren't afraid of anything. Now we could bear witness to the National Socialist Revolution. We swore an oath of loyalty to the Leader and we will keep it as long as we live.' Hertwig was eventually dismissed from his job for 'speaking out' against individuals he described in his letter to Hitler only as 'Reactionaries', who he felt were part of a 'class of lords taken over by the Third Reich'. Since then he had remained unemployed.

Either Hertwig had opposed the Party bigwigs and denounced actual abuses in Thuringia, or he was such a fanatic that he became insufferable even to the Nazi Party administration. Some of these rabid supporters saw a 'Jewish–Masonic world conspiracy' at work everywhere, and detected opposition to the regime in anyone who was not as radical as they were. Despite their adherence to National Socialism, such individuals were problematic for the Party.

Hertwig received a reply from Hitler's private office on 23 May 1934.

Dear Mr Hertwig!

The Leader sends you and your four brothers his sincerest thanks for your good wishes on the occasion of his birthday.

The little work The Blood Brothers gave the Leader special pleasure. Unfortunately from here it is not possible to provide support for the publication of the work

With a German salute!
A. Bormann

Marie Bennewitz from Chemnitz in Saxony wrote on 18 April 1934 with a somewhat more reasonable request. She asked Hitler's sister Angela Raubal to present her letter to Hitler in person. In addition, she asked for a signed portrait of the Reich Chancellor. On her stationery an image of Horst Wessel had been printed.

To our revered Mr Reich Chancellor and great Leader of the wonderful National Socialist movement!!!

Hail Victory!

Dear Mr Reich Chancellor!

It is my heart's desire to send you once again this year, on the occasion of your birthday, the most sincere wishes for happiness and blessing. In the coming year may our Lord God give you strength and health and continue to protect you as he has up to now. Dear Mr Reich Chancellor, you will again receive thousands of letters of good wishes and gifts, but you must not be angry about this, because we National Socialists want only thereby to prove to you how much we all love you and how much we revere you and that we give you our full trust. It is just a bit of a shame that you cannot read all these letters, which would sometimes bring a smile to your lips at what might be childish good wishes. In earlier years only a few of your loyal comrades may have been aware of your birthday, I myself have known about it since 1931. Therefore in 1932 I congratulated you for the first time, precisely at the difficult and sad time when eight days earlier our SS and our Stormtroopers were dissolved, I always think back to how upset we all were. Thank God that since that terrible time everything has taken a turn for the good. Through your tireless battles and your persistence and your love of the truth you have succeeded in having nearly the whole people behind you, and thus now the whole people also celebrates your birthday from the bottoms of their hearts and wishes you the best, Mr Reich Chancellor! We are all so proud and happy to be guided by your powerful and purposeful hands.

With a great 'Hail Victory!' please receive,
Mr Reich Chancellor,
German greetings from Chemnitz from
Mrs Marie Bennewitz
An old German mother

The action stamp on the letter is 'Thank', meaning that she probably received the picture she asked for.

Edith Hertel from Berlin combined good wishes for Hitler with a request for an autograph. She addressed her letter to Angela Raubal, Hitler's sister.

Dear gracious lady!

For the great kindness of forwarding the enclosed post to your brother, my most respectful and dearest thanks.

> *With the greatest esteem*
> *Edith Hertel*

The letter was received on 12 May as part of a bulk delivery from Obersalzberg, Hitler's mountain retreat near Munich in Bavaria. Hitler's home, the Wachenfeld Haus (later known as the Berghof), was located here, and in 1939 the Eagle's Nest, a chalet on a mountain spur called the Kehlstein, was given to Hitler as a 50th birthday present.

The letter was given the entry number 4712. A handwritten note reads 'Thank 16.5.34', but the usual indication 'picture' is missing. Here is the letter to Hitler Edith Hertel enclosed:

Dear Mr Reich Chancellor,
Our Leader!

Being unfortunately only a small part of the millions of the German people, I nonetheless very humbly take the liberty of also communicating to my Leader the sincerest wishes for happiness and blessing on this day. With the dearest inner wish that through our venerable and noble-minded Leader's generous power and readiness for self-sacrifice, the German people will be guided to the place where it has belonged from the time of our oldest ancestors; I daily pray to the dear Lord to keep our highly respected Mr Reich Chancellor and Leader of a nation healthy and alive for a long time. I share in this wish and with this great prayer from the bottom of my heart. May God preserve our truest noble Leader!

I request a great kindness, something written in his own hand by our Leader, Mr Reich Chancellor Adolf Hitler, on the enclosed card.

With the greatest respect,
Edith Hertel

The widow of the automobile inventor Carl Benz from Ladenburg, western Germany, wrote on May 1934. In her letter, which was written on handmade paper, she also thanked Hitler for a signed picture:

Dear Mr Reich Chancellor!

Profoundly moved in the depths of my heart, I would like to express my very warmest thanks for the picture with your signature on it, which is so valuable to me, and which was forwarded to me by Mr Director Werner of the Daimler-Benz works in Mannheim. Nothing could have given me greater joy on my 85th birthday than this kind attention of yours. This image of our beloved Leader and the saviour of Germany will hang in a permanent place of honour in my house.

Please accept, dear Mr Reich Chancellor, the most deeply felt thanks of an old woman who is already seeing so many wishes of our German people being fulfilled in your selfless works and who can conclude the evening of her life with the satisfaction of knowing that Germany's welfare is in sure hands.

May God's blessing continue to accompany you!

Hail to our German Fatherland!
In sincere esteem
Mrs Bertha Benz

The schoolboy Nikolaus F. also requested a picture. On 7 March 1934 he wrote on lined paper, carefully ripped out middle sheet of a school notebook, in a beautiful hand:

Dear Mr Reich Chancellor!

Since on 14 May 1934 I will complete my 10th year of life, I take the liberty, as a German pupil in the Saar, of directing a very sincere request to you, highly esteemed Mr Reich Chancellor. I have already heard so much about you and also read about you in the newspaper, and I have a single wish, that you might give me a large photograph of yourself for my birthday. Since because of unemployment and great need nothing goes into my little savings box at the moment, I cannot make this request of my parents.

That would be my sole German wish.

In the hope that my little letter is not unwelcome to you, I remain with a

> *German salute*
> *Hail Hitler!*
> *Your German child of the Saar*
> *Nikolaus F.*

The reply from Hitler's private office was brief:

Dear Nikolaus!

I gratefully acknowledge the reception of your letter to the Leader dated the seventh of this month. We will be glad to fulfil your wish. I am sending you enclosed a picture of the Leader.

> *With a German salute*
> *A. Bormann*

What is interesting about Nikolaus' letter is that he was not living in Germany at the time, but instead in Bliesmengen, in the neutral Saar area. Despite this, he repeatedly emphasized his Germanness. Nikolaus' letter was just one of an increasing number of letters Hitler began to receive from Germans living abroad.

A year earlier, Hitler had received a letter from Reich Association of Loyal East and West Prussia. Their letter discussed their birthday gift to Hitler, which was a reproduction of the referendum monument in Marienburg, East Prussia. This monument commemorated the referendum held on 11 July 1920, in accordance with the Versailles Treaty, in which the population was asked whether they wanted to join Poland or remain in Germany. The majority of residents chose to remain German. After the Second World War the town was integrated into Poland, and is today known as Malbork. They also asked whether Hitler would be an honorary member of their society.

Dear Mr Bormann!

Your message arrived today, telling me that the reproduction of the referendum monument in Marienburg, the marble column with the bronze rider given the Leader by the Reich Association for his birthday, now stands on his desk and is thus as appreciated as I had hoped it would be. This has given exceptional joy to me and everyone else whom I have told about it. Insofar as you have contributed to this commemorative monument being put in the most worthy place, I want to express my especially warm thanks to you as well. The column is meant to be the visible sign of the very close bond between East Prussia and the people and the Reich and with the chancellor, who, as we all know, is particularly partial to the German East and within it the province of East Prussia.

On the occasion of the Leader's birthday we have written a letter, a copy of which is enclosed. As you will see from the letter, we are requesting that he allow us the distinction of being included in the circle that binds East Prussia with the chancellor by accepting in this special case nomination as an honorary member, even though he usually declines such honours.

In the event that you, esteemed Mr Bormann, who have the good fortune to be among the Leader's trusted advisers, might be able to ask him to be our honorary member alongside our great compatriot Mr Reich President von Hindenburg, we would owe you the greatest conceivable gratitude. The Leader may be assured of the loyal obedience of the Reich Association.

Hail Hitler!
With eminently high esteem
your very devoted
Hoffmann

Hitler declined his offer of membership, but did reassert his dedication to the German East:

Today I received the copy of your letter of 20 April of this year, the original of which apparently was lost by an unfortunate accident amongst the ten thousand letters that came in on the occasion of my birthday.

I would like to offer you, even belatedly, my warmest thanks for the good wishes and especially for the reproduction of the referendum monument in Marienburg.

The future of the German East and its close connection with the motherland, which you have made your primary task, are also especially close to my heart. However much I was pleased by your proposal that I accept honorary membership in the Association, even in this case I must ask you not to nominate me.

With a German salute
Adolf Hitler

On a piece of cardboard ripped off a package of thread, Stormtroopers and SS men being held in the Salzburg prison in Austria, presumably as a result of the February Uprising, a civil war between socialists and fascist-conservatives, wrote on 18 April 1934 to congratulate 'their' Leader Adolf Hitler on his birthday. The good wishes were signed by twenty prisoners, and in a fine hand one of them had written: 'we persevere!' Then followed a postscript, which is only too understandable: 'Unfortunately we had nothing else at hand.'

Hugo Herberg from Bonneweg in the Grand Dutchy of Luxemburg also sent Hitler birthday greetings. For him Germany and not Luxemburg was the beloved Fatherland and thus Hitler his true leader.

Dear Mr Reich Chancellor!

On the occasion of your birthday the sincerest good wishes from beautiful Luxemburg. I wish that you might stand for many years yet at the pinnacle of our beloved Fatherland and succeed in creating work once again for all the unemployed.

I will never forget your birthday, since my dear father was also born on 20 April. He is president of the German Men's Chorus Association. We are also members of the German colony.

Now I have a request to make of you.

Please send me a picture of you; here one cannot buy such a thing. If you grant this wish, you will give me great joy.

With a German salute
Hugo Herberg
Luxemburg-Bonneweg

Herberg received his picture. On 11 May Albert Bormann wrote:

Dear Mr Herberg!

The Leader asks me to express his warmest thanks for your letter and good wishes on his birthday.

In the attachment you will find the picture of the Leader you desired.

With a German salute!
Albert Bormann

Annelene K. was another German living outside the borders of the state who looked to Hitler as her Leader. She was from Heydekrug in the Memel territory in what is today Lithuania. This area was defined by the Treaty of Versailles in 1920 and was intended to remain under the control of the League of Nations until a point in time when the population could choose whether or not to return to Germany. It was occupied by Lithuania in 1923 and then by the Germans in 1939. After the war it was then annexed by the Soviet Union, but has been part of Lithuania since 1991.

On 7 May 1933 she wrote to Hitler and demanded that he take action against Jews and Lithuanians in her homeland. Derisively, she called the latter 'Szameites', that is, people who could not speak 'proper' German.

Dear, good Uncle Hitler,

We have been waiting a long time for you to come to our Memel territory. From the smallest child to the biggest man, Jews and Szameites not included, everyone here shouts, full of enthusiasm, only 'Hail Hitler!' We would all be very, very happy to return to Germany. The Jews and Lithuanians all have to leave, right? They are getting terribly uppity here. When I say 'Hail Hitler!' they try to beat me up or they shout 'Hail Haag!' because not long ago a disgraceful judgement against the Memel territory was handed down in The Hague.

Our 'Commandant' has strictly forbidden the wearing of swastikas or similar insignia here. We are also not allowed to say Hail Hitler, and if we do we are taken straight to the Bajohren prison and locked up there. Yes, dear uncle Hitler, here we are in a kind of prison. Come as soon as you can and save us from the Jews and Lithuanians. Here the Jews are not only taking our bread away from us, but even sacrifice Christians at Easter time. Every child is afraid to go into a Jewish shop before Easter. That is dreadful. If our newspaper writes something that the Lithuanians don't like, then the newspaperman is immediately punished with a high fine or imprisonment. So dear uncle Adolf, come very soon.

I am going to try to send this letter to my uncle, Richard Maul in Tilsit [in modern-day Russia], and I hope that the dear Lord helps me so that this letter reaches you. Should you be so kind as to write to me, then don't send the letter directly to me, but rather to: Richard Maul. Uncle Maul will forward it to me, because I have asked him to do so. If the Commandant were to find out about it, he would have me shot dead, but I am not afraid, I will act like Horst Wessel, whose song not only I but all the young people here sing every day.

Now dear uncle, don't talk about this letter on the radio either, because the Lithuanians are very eager to hear your beautiful radio speeches.

Heartiest greetings from the youth of the Memel territory and especially from your little 13-¾-year-old niece

Annelene K.

Annelene K. was of course not related to Hitler, even if she called him her uncle and saw herself as his niece. She received no answer from either the Chancellor's Office or Hitler's private office.

Alice Zimmermann of Vienna, Austria who wrote on 5 November 1933, also asked Hitler for help. She felt that living in an Austria that was separated from the German Reich was 'hell':

Dear Mr Reich Chancellor!

A fortnight ago I came to Berlin on a visit because I could no longer stand being in Vienna and because I wanted to breathe pure fresh air again.

On 27 November I was in the Sports Palace [this was a multi-purpose winter-sport venue and meeting hall in Berlin that had been built in 1910. It could hold up to 14,000 people and is most famous for the speeches and rallies held there during the Third Reich] – I heard you and saw you for the first time in my life; but during this fortnight I also became familiar with the whole cheerful, fresh activity in the new young Germany!

And now I ask you, revered Mr Reich Chancellor, in the name of all German Viennese women, to come to us and help us, we want to be happy and free and German too! We all adhere loyally to the swastika, we secretly continue to pay our dues and to help our needy Party comrades as much as we can. – Perhaps you will be happy to hear this, Mr Reich Chancellor.

Should you have any assignment or greeting to give the women of Vienna, my cousin, Mrs Elfriede Friesel, Berlin, with whom I am currently staying, will communicate it.

I myself must return to Hell tomorrow – and perhaps soon into a concentration camp – because I want to be German. May the Lord God preserve your strength and health!

That is the earnest prayer of all of us Germans in Vienna!

Party member Alice Zimmermann
Inzersdorf near Vienna

Hitler and the Nazi Party were already hatching a plan to take over Austria. But obviously, Hitler did not divulge this information to Alice

Zimmermann. Even Hitler's sister knew nothing about the impending putsch, as we can see from her letter of 16 June 1934. She does, however, note the good relations Hitler enjoyed with Mussolini's fascist dictatorship in Italy:

Dear Adolf!

I send you my heartiest good wishes for your birthday tomorrow.

All our thoughts on this day were about Italy, and I was particularly happy about the fabulous reception there. If only the poor Austrians could also be helped. They often have to endure inhuman things, and they accept everything in their hopes in you.

All the best and sincere greetings from your sister

Angela

This international support for the development of a larger, ethnic German Reich would become increasingly important as the decade went on. But at this point, the new Chancellor was happy to file it away with the widespread veneration he received from Germans within the Reich during the founding years of the Third Reich.

6

PRIVATE PETITIONS AND POLITICAL
REQUESTS

Hitler did not only receive letters of veneration, presents, and requests for pictures. In developing his image as Germany's protector of morals and decency, as well as the guarantor of order and security, he cultivated the idea that his population could trust him completely. Many of them clearly did. As a result Hitler also began to receive letters that asked him to intervene in private matters.

The Stormtrooper Herbert Findeisen wrote to Hitler from Freiberg in Saxony on 1 January 1934:

To my Supreme Leader
Reich Chancellor Adolf Hitler
Chancellor's Office, Berlin

My final call for help!
I stand today as a 23-year-old Stormtrooper at the end of my young life and must take a second person with me into death, namely my beloved. Therefore I am addressing my last call for help to you, esteemed Mr Chancellor, trusting in you as in my own father, who unfortunately already fell victim to the war in 1914.
My request is the following: three years ago I was ordered to make support payments for two children, which has deprived me of any

further advancement in my life, in part through no fault of my own. Now I have been for two years in a relationship with a girl who is twenty years old, and we are both so much in love that only death can separate us. I would like to marry my beloved, but my parents-in-law absolutely refuse because of my support payments.

Esteemed Leader and chancellor, please be father to me a little bit, and help me be happy with my beloved. I would very much like to take part in the further awakening of our German Fatherland, and help fight for our Germany. I hope that my last request and call for help will not be entirely in vain, and that you can already today ensure that in our marriage there will never be a day on which we shall not thank our helping father.

With a German salute
Herbert Findeisen

Since the Party line insisted that Hitler would not get involved in private matters, Findeisen's letter was marked with a red line and the notation 'to be filed'. It is impossible to know whether Findeisen actually killed himself. His was not the only such threat – it appears that there were multiple incidences of suicide being threatened as a type of blackmail.

On 14 April 1934, the letter written by Susanne Hesse from Kraschwitz in Thuringia also went into the files without an answer:

My Leader!

Please forgive me if I take the liberty of asking for a little of your precious time. In my distress I no longer see anything else to do and I will be as brief as possible. I am an ordinary blonde girl, the daughter of an equally ordinary and genuine German farmer, and I have always wished to become the wife of a capable young farmer, on whose land I can then work and produce as much as I want amid a family of blond boys and girls (I would like to have at least ten of them). I am competent in all branches of domestic economy – I have now found such a nice man. Unfortunately, however, his mother does not give her consent to our marriage . . . because he is of aristocratic descent and I am only an ordinary farm girl. His name: Alf-Dietrich Baron von Stryk. He currently manages the two manors of Kaufungen and Wolkenburg in Saxony, which are owned by Count Gert von Einsiedel of Wolkenburg Castle in Saxony. He is a long-time Party member and now leader of the Wolkenburg Storm Battalion cavalry unit. Since his mother denies permission, he is consequently without means (I assume this, because I have not spoken with him again since the talk with his mother, and he has only [sent] me a farewell letter, without giving any reason), and our plan to take on a settler's holding of at least 150 acres of land will fall through, because my father can contribute at most 10,000 marks, and that is not enough. You will say, take a smaller settler's holding. Very esteemed Mr Reich Chancellor, Alf has always been on noble estates, and as a result he would never be able to get used to such conditions; thus that would lead to nothing good. Oh, couldn't you help us somehow. I ask you most earnestly to do so. If you want to know whether what I have said is true, the Reich Leader of the Peasants [and Minister of Food and Agriculture] Darré knows him personally very well, and has already offered him his help. However, only my parents know about our relationship. Can't Mr Darré use him somewhere? Oh, how I would rejoice and be grateful to you from the depths of my heart. If I can't have Alf, I shall never marry. Oh, please help us out of our emotional distress. If there is any possibility of helping us, I sincerely request that nothing be allowed to become public, and if at all possible that the Baron also not learn about it. He might never be able to understand my begging letter. But what won't people do for love. – May I then expect an answer? So for the moment make nothing, please, please, nothing public, my parents must not learn about it either in any case. No one knows about my letter and no one must know about it.

With a German salute and Hail Hitler
Susanne Hesse

P.S. The Mr Reich Chancellor might think that I am insisting on marriage because he is a Baron. Oh no, I care about that not at all. I am just so very much in love with him that I cannot be responsible for anything that might happen if nothing comes of this. Otherwise I would not have dared to write to you. So please forgive me this letter, and help me please if it is at all possible.

Suse Hesse

Susanne Hesse received no reply, and Alf-Dietrich Alexander Reinhold von Stryk married the daughter of a Westphalian factory owner. He was reported missing in Russia in 1944, and in 1953 he was declared dead.

The girl from Thuringia was not the only one who wanted to request something for her beloved. Existential questions were only seldom involved. For example, a woman from Mannheim whose fiancé was just taking the second national bar examination, asked Hitler to employ her future husband in government service. Otherwise they could not marry or found a family. As a lawyer he would earn so little that he would have to sub-let an apartment, and then the marriage would not take place.

The case of Elsa Menzel, who wrote to Hitler on 7 December 1933 from Berlin-Friedenau, was considerably more serious:

My Leader!

In my extreme need I turn to you, my Leader. About five weeks ago my husband, Colonel Paul Menzel, was arrested on his way to the supreme Stormtrooper leadership in Munich on the ground that he had embezzled Stormtrooper funds. In a few days the Gestapa [the Secret Police Office, founded by Hermann Göring in April 1933 and headed by Heinrich Himmler from April 1934, which later became known as the Gestapo – the acronym for Secret State Police] was able to establish that my husband was completely innocent. Nevertheless, at the instigation of Group Leader Ernst my husband had to remain in the custody of the Prussian military police. Since the Group Leader refused even to discuss the matter with me, I have no remaining recourse other than to appeal to you, my Leader. My husband's existence was annihilated, the family was destroyed, and the state of my husband's health and of my own is catastrophic.

I beg you, my Leader, to concern yourself with the fate of my husband, who is a National Socialist of the most ideal kind.

With deepest esteem,
with a German salute!
Mrs Elsa Menzel

An employee of Hitler's private office noted on her letter 'ask Gestapa'. The same day, Head Adjutant Brückner got in touch with the secret police office and asked for an explanation. His letter has no formal salutation but instead begins immediately with the description of the matter at hand:

Mrs Elsa Menzel, Berlin-Friedenau, has appealed to the Leader in a letter. She claims that her husband, Colonel Paul Menzel, was arrested on the charge of having embezzled Stormtrooper funds. During the investigation by the Gestapo the complete innocence of Party member Menzel is supposed to have been established. I ask that you inform me as soon as possible whether Mrs Menzel's account corresponds to the facts, because her husband is still being held in custody by the Prussian military police.

With a German salute
Brückner

An action note in shorthand is found on the letter of 14 December 1933. Colonel Menzel was in fact released from custody. The case of Paul Menzel makes it clear that despite all the bureaucratic restrictions it was possible to make one's way into the proximity of the 'Leader'.

The letter from Ernst Feist of Freiburg in Silesia shows that at least 'veterans' got a hearing. So-called old fighters, individuals who had joined the Nazi Party before the parliamentary elections of 1930, received employment and promotion benefits after 1933. They were often also helped out in times of need in recognition of their work for the Party during its difficult early years. On 10 January 1934, Feist asked for a loan.

Re: request for the granting of a loan.

A similar request was already addressed through the SA [Stormtrooper] service at the beginning of October, concerning which I have thus far heard nothing. I am 26 years old, have been a Stormtrooper since early 1930, and was married in November 1933. I am currently employed in my father's business and I would like to make myself independent as soon as possible.

My father, who had to flee Upper Silesia as a refugee in 1919, lost his whole fortune and received no compensation, so that he is now not in a position to support me monetarily, since he must support my six siblings on his present income. For this reason I request that I be granted a loan in the amount of 3,000 marks, which I will pay back in monthly instalments. As security for this loan, my father will deposit his life insurance policy taken out in 1925 in the same amount.

Hail Hitler
Ernst Feist

The Chancellor's Office forwarded the letter to Hitler's private office. The letter bears an action mark, which proves that someone took care of the old Party member. Presumably an employee in the private office called the district leadership in Freiburg and asked that Feist be helped by the district savings bank. The Nazi Party did not establish its own banks, but immediately after it took power it placed Party members in all the public credit institutions.

Mrs Elisabeth Barth, a widow from Chemnitz in eastern Germany, wrote on 4 March 1934 about her poverty, which she felt had been caused by Jews. She may have been serious enough in her anti-Semitism to have actually blamed the Jews for her worries. Alternatively, she may well have thought she was more likely to get a reply from Hitler if she framed the letter in that way.

Mr Reich Chancellor Hitler!
Dear Mr Reich Chancellor!

I offer many apologies for taking the liberty of bothering you in person, but I am in such deep desperation and have been unable to find advice and help anywhere.

Everyone claims he is not in a position to help, and from the Mr Reich Interior Minister, to whom I have written on various occasions, I have received no answer at all.

In my exceptional case, however, something must happen or one cannot go on living under such conditions.

To help you understand, I shall briefly describe my situation:

A Jewish woman destroyed my twenty-year-long marriage, and I subsequently divorced my husband. My former husband was judged to be the sole guilty party, and therefore was ordered to support me until he died. After the divorce he immediately married the Jewish woman. However, at that time his official position had already been cancelled, effective from 1 April 1912. The marriage took place on 12 February 1912, and he resumed work [in private industry] on 1 April 1912. From 1912 to 1931, that is, for twenty years, he worked in industry, and never again in state office. On the basis of this six weeks of work by my late former husband, the Jewish woman can claim, in accord with the *Marxist law*, a widow's pension from the Prussian state. The Prussian state still continues to pay the widow's pension to this Jewish woman, who also receives a widow's pension from the employees' insurance fund, because my late former husband was also insured after twenty years of work in industry. The Prussian state pays me a widow's pension of only 38.33 marks per month, so that I receive not even as much as a welfare recipient and am also dependent on the payment from the welfare office, and even here, because this payment is not considered as welfare income, only with a 5-mark monthly deduction. A welfare retiree receives 42 marks a month, and here too I am fobbed off with 37 marks.

Although according to the law the guiltlessly divorced first wife is supposed to receive a widow's pension in the amount of the legal widow's pension provision, I am fobbed off with this starvation amount, whereas this *Jewish woman* is paid twice, a widow's pension from the

Prussian state and a widow's pension from the employees' insurance fund, which comes to about 130 marks per month after the various deductions. It is presumably not in accord with the policy of National Socialism that in the sacred Third Reich a Jewish woman is given such an advantage over an honourable German woman. Surely on grounds of fairness alone I can justifiably claim the pension to which I am legally entitled, because first of all in my twenty-year marriage I had to do without to pay for the pension, and secondly because my divorced husband was supposed to support me until my death. Therefore I have a right to this pension even after the death of the deceased. I note that my divorced former husband was of old Aryan descent, as I also am.

Veterans who know the conditions I am living in are extremely surprised that even today the state is paying this kind of pension to such a common Jewish woman without her needing to lift a finger, whereas the old, long-standing, unemployed fighter for the Nazi Party still has to scrape by on unemployment payments.

This is not in accord with the battle against Judaism, and therefore I have been advised to present my case personally to the esteemed Leader.

I have already sent my explanations regarding this matter to the then Reich Commissioner for the Prussian Ministry, on 11 April 1933, further explanations to the Minister for Economics and Labour in the Prussian Ministry on 14 June 1933, and once again on 15 November, after querying. On 19 September and on 13 December 1933 I wrote to the Reich Interior Minister, Dr Frick, who has the power to change the relevant law, but received absolutely no answer. On 26 January I wrote once again to the aforementioned and enclosed five medical attestations, and again up till now I have had no reply.

I note that the state of my health has now declined so much that I cannot even take care of my household without help. Unfortunately I no longer have the money to pay for further attestations. When I, as a German woman and mother, am not considered equal even to a Jewish woman, who receives two to four times more financial support, that is not only an unacceptable cruelty, but also does not correspond to the justice of the National Socialist state.

Therefore I cannot believe, after what the highly esteemed Reich Chancellor wrote about Jews in his book, [that he] endorses this

privileging of a Jewish woman, and I hope that through the generous mediation of the Reich Chancellor a final decision will now be
made, for which I offer in advance my sincerest thanks, along with
my best wishes for the continuing well-being of our beloved people's
chancellor.

> *With a German salute and*
> *'Hail Victory'*
> *Elisabeth (widow) Barth*

Overt hatred of Jews is found again in a letter from Richard Fichte,
also from Chemnitz, who wrote on 2 February 1934 to 'the Reich government, personally to Mr Reich Chancellor Adolf Hitler'. His letter
clearly shows which economic conditions led him to make a protest.

Dear Reich government,

In a matter that enrages every German businessman, as an old people's
campaigner for the Third Reich I turn to the Reich government to
request it to keep Jews in the Third Reich from being in a better position with respect to their purchases than businessmen with German
blood.

Foundation: the Reich Association of the German glass container
industry, lead glass professional group, Dresden, Berhardstr. 35, has
distributed sales discount lists that are valid for the whole sector.
Afterward are listed the individual firms that fall under the three discount lists.

Under list 1 come all the German small businessmen in the sector,
who receive a 5% discount.

List 2 holds for all middle-sized and large specialized businesses in
the sector, which are entitled to a discount rate of 7%.

List 3, which provides for a discount rate of 10%, holds primarily
for Jewish department stores, Jewish firms, and large enterprises, the
ones on which a very sharp eye was to be kept in the Third Reich. From
this it seems therefore that in the Third Reich Jews can still buy considerably more cheaply than businessman of German blood. I am convinced that the Reich government will be able to prevent this disgrace.

Because in fact it is almost only Jews, that is Jewish large enterprises, that fall under this discount list with a 10% discount. As a business-man of German blood, I immediately contacted the Reich Association of the German glass container industry and vigorously attacked this regulation. The result amounted to zero . . .

Today I have therefore sent the Reinerzer Crystal Glass Factory a letter (copy enclosed) that I am also making the object of my complaint to the Reich government.

Please step in immediately and with the full rigour of National Socialist consistency to forestall the violent reaction that must result in the German-blooded business world when it learns that even in the Third Reich it is beaten down to the advantage of the Jews.

I ask the Reich government for a fundamental decree according to which no Jewish business may be put in a better position than German businesses with regard to discount rates. This decree is fundamentally necessary in order to prevent National Socialism from being vitiated by subordinate organs.

I need hardly add that I have been led to address this outcry to the Reich government solely on nationalist grounds.

With a German Hitler salute
your very devoted
R. Fichte

The government of the Reich, i.e., Hitler, had no intention of influenc-ing the discount lists of any glassworks. Fichte's letter went into the files, as did all his others. Instead, the decision was made to 'Aryanise' larger Jewish enterprises. Under the new owners appointed by the Nazi Party the situation of small retailers did not change. Businessmen like Fichte whose livelihoods were threatened had always supported the Nazi Party but did not profit from the latter's seizure of power or from the expropriation of Jewish large business owners.

The fact that a social revolution had not yet occurred also irritated the Local Peasant Leader Jakob Falkenstein from Hüttenfeld in Hesse, western Germany. He wrote a letter to Hitler on 5 February 1934 in which he described the local conditions quite precisely:

My Leader!

I know that you have to work a great deal: night and day, therefore I will also be brief and ask you, my Leader, only to provide information on a few points that no one else can give me. We have a little village of 500 inhabitants. But in our locality people are dissatisfied as never before.

1. Farmers: In every earlier election they all voted for our Nazi Party. Today they are no longer satisfied, because they have still not seen any results. The farmers read in the newspapers that things are advancing, and hear it in assemblies, but they want their personal selves to be put in the foreground. Here we have had a few unemployed, but since November they have been working again, are earning their potatoes and their bread themselves, and nonetheless to a large extent have been able to receive aid. This is a bitter disappointment for the farmers who contribute potatoes, grain and all kinds of things that are received by the others, who go for walks and laugh at the little farmers in the summer.

2. The Jewish question. Dairying is the main local occupation. [And in this area the vast majority of cattle dealers were Jewish. As a result] no one but the Jew can provide cows to milk, insofar as people have no money, and the Jew gives them cows. As Peasant Leader, no matter what I do is of no avail; even the Storm Battalion Reserve does business with Jews.

3. Workers: in our locality we have a Baron von Heyl who owns two estates. He employs workers, for the most part Stormtroopers, and pays them 24 marks every fortnight without food and lodging. When everything is deducted the poor people, who faced death to fight for the Third Reich, have nothing left and still have to feed their families and pay the organization, the Stormtroopers, and all kinds of other things, whereas others who have previously done nothing, for whom the money was not enough, took a Marxist attitude, and seriously mistreated our Stormtroopers, now have highway jobs and receive double pay.

The result: dissatisfaction.

4. Refinancing: if anyone who has fallen into debt through no fault of his own files for bankruptcy, the creditors say he is trying to steal their money. Everything one tries does not succeed. But I, my Leader, remain as the only veteran among these people in the locality. I have to say, if I didn't have a firm belief in you – yesterday, today, and tomorrow – I think I would long since have gone mad, everyone wants information, mostly this and that.

I therefore beg you, my Leader, to be so good as to give me guidance as to how I should go on.

Requesting a prompt reply
Jakob Falkenstein
Much luck with a difficult task, Hail my Leader!

The letter was filed without reply. However, the adjutant's office was informed of the protest and perhaps Hitler was also notified.

7

DISSENT

The mail received from the people in 1933 and 1934 did not consist solely of expressions of veneration or private petitions written by Hitler supporters. Interestingly, the letters also reveal a surprising level of protest and dissent from Germans and from others living abroad.

The writer, Harald von Koenigswald, whose unsparing reports on Soviet terrorism in East Germany made him known to a wider audience after 1945, wrote several times to Albert Bormann seeking an improvement in the situation of certain persons. For example, in April 1933:

Dear Mr Bormann!

Although I know that you are now so overloaded with work and that I recently approached you regarding another matter, today I must once again ask you for your mediation. But you yourself know how responsible one feels for hardships that in principle require that steps be taken, when they affect people who have devoted their whole lives and all their energy to the nation.

I refer to the Imperial undersecretary of state Prof. Dr Göppert, who comes from an old Prussian family of public officials (Frederick the Great often stayed in his ancestors' house). His daughter has Jewish blood as the granddaughter of Prof. Hirschfeld, who was greatly respected in his time and was a friend of Theodor Mommsen [a German classical scholar and jurist] who dedicated his book on constitutional law to him. Miss Göppert has been put on leave as a student teacher, and that is very painful for his Excellency Göppert, who as a lecturer in law at the University of Bonn always strongly emphasized his nationalist attitude, especially during the time of the separatists and the French on the Rhine.

Would it now be possible, in consideration of the personal qualities of his Excellency Göppert, to allow his daughter to continue and complete her training by advising the Attorney General of District Court I? She does not plan to enter government service later on, but rather to use her knowledge in private, scientific work. I would be very grateful to you if you could let me know whether something can be done about this case, and would be very glad to hear from you again, even without such an occasion, and remain, with warmest greetings also from my wife

Your Koenigswald
21 April 33

Bormann did not reply. Whether anything could be done for the student teacher in 1933 is also unclear. In any case, she survived the Nazi terror.

Despite the increasing irrelevance of former governmental structures, many Germans held on to an idea of law, political legitimacy, and civil rights in cases such as Koenigswald's. Considerable numbers of Germans, for example, still saw the decrepit President of the Reich, Paul von Hindenburg, as a nonpartisan authority, and addressed their petitions to him. Usually the petitioners were simply told that the Reich government or some other authority was responsible for the matter in question.

Erich Ludendorff, Hindenburg's chief of staff in the First World War, and former Nazi supporter, also wrote increasingly desperate, enraged letters drawing attention to conditions in the Reich. He repeatedly informed Hindenburg of the arrest of members of his Tannenberg-Bund, a far-right German political society he founded in 1925, after his disastrous Presidential campaign. He combined

this specific complaint with a more fundamental criticism. The tone
Ludendorff adopted is astounding. With reference to the case of a
journalist in Breslau who had been arrested, on 18 August 1933 he
sent Hindenburg a handwritten letter telegram without any formal
salutation:

Strick/Breslau free again, was terribly mishandled. How can you allow
such things. Don't you still feel the fear and desperation of the tor-
mented people? Put an end to this unbearaby dreadful condition of
lawlessness. You have the power and the duty to do so.

On 16 August Ludendorff reported further abuses and the shocking
case of a pregnant woman whose anxiety after the arrest of her husband
caused her to lose her child, and two days later he protested against the
continuing arrests. On 25 August 1933 he wrote to the President of the
Reich: 'the illegal attacks and arrests have not ceased in the German
Reich, of which you are the head and whose constitution you have
sworn to uphold'.

Once again Ludendorff described a few cases and then went on:
'that is what the legal conditions in the German Reich have come to.
This telegram will probably also not be given to you, even this will be
kept from you, but your entourage should understand that the people's
turning away from the state and its despair regarding the uncertainty
of law and the economic emergency is steadily increasing'. In referring
to Hitler's entourage, Ludendorff probably had foremost in his mind
State Secretary Otto Meissner, who had been the head of the Office of
the President of Germany for the entirety of the Weimar Republic and
still was, despite attempting to resign once the Nazis came to power.
Meissner had a copy of both letters and the enclosed materials made
and delivered the dossier to the State Secretary of the Chancellor's
Office, Hans Heinrich Lammers. He did the same thing with the last
letter that Ludendorff sent Hindenburg on 18 November 1933:

Mr Reich President!

Two days ago I informed you of unprecedented incidents. Such incidents are piling up in a terrifying way.

Today I am writing to tell you that during the night of 12–13 November, in Hedwigskoog, a farm owner called Wollatz had his farm broken into by ruffians, who attacked this German and godfearing man. He fled from the criminals. His wife, and mother of five children, was reduced to a sorry state. She fled in her nightshirt to her parents who live far away. The eldest child was threatened with a revolver, and is still trembling. 145 marks were stolen. Farmhands were mishandled. The perpetrators, who belong to the SS, have not been arrested, even though a complaint was filed.

That is the shape that things repeatedly take in the Reich that you govern. Law is increasingly trampled underfoot, despite all the talk about legal conditions and the introduction of a new legal code. The physical freedom of Germans is being threatened in an unprecedented way. Today, when 'cultural chambers', i.e., 'leaden chambers' are being established for German intellectual life, the last remains of intellectual freedom are being buried in a way that was not the case even in the Jesuit state of Paraguay and in Germany during the darkest Middle Ages.

When someday the history of the German people is written, then the end of your presidency of the Reich will be described as the blackest age in German history. I know that my letters to you are of no avail. After all you needed only to order the Army to put an end to these unbearable conditions among the people. But I am confronted by the serious reproach of my life, that it was only through the advice that I gave you, and through my acts, that you were able to become the Reich President of the now unfortunate German people.

Long live freedom! May this cry ring in your ears until you close your eyes.

Ludendorff

Meissner received confirmation that the dossier had been received.

Whether most Germans at this point would have felt themselves to be 'unfortunate' is certainly up for debate. It points to Ludendorff's continued inability to read Germany's political mood correctly. Ludendorff fell silent in November 1933. Personal discussions with Hitler, and with fellow participants in the 1923 putsch, led to nothing.

But Ludendorff's supporters did not cease to criticize the Nazi Party, which they regarded as much too socialist. The Nazi leadership was, probably wrongly, concerned about the threat posed by Ludendorff and his supporters and kept them under surveillance as a result.

Ludendorff was not the only one concerned about developments in the regime, particularly the rough treatment of some Germans. On 25 March 1934, Editha Badke from Berlin wrote to Hitler regarding her husband, who had disappeared:

Dear Mr Reich Chancellor!

I am writing to you for the third time. It cannot be true that you are not willing to listen to my request. No, I assume that you did not personally receive my letters of 16 January and 26 February of this year, otherwise I would have received a reply. But the torment increases from month to month. How can it be that my husband has already been imprisoned for five months without any prospect of a trial? If he had committed a serious offence, I could understand this; but as it is it is, incomprehensible to me. He has always been cooperative, and everyone who knows him can give him a good recommendation. I assure you again and again, that we are willing to accept whatever you give us. We also do not want to complain that in this year we have still not found work, because it is certainly very, very hard to provide jobs for millions of people who are unemployed. I grant that in their need people are often indignant. But when there are all kinds of things to buy and I have no money and [one] has known only poverty ever since childhood, then one does have doubts. But I have recovered my trust in a better future, and therefore I am willing to accept everything, only I ask you, be lenient and give my husband his freedom back.

With great confidence and thanks
I remain, with a German salute
Editha Badke

One wonders whether Editha Badke's husband, who it seems was perceived as some sort of political opponent, was even still alive when she wrote her letter of protest to Hitler.

Also filed away was a letter written on 3 May 1934 by Anna Banz from Kaufbeuren in Bavaria, whose husband had been dismissed in accord with Paragraph 6 of the Law on the Rehabilitation of a Professional Civil Service. This paragraph permitted dismissals for the purpose of 'simplifying administration', but was regularly invoked when it was a question of freeing up a position for a Party member.

Dear Mr Reich Chancellor!

I sent the enclosed to Berlin for your birthday. Now it has been sent back to me by the post office.

I am trying once again to send you the picture of my son.

My earnest request that my husband be given back his position as a postal secretary in the Postal Service has unfortunately been rejected. I no longer dare to ask you once again, esteemed Mr Reich Chancellor.

Unfortunately, I cannot rid myself of the feeling that the dismissal in accord with paragraph 6, on account of debts, of a man who supports three children and also took part in the 1914–1918 war, has done my husband and the whole family a great injustice.

With a German salute!
'Hail Hitler!'
Most devotedly
Anna Banz

Anna Beeger from Grimma in Saxony sent Hitler a picture of her youngest son, whom she claimed was an enthusiastic member of the Hitler Youth, and asked him personally to investigate the suicide of her 'good husband', a foreman. She addressed the letter 'to our beloved Leader!' Desperately, she described going without success from one office to another, from the attorney general's office to the SS and from there to the police. Since she received an answer from none of these, she was now, in April 1934, describing the case. She enclosed her husband's statement about an incident that had taken place on the evening of 1 July 1933:

The undersigned hereby takes the liberty of explaining as follows the
incident that took place on 1 February at the marksmen's festival.
Around eight p.m. I met one of my fellow workers, who joined me,
along with his wife. Although he had earlier been a communist, I do
not know what his current attitude is, since we did not talk politics
at all. Until 12 midnight he was at my place, then he went home. Up
to this point no one has accused me of anything, but should this be
important, I hereby most respectfully ask forgiveness. I assure you
that in the future I will no longer say anything to such a person. At
12 o'clock I met an acquaintance I used to sing in the chorus with,
Gustav Küne. We went together to the Schützenhaus [bar] and drank
a few beers. All of a sudden Stormtrooper Grüneberger came up to
my table and said: 'You can buy one for me, too.' Without giving it a
thought, I bought him a beer. A few minutes later he came back and
said aggressively, 'You have to buy one for my Troop Leader, too.'
At that I replied: 'Not that way, he has to come himself.' I assume
that the second beer was supposed to be for the Stormtrooper Kanis.
That was when the taunting started. If Mr Kanis accused me of saying
'I'd rather buy one for the Communists', I deny that. I suppose he
must have imagined this to take revenge on me for not paying for the
second beer. I also take the liberty of enclosing a statement by Mr
Küne that the phrase 'I'd rather buy one for the Communists' was not
uttered at all. Since the taunting was too much for me, I left. At this
point they must have lost sight of me, because after a while, when he
saw me again, he started right off with the words: 'Now I've got you,
you jerk, I've been looking for you for a long time', and right away
they started beating me. I was attacked from all sides, and Mr Kanis
kept hitting me, and they [partly] pushed me, partly dragged me to
the Muldenwiese. Here the beating began again. Mr Kanis demanded
that I confess that I had used the word 'Communists', and because I
refused, they kept hitting me so long that in desperation I finally said
'yes'. Suddenly Mr Fleming appeared, and everything immediately
stopped. He asked Mr Kanis what he had against me. He [Mr Kanis]
then told what had happened, that I had said: 'I'd rather buy one for
the Communists', which I had admitted. When Mr Fleming asked
whether that was correct, naturally I admitted that I had said 'yes',
because I thought that, if not, it would all start over again. Then Mr

Fleming told me to go home, and I immediately obeyed. At the same time, I enclose further eyewitness testimonies, from which you will be able to see how roughly and brutally Mr Kanis has dealt not only with me, but also with other people.

I would also like to describe for you my attitude towards politics. First of all I would like to point out that as old as I am, I have never yet been involved in politics, and I am not now. However, I immediately joined the National Socialist Factory Cell Organization. [This was a Nazi workers' organization, founded in 1928. It became the official Nazi union and workers organization after 1932. It was absorbed by the German Labour Front (DAF) in 1935.] If perhaps you might think that I am not satisfied with the current government, I hereby point out that in my building I have two children – thirteen and sixteen years old – who adhere body and soul to the Hitler Youth. And I am happy about that. If I were not I would long since have forbidden it. I will now close my report, and you may judge, sirs, whether I have done anything offensive.

Very respectfully yours,
P. B[eeger]

While the husband put his statement on paper, his wife sought out witnesses to the event. She came home with a series of witness statements. The following day she gave them to the local policeman, a man called Wappler. She described to Hitler what happened next.

That morning I went back to Mr Wappler, in order to find out what was happening. Mr Wappler told me that the investigation ... was underway and that my husband must go there for questioning. I asked Mr Wappler whether my husband could not be questioned here. Mr W. replied that he could make no exceptions. As a result my husband assumed that he would be picked up tomorrow morning. He thought that even today he might be taken away from work. In order to spare his family this disgrace, he hanged himself.

Grimma, 11 July 1933

A Jewish master craftsman reacted to the Stormtrooper's terrorism
with a letter of protest. Heinrich Herz from Hamborn am Rhein wrote
on 27 April 1934:

Very esteemed Mr Reich Chancellor!

On the assumption that you, respected Mr Reich Chancellor, will
understand my situation, please permit me to inform you of the following: I have repeatedly appealed to various authorities, but have received
a reply from none of them. Since my last attempt on 12 December 1933
also remained unanswered, I am turning to you, respected Mr Reich
Chancellor, since my intuition tells me that you, respected Mr Reich
Chancellor, will not accept this. I look on the events of the last years full
of admiration and trust, and I am inwardly a good German who cares
about the welfare of his country with every fibre of his being.

But with all this admiration a drop of wormwood has slipped into my
heart, and I ask myself over and over why that is so. I am very far from
complaining, and have fought evil and immorality all my life. Honesty
and genuineness were and are my supreme duty. I marvel with satisfaction at the eradication of profiteers and bigwigs, no matter from which
camp they came. But what I cannot say I am satisfied with is the one-
sided treatment of thousands of my co-religionists, whose feeling and
thinking are just as German as mine. How much I should like to help
build up my beloved Fatherland, if only an opportunity to do so were
offered me.

Just as you have battled for years to achieve your goals, respected
Mr Reich Chancellor, so I would like to lead the battle for my co-
religionists and not rest until I emerge victorious from this fortress. It
is true that I am a simple master craftsman and have never experienced
anything but disappointments in my life. My whole life is just a series of
sorrows, which has, however, sometimes been shot through by a ray of
sunshine. Hardened by my fate, I have become a fighter, and I want to
use the time remaining to me to try to get closer to you, respected Mr
Reich Chancellor.

I am firmly convinced that you, respected Mr Reich Chancellor, will
soon acquire a different opinion of a large part of my co-religionists;
indeed, I would claim of by far the greatest part. If I personally lack the

means to fight for our cause, this should not prevent me from using all my strength on behalf of my ideals. I want to begin with my first task, and that is regaining the lost rights of Jewish master craftsmen. As long-time head of the Hambron Plumber's Guild, I believe I am called upon to undertake this task. And now a brief outline of my life.

As the son of a master craftsman, I attended the elementary school in Bad Nassau. I lost my mother when I was seven. At fourteen, I was apprenticed to a small master plumber in Wattenscheid in Westphalia [in western Germany]. My apprenticeship was for three years. Since my blessed father lacked the means to clothe me, this contract was extended to five years, and for my work I received full room and board and clothing. When I was nineteen, I ended my apprenticeship and worked as an assistant in various large workshops. At twenty I became a soldier and was discharged at twenty-two as a sergeant-candidate. After several years of working in Aachen and Eschweiler, in my twenty-fourth year I married a co-religionist, a very poor but hardworking girl. Seven children were born of our marriage, of whom one died young and two daughters died at the ages of twenty-two and eighteen. I founded my independent existence in Eschweiler, and after six years moved to Hamborn, which was then a flourishing community. Taking great pleasure in my work, I carried out the tasks that were sent me and in 1912 I was able to build my own house. However, there were setbacks then as well. But each time I recovered, because my customers were satisfied with my work. In January 1915 I went to war as a member of the Prussian militia and returned after the armistice as a sergeant, safe and sound. Like many others I also had to start over from the beginning, and my wife's task consisted in having my children learn some respectable trade. Two of my sons entered my own trade and for one of them [the] eldest, I sacrificed to send him to the state mechanical engineering school in Cologne, where he passed his engineer's exam with a good score. One son who had special talent studied music. In 1930 I voluntarily resigned my office as head of the Plumbers' Guild, even though I had been unanimously re-elected, but I remained a member of the Guild's examination board.

Before the outbreak of the National Revolution I was on a firm footing. Like a lightning bolt out of a clear sky the storm swept over me. I lost all my customers. No government agency, no commune, not even a private individual offered me a contract, even though I had never had differences of opinion with my public and private customers. My grown-up sons were thrown out of work, and at times I have been dependent on public welfare. Despite the many directives issued by Mr Minister Frick [a prominent Nazi official who was Reich Minister of the Interior during the Third Reich] and others, my long-time public customers have not returned, and the private customers only do so hesitatingly, because they think, though I cannot prove this, that they might get in trouble with the subordinate Party organs.

And now, respected Mr Reich Chancellor, judge whether I have deserved this? My wife, whom the time of hardship has made ill, was told by her doctor to undergo a four-week rest cure in the Sauerland [a rural section of Westphalia that is hilly and covered with forests]. My health insurance has lapsed because I have not made payments, and I have had to let go thousands in life insurance, etc.

Very respected Mr Reich Chancellor, use your authority to give us hope that we can live again. I shall thank you thousands and thousands of times for it.

Heinrich Herz

Not all letters from Germans who were branded as Jews after 1933 were as self-confident as the one from Heinrich Herz. But all these letters demonstrate how integrated into German society these Jewish citizens were – and how German they felt themselves to be. The growing discrimination against them thus came as a surprise to most. The growing exclusion of Jewish Germans was particularly hard for those who learned only after extensive research that they had Jewish ancestors.

For example, the Berlin artist Rudolf Jaenicke had supported the Nazi Party since 1932. Only when he wanted to work as a Party official did others discover a Jewish grandmother in his ancestry. Thereupon the Nazi Party refused to employ him. In his petition to Hitler he emphasized his otherwise good Evangelical ancestry and his Christian way of life. Then he added his request:

Our great beloved Leader Adolf Hitler! I ask you now for advice. Must I give up everything? We are also people and perhaps better than some others. Must I leave the Nazi Party, etc.? I can't see why. But in spite of all, my sincere belief in our German Fatherland, in the National Socialist idea, and above all in you, great Leader, that belief cannot be taken away from me.

And so, great beloved Leader,

Mr Reich Chancellor Adolf Hitler!

Please help us, too.

For this is God's work, and we believe in the one whom he has sent to us.

> *Hail Hitler!*
> *Rudolf Willi Ernst Jaenicke*

Oh, if only I could speak to you personally.

Hitler's private office replied on 5 April 1934.

Dear Mr Jaenicke!

Your letter to the Leader of the 23 March was received here. I regret to tell you that this office can do nothing about your case. I therefore recommend that you approach your local group, which may be able to help you in some way.

> *With a German salute!*
> *Albert Bormann*

The documents you sent are enclosed.

Organized protest came from the Jehovah's Witnesses, a Christian separatist group founded in the late 1870s by Charles Taze Russel. Jehovah's Witnesses believe that God will imminently end human life on earth, establishing a pure society consisting only of true believers. Evangelical work is considered crucial and all Witnesses must undertake it. At this time Witnesses did not take part in national elections on principle. They also refused to make the Hitler salute and did not display flags on their houses. Their pacifist attitude could not be tolerated by the National Socialists, and the Party and the Gestapo constantly harassed them. Prohibitions on publication and assembly were issued and then cancelled, and local police forces were instructed to arrest all the offensive missionary members.

In September delegates from many European congregations met in Basel, Switzerland, and decided to defy the Nazi regime. Their refusal to compromise is reflected in the adaptation of a saying about the persecuted Hebrews in Babylonian exile: 'see not only the fiery furnace – see also the deliverance therefrom'. The Jehovah's Witnesses present in Basel obliged the members of their congregations to continue their ministry in prayer groups and their missionary work. The Basel Congress, which was attended by over 1,000 Germans, also suggested that a letter of protest be written. On 7 October 1934, many congregations therefore wrote to the government of the Reich or to Reich Chancellor Adolf Hitler himself:

To the Government of the Reich, Berlin

Jehovah's word, as it is given in the holy Scriptures, is the highest law, and it is our sole guiding principle, because we have dedicated ourselves to God and are true, genuine followers of Jesus Christ.

During the past year, in contradiction to God's law and in violation of our rights you have forbidden us to gather as Jehovah's Witnesses in order to explore God's Word, pray to God, and serve him. In his word God commands us to meet (Hebrews 10: 25). Jehovah bids us and says: 'You are my witnesses [that] I am God . . . go and say this to the people' (Isaiah 43: 10, 12; Isaiah 6: 9; Matthew 24: 14).

There is a direct contradiction between your law and God's law. Since we follow the counsel of the true apostles, 'we must obey God rather than men' (Acts 5: 29) and that is what we shall do.

We therefore hereby inform you that we will follow at any price God's command that we meet together in order to explore his word and that we pray to him and serve him as he has commanded us. If your government or government officials do us violence because we are obeying God, then our blood will be on your head, and you will have to render account for it to God the Almighty. We have nothing to do with political matters, instead we are fully devoted to the Kingdom of God under the rule of Christ, his king. We shall not torment or harm anyone. We should rejoice to remain at peace and do as much good as we can to all people. But since your government and your officials continue their attempt to force us to disobey the highest law of the universe, we are compelled now to inform you that we wish to obey Jehovah through his grace and that we trust him entirely to deliver us from any oppression and all persecution.

Jehovah's Witnesses
Bad Dürkheim

The wording of the letter of protest was, apart from small variations and spelling errors, always the same. At least fifteen letters, including several from Saxony and from southern Germany were found in a file from Hitler's private office in the special archive in Moscow. The letters of protest sent to Hitler from outside Germany were also always the same, as in the telegram from Enschede in the Netherlands:

To the Hitler government, Berlin, Germany

Your ill-treatment of the Jehovah's Witnesses enrages all good men and disgraces God's name. Stop persecuting Jehovah's Witnesses, otherwise God will destroy you and your national party.

Th. Bykerth
Secretary of the group

At least twenty of these letters came from congregations of Jehovah's Witnesses in Belgium, Switzerland, France, the Netherlands, Luxemburg, Great Britain, and Denmark. On 9 October 1934, Jehovah's Witnesses from Cleveland, Ohio wrote to 'Chancellor von Hitler, Berlin, Germany':

KLASSE	KT-BEST.		KT-AZ	NR
			ENSCHEDE	

AANTAL WOORDEN	DAG *7 Oct 1934*	UUR .en MIN.	DBVS	

A. Overseinen . . . ƒ
B. Antwoord . . . „
C. Ontvangbewijs . . „

AANGENOMEN DOOR :   GIRO-NR

RIJKS-TELEGRAAF

Overgeseind naar...................
In draad................., den .... 193......
te ....
door :

Samen . . . ƒ
Bij Terug betaald den ƒ

JE-MAINTIENDRAI

TELEGRAM

Enschede, 7 Oct, 1934.

An die Hitler-Regierung
Berlin (Deutschland)
Ihre schlechte Behandlung der
Zeugen Jehovas empört alle guten
menschen und entehrt Gottes Namen.
Hören Sie auf Jehovas Zeugen weiterhin
zu verfolgen, sonst wird Gott Sie und
Ihre nationale Partei vernichten.

F Bijkerk
Schriftführer der Gruppe

HET ONDER DE STREEP GESCHREVENE WORDT. NIET MEDEGESEIND.

NADRUK VERBODEN.
MOD. T I A L. 1012/'34.

NAAM EN ADRES VAN DEN AFZENDER :

TELEFOONNUMMER VAN DEN AFZENDER :

The protest against the persecution of Jehovah's Witnesses was worldwide and well organized. But instead of changing its political targets, the regime responded by extending its repression. Hitler's chancellery forwarded almost all the letters to the Gestapo, which arrested the writers and sent more than a thousand of them to concentration camps. A few letters remain in the files – like this telegram of protest from Enschede in Holland.

Source: RGWA (Moscow)

Mr Hitler. A warning! Give Jehovah's Witnesses their freedom and allow Kingdom work to continue, lest you experience the Lord's vengeance.

> *Yours for*
> *Christ's Kingdom*
> *Lila de Long*

The protest directed to Hitler had massive consequences. All letters and protests from Jehovah's Witnesses – how many there were can no longer be determined – were collected and organized in Hitler's private office. Hitler's office forwarded at least a thousand of these letters to the Gestapo for, as the cover letter put it, 'further processing'. The secret police acted in December 1934, and in January 1935 a further wave of arrests followed. Of the approximately 30,000 Jehovah's Witnesses in Germany about 10,000 were arrested during the twelve years of the National Socialist dictatorship; 2,000 of those were incarcerated in concentration camps, where about 950 died. In comparison with the millions of victims of the Nazi regime this number may seem small, but it testifies to an act of collective, ruthless self-assertion that compels respect.

The Nazis' establishment of a dictatorship and the injustice connected with it were in no way accepted without complaint. In particular, judgements that were technically legal but obviously unethical caused a wave of protest letters. In this case both Germans and foreigners addressed Hitler personally in attempting to bring about either a reprieve for someone condemned to death or a pardon.

One well-documented case demonstrates this particularly well. The Moscow files contain 118 letters with more than 2,000 signatures of protesters against the planned execution of the Communist Etkar (or Edgar) André. André was leader of Hamburg's Red Front Fighters' League, which was the German Communist Party's paramilitary organization, founded in 1924. It was banned in 1932 after repeated street fights with Nazi Stormtroopers.

André had been arrested after the Reichstag fire, presumably using the new powers of the Order of the Reich President for the Protection of People and State, which gave the Nazi authorities the legal ability to arrest political opponents without needing a specific charge. In 1936 he was convicted by the criminal division of the regional high court in Hamburg of preparing to commit high treason accompanied by murder, and was later guillotined. His killing was undoubtedly unjust. Since participation in the murder of a Nazi activist could not be proven in the trial, the judges argued that because he was the highest leader of the paramilitary group, André was automatically responsible for the actions of other members.

The condemned man's wife fled to Denmark, where Communists and human rights activists organized a campaign to win him a pardon. In Denmark, the Netherlands, France, and Czechoslovakia, there was a wave of protests in August 1936, partly using pre-printed resolutions. The size of the protests was astonishing given the situation at the time.

Among the signers of a pre-printed text was the then world famous writer Martin Andersen Nexö. Nexö was the first mainstream Danish author to focus on the working classes in his writings and is remembered as the first major Danish Communist writer. He was arrested in 1941, during the Nazis' occupation of Denmark. When he was released he went to Sweden and then on to the Soviet Union, where he made anti-Nazi broadcasts to Denmark and Norway. After the Second World War he moved to Dresden, in East Germany, and was granted honorary citizenship.

The text he used not only opposed the Nazi regime's treatment of André but also the unjust judicial system in general:

To the government of the German Reich and to Mr Reich Chancellor Hitler, Berlin

We undersigned Danes call upon the government of the German Reich and Mr Reich Chancellor Hitler to grant amnesty for the prisoners currently held in German penitentiaries on political, racial, or religious grounds.

We know that in Germany it is considered important that we here in Nordic countries have sympathy and understanding for the German people. We therefore see ourselves as authorized to point out that in our countries, where humanity and justice are valued especially highly, such an amnesty for political, racial, and religious prisoners and the

– often promised – abolition of the concentration camps is seen as an unavoidable humanitarian demand. At the same time we gladly express our sympathy and support for the European amnesty conference for political prisoners in Germany, which has been called by well-known public figures from around the world.

Martin Andersen Nexö

Others wrote their own letters to Hitler protesting the situation. An aristocratic German woman living in Switzerland asked Hitler for legal leniency. The board of the SPD Party in Basel made a 'blazing protest in the name of humanity' and wrote to Hitler on 8 July 1936:

Mr Reich Chancellor,

The workers and a large part of the population of Basel learned with horror of the judgement handed down by the criminal division of the Hanseatic Regional Court against Edgar André.

The people of Basel see in it not atonement for past criminal acts, but rather an act of vengeance on the part of the ruling party against one of their opponents. Against this we make a blazing protest in the name of humanity.

We will also not let our protest be countered by the claim that we have no right to get involved in German internal affairs. When a person we believe to be innocent is to be executed solely because of his ideas, then national boundaries no longer matter. Humanity itself must take a stand and try to prevent the intended injustice. Mr Reich Chancellor, it is in your power to prevent the judicial murder of Edgar André.

We call upon you, and in this we have the support of the Swiss people and the people of Basel, to make use of your right of granting pardon and save Edgar André from the executioner's axe.

We also demand justice and therefore freedom for the other victims of your Party rule – Carl von Ossietzky [a radical German pacifist writer from Hamburg who was arrested by the Nazis after the Reichstag Fire and detained in a concentration camp. He was awarded the Nobel Peace Prize in 1935. Ossietzky died in 1938 from a combination of tuberculosis and the long-term effects of his incarceration.],

Thälmann [Ernst Thälmann was leader of the Communist Party of Germany during most of the Weimar Republic. He was arrested by the Gestapo in 1933 and held in solitary confinement for eleven years. He was shot in the concentration camp Buchenwald in 1944 on Hitler's direct orders], and many others.

With special esteem
The Social Democratic Party of the city of Basel
President of the Parliament E. Herzog Nat. Rat.
Party Secretary Schneider Nat. Rat.

Letters of protest also came in from New York, Prague, Ostrau in Czech-Bohemia, and London. The letters from Communist factory cells and the collections of signatures were framed in the usual rhetoric. On 21 July 1936, however, a few young people from Blackpool (Lancashire, UK) also wrote to Hitler. Interestingly, they chose to write their letter in German:

Dear Mr,

From England we say – Release Edgar André and Ernst Thälmann!

Marie Smith
John Wells
Lucille Morton
William Wallace
J. Jones
B. Griffiths

A letter from a woman in Friesland in the Netherlands seemed to Hitler's private office worth specifically informing Hitler about. Albert Bormann reported to Hitler: 'The writer admires the Leader of the German people and his great deeds. Before the war she had an opportunity to become acquainted with the German people, and has always had great admiration for it. Now she asks the Leader to pardon Edgar André because of [public opinion] abroad.' Someone from Switzerland wrote Hitler a single sentence: 'There has been enough murdering.'

Also filed away was a letter from an Alsatian written on 9 September 1936:

Mr Reich Chancellor,

In this letter I want to tell you again exactly what international human-ity thinks of the injustice that you have done our beloved Edgar André, who because of his outstanding character and free-thinking was beaten to death. You also talk about brothers killing brothers in Spain – naturally your accomplices of Franco are the aggressors. [Here the author is referencing Germany's assistance of General Franco's right-wing forces during the Spanish Civil War.]

We understand. Just look at Germany – what a Hell for freedom fighters. Decent people like these are destroyed and how they are mur-dered – yes it is known to the world. That is why International Labour stands behind our beloved Edgar André, who had even proven his innocence, but because he doesn't think the way you do he must die.

Justice, justice lasts longest.

Yes, Spain will uphold its republic. It will win, it must win. Then the war you have in mind can be declared the final salvation.

No you want to scare the world with the Bolshevist regime
No we're not afraid we're waiting for it with longing
You all know it.
Be quick and declare your war you see it and feel it.

An Alsatian Militiaman
who with his whole heart
fights alongside Spain
all alone I have collected 476 francs
in 10 days
Free Edgar André
Hail Thälmann

8

EXPRESSIONS OF LOYALTY

The campaigns of Hitler's opponents opened the eyes of many people abroad who had up to that point been uncritical of the Nazi regime. Although some Germans did themselves protest, they were largely isolated and ineffective. The Nazis did not of course let on that such protests were taking place at all. Perhaps greater numbers of Germans would have protested the regime's increasingly brutal policies if they had known that similar sentiments were being expressed abroad.

But there were few letters of protest even when the regime attacked its own supporters. Between 30 June and 2 July 1934 the Nazi leadership undertook a violent purge of the paramilitary organization the Storm Battalion, killing at least 85 Stormtroopers, including the Battalion's entire leadership. Over 1,000 others were arrested, using the same powers that had allowed for the arrests of communist opponents a year previously. Most of these individuals, however, were themselves Nazis. The purge, known variously as the Night of the Long Knives and the Röhm-Putsch, was undertaken by Hitler because he saw the dominance of the Stormtroopers and the popularity of their commander Ernst Röhm as a threat. The fact that Röhm had been a member of the Nazi Party since the early 1920s was not enough to save him. Hitler hesitated at the idea of murdering Röhm, and instead gave him the opportunity to commit suicide. Röhm refused, and was subsequently shot in the chest at point blank range. The Stormtroopers, who, under Röhm's cultish leadership, envisaged themselves as leading a further revolution and absorbing the German Army into a national militia, were a clear threat to Hitler's authority. The Storm Battalion's desire to replace the Army also threatened the military establishment, an institution whose support Hitler needed for his foreign policy goals, and one which still required Nazification. Although the Night of the Long Knives seemed to some Germans to be a shocking act of brutality, for many others, Hitler and the Nazi Party had seemingly restored law and order in reigning in the unruly Storm Battalion.

While there were few letters denouncing these actions, many Stormtroopers wrote to Hitler to profess their loyalty to him.

Stanislaus Jaros, from Lobstädt in Saxony, a Party member and a member of the Stormtroopers since 1930, sent his oath of allegiance to Hitler on 13 July 1934. He indicated that he was relieved by a radio speech in which Hitler explained the assassination of Röhm and other Stormtrooper leaders, and believed what Hitler said word for word.

My Leader and People's Chancellor!

I followed your speech from the Reichstag building, sentence for sentence with a pure heart and deep reflections. It penetrated my heart and soul like a deliverance, a salvation for the whole German people. My heart bled inwardly, and tears came to my eyes.

I congratulate you, my Leader, on your energy and your prompt decision by which you have saved us from this bitterly difficult fate and called to account the mutineers and condemned them to just punishment.

May Almighty God continue to give you the energy to protect us Germans from every fate.

I am prepared, like my father, even to sacrifice my life, when Germany is involved and you, my Leader, call.

Hail, my Leader
In true loyalty, Stormtrooper and Party member
Stanislaus Jaros

Very few Germans were willing – or desired – to criticize the regime. Some were convinced by the Nazis' political programme; others feared for their lives. Out of more than 100 letters preserved from 1935, only one letter could be interpreted as a criticism of the regime. The sender complained about local Party officials' agitation against the church. The others asked for Hitler's autograph, donated money for the winter-aid programme, or congratulated him on the anniversary of his accession to power. All were eager to demonstrate their loyalty to the regime and affection for Hitler.

For example, a woman from Berlin sent flowers to the Chancellor's Office on 30 January 1935. On the attached card she had written:

Dear Leader!

As a small sign of great love and gratitude these roses for your day of remembrance are sent you by

Your Party comrade Anna Kellermann

Hitler's office replied on 5 February 1935:

Dear Party Comrade!

The Leader wants you to know that he is grateful for the flowers and good wishes. You have given him real pleasure.

With a German salute!
[unreadable]

The master hairdresser Curt Rudolf Kempe from Seiffen in the Ore Mountains, also known as the Erzgebirge, on the border between Germany and the Czech Republic, had a very unconventional idea, which he communicated to Hitler's office on 4 April 1935.

As a resident of the Ore Mountains, I want to see our Leader, and I ask very politely whether it is possible that I could come to Berlin and see our Leader. In addition I would also like to ask very politely whether if I am allowed to see our Leader it might be possible that at the same time I could also cut his hair?

I am a professional hairdresser, 46 years old. It would be for me the happiest moment of my life if this were also possible. I would gladly bring with me from here the tools that would be needed.

I would also be prepared, if the condition were set, to walk from the Ore Mountains to Berlin. I would very much like to fulfil this condition.

It could not happen that I would not cut our Leader's hair correctly, because I was able to acquire sufficient knowledge in my profession in order to meet any demand, through years of work as an assistant abroad. I am also very willing to submit my curriculum vitae, which I had certified by the community authorities.

I request very obediently that our Leader be made aware of this letter so that our Leader can make his decision.

Likewise I request very politely that should you give me permission, you inform me promptly, since it would in any case take a fortnight to walk from Seiffen in the Ore Mountains to Berlin.

Should my letter to you seem untrustworthy, I beg you to seek information regarding me personally from the local Seiffen Nazi Party group and from the Seiffen community authorities.

Hoping that my wish can be fulfilled and that I will receive a reply to the effect that I shall be allowed to cut the Leader's hair, and with the request that should it be possible, you would let me know the exact time and place where I should appear.

Hail Hitler!
Curt Rudolf Kempe
Master Hairdresser

A family from Berlin described for Hitler a dispute that had taken place between their two children. On 12 April 1935 the parents reported the dispute in the form of a humorous narrative and gave it the title 'Children's logic! Oh, these children!'

Oh, these children! Today of all days, when their poor mother has just turned 29, these kids make her aware of her future calling as a mother-in-law. And whose mother-in-law I am supposed to become! Listen and be amazed:

My seven-year-old daughter is once again too lazy to help clean up in the children's room. Her big brother has to do everything all by himself; her little brother has deliberately slipped away. He doesn't like cleaning up either. And the big brother's patience is also not very extensive. 'You, Gina, help a little this time. You can really put away your doll stuff all by yourself, and kindly clean up the dishes too.' 'No,' says the Gina-swallow, 'I'll start working when I'm grown up and have a husband.'

'Ooh, you'll never get a husband, Princess Lazybones!' 'That's what you think, you stupid idiot! I'll get the best husband in all Germany.' 'Hmmph, who is that then, if you know already?' 'What, you want to join the German Youth [the subdivision of the Hitler Youth for boys aged 10–14], and you don't know who the very, very best man in Germany is? And you want to be a Hitler Youth?' 'Listen, Gina, you're getting really out of line! Of course I know who the best man in Germany is, but I don't know who the best one will be when you finally want to marry a man.' 'When I want to and when I'm big enough, then he will still be the same as he is now.' Aribert stood there flabbergasted and speechless. 'You don't want to marry our Hitler?' 'Just Hitler, no one else,' the little girl says proudly. 'I want no other husband.'

'Daddy, Daddy, come here! Daddy, Daddy!' The father comes rushing into the room, wondering crossly who has a bump on the head and who is going to have to be spanked for it. 'Daddy, just think, Gina wants to marry the Leader! And she's only seven years old! Our Princess lazybones wants to marry the Leader! Gina, Gina, he'd die of hunger if he was your husband!!! Oh, the poor man!' Aribert is beside himself with laughter, he can't get over it. Little Gina stands in the middle of the room, furious and offended. 'You don't have to shout so stupidly, I'll get him. Right now he still doesn't have time to get married; but when I'm grown up, everything will already be going much better, and then he won't have so much to do. Then I'll become his wife.'

'But Gina,' says the father, smiling. 'He doesn't know you. You don't know whether he would love you or not.' 'He has already loved me as long as you have', the little lady says boldly. And then she cries with rage and bitterness: 'All his men have got wives and children, he is the only one who is all alone. I love him so much, and I am so sorry for him.' We are astonished: all his men have got wives and children? 'Well yes, Dr Goebbels has got a wife and children, and now the other one has also got a wife in the cathedral.' 'Who then, little swallow?' the father asks. Gina stamps her little foot, exasperated by so much stupidity. 'But Daddy! I mean the man who is also his friend, and whose trousers have such colourful sides. And then he's always wearing something as if it were raining.' Now it begins to dawn on us! 'You mean Hermann Göring?' The father says, at a loss: 'But darling, you don't need to feel sorry for the Leader for that reason. He's happy when his friends are happy.' 'Hmm, are you happy too, Daddy', Little Gina says, giving her father a sideways glance, 'when everybody else gets something wonderful and you are the only one who doesn't? Are you really happy then, without being sad, because you haven't got anything?' 'But Gina, do you mind!' says the father indignantly. 'And so I'll marry him! Why should he remain alone? If he is the very best man in Germany, then he will also have the very best children.' 'And', Aribert scoffs, 'the very best wife, and that's what you claim to be, Gina?!' 'Shut up, old stupid Aribert! You shouldn't always annoy me so much. I am not the best wife; but I love him, and I don't want him to be all alone.' 'My darling', the father says earnestly, 'he is not alone. He has all of us, men, women, and children in Germany and far beyond it. We all love him. That is worth more than the love of just one person.' 'Yes, I already know all that, and that is all true, Daddy. But he also has to have someone who really and truly loves him. When I am his wife, then I shall set the table for him, he will always have flowers, and I shall caress and kiss him.' 'Gina, you dummy', Aribert says, 'when you're grown up, Hitler will be old. He'll still be our Hitler, but a man like that is not for a woman. Then he will no longer have any teeth, and his hair will be falling out too. He won't be handsome any more, and . . .' 'Phooey, you're an old toad', sighs our little swallow. 'Daddy, that isn't true! He'll still be just as handsome as he is now, won't he, Daddy? You darned old rascal! Once I'm with him, we shan't ever invite you over. And if you get married, you'll get a stupid old witch.' 'Now, that's enough!' says the father. 'Leave the little girl alone! Get out of here, Aribert!' He takes the dumb little girl in his arms, and she cries herself to sleep. As the little swallow is laid in her little bed, she murmurs drowsily, 'and

I will be his wife'. Then she sticks her thumb in her mouth, and falls sound asleep.

Outside, in our tiny little garden, Aribert and Pips are hopping around and singing a rhyme of their own:

Gina wants to marry Hitler
ohoho!
Gina will someday be his wife
ohoho!

Then Father comes, grabs his two boys by their collars, gives them a shake and says: 'Off to bed! And if either of you annoys little Gina – you know how – he'll have to deal with me.'

On 5 June 1935 Albert Bormann replied:

Dear Mrs S.,

Your nice, lively little episode has given the Leader real pleasure. The Leader wishes to thank you for the birthday greetings that you sent at the same time.

With a German salute!
[no signature]

The family had not explicitly congratulated Hitler on his birthday, but the letter came in April, and so it was assumed that that was their intention. In August 1935, the family sent flowers and a letter from the children to the Party office.

Dear Leader!

We wanted so much to see you. I love you so much. Please write to me.

Many regards.
Your Gina.
Greetings.
Aribert S.

In October, the mother enquired whether she might have two pictures of the Leader for Aribert and Regina. She was assured she could, but evidently the letter of reply did not include them.

Dear Sir!

I would like to thank you for the lines you wrote to my children Aribert and Regina. The two of them have been pestering me for weeks, asking me to write you. They want me to say that at the bottom of your letter was written 'Enclosures'; but there was nothing enclosed but the letter, the top of which was stuck to the envelope. The children think that you meant to include a picture of the Leader for them, which might have been inadvertently not enclosed. Over whose bed the picture is to hang is already the subject of an intense battle. We already have an especially fine picture of our Leader in the living room, but for the children that is too much general property. Furthermore, Gina says very disdainfully: 'In that one he still has mother-of-pearl buttons on his brown shirt! He no longer needs anything like that.' Therefore I have carried out my commission by writing this letter.

Hail Hitler!
Ella S.

It is not surprising that Hitler's office mistakenly assumed that birthday greetings had been included in the family's April letter. Hitler was now accustomed to receiving a large number of birthday greetings from Germans. What was new, however, was that gifts of money also came in. On the one hand, these were donations that Hitler was supposed to distribute to needy 'fellow Germans'. On the other hand, there were cheques that were supposed to make Hitler well disposed towards something, that is, bribes. The senders did not realize, however, that Hitler preferred to bribe other people. For his presents to generals and high officials, partly in the form of lavish gifts of money amounting to several hundred thousand marks, he had the head of the Chancellor's Office change even the Civil Service Law.

However, poems were still the preferred form for birthday greetings. A Stormtrooper Assault Leader named Albert Kässmeyer from Ulm in

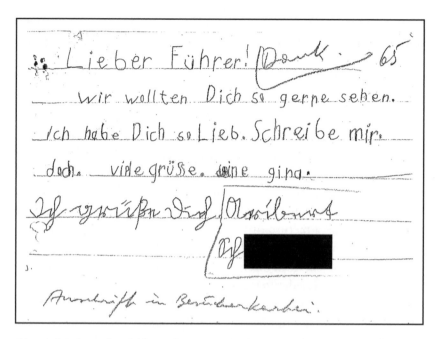

Gina and Aribert, the children of a poor Berlin family, revered Hitler more than
anyone. Their father described Gina's desire to marry Hitler very humorously. The
private chancellery informed him that the Chancellor of the Reich found this story
amusing.

Source: RGWA (Moscow)

southern Germany, who was Regiment 120's senior paymaster, sent
Hitler verses he had composed himself. In the accompanying letter,
dated 5 April 1935, he emphasized that the preceding year he had
already tried to send Hitler a poem through official channels. However,
it had been sent to the Stormtrooper publishing house in Munich,
probably because it was thought that the latter was responsible for
songs and poems. Kässmeyer wrote: 'This year as well I have not failed
to remember my Leader. Once again I have written a poem and sent it
through official channels, but Regiment 120 returned it to me with the
comment that I should send it to you personally. May God grant that
my beloved Leader be in the best of health. Long live my Leader! Long
live our eternal Germany!' The poem was entitled 'Hail Victory' and
was dedicated to 'My Leader on his birthday 20 April 35'.

Another poem was sent by Nikolaus Kahlke, who was, as he him-

1. The head of the Hitler Youth, Baldur von Schirach, summed up the relationship between Hitler and the German people in a poem:

There are four thousand of you behind me, and you are me and I am you.
I have experienced no thoughts that have not quivered in your hearts.
And when I speak words, I know not one that is not at one with your will.
For I am you, and you are me, and we all believe, Germany, in you!

The letters written to Hitler by the people confirm this impression. Yet there was also protest and open criticism of the Nazi Party and of Hitler himself.

© Bayerische Staatsbibliothek München/Fotoarchiv Hoffmann

2. Hitler in the photography studio in 1927. The contrast with the photo taken in 1934 (picture no. 1) is obvious: the pose of the energetic tribune of the people was calculated but nonetheless produced its effect.

© Bayerische Staatsbibliothek München/Fotoarchiv Hoffmann

3. Rudolf Hess, who had been Hitler's private secretary since 1925, dealt with the post largely on his own, and regularly presented important files to the 'Führer.' Here, on vacation in Obersalzberg.

© Bayerische Staatsbibliothek München/Fotoarchiv Hoffmann

4. From 1931 on, Albert Bormann worked in Hitler's private chancellery. After the redistribution of work areas he headed the private chancellery and dealt with letters from the general population.

© Bayerische Staatsbibliothek München/Fotoarchiv Hoffmann

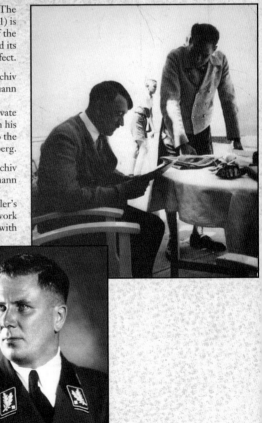

5. Prague, March 1939. The photo shows Hitler's typical governing style: various department heads present their requests, Hitler decides. From left to right: Adjutant Julius Schaub, Interior Minister Wilhelm Frick, the head of the Reich chancellery, Hans Heinrich Lammers, and Ministerial Director Wilhelm Stuckart. In front at right (with her back to the camera) the recording secretary, Christa Schröder.

© Bayerische Staatsbibliothek München/Fotoarchiv Hoffmann

6. A similar scene in the Führer's headquarters. During a walk taken on 5 June 1940 at the Rocky Nest (the codename for one of Hitler's headquarters, located in west Germany), the head of the presidential chancellery, Otto Meissner, reports on events in Berlin. In the middle, Adjutant Julius Schaub.

© Bayerische Staatsbibliothek München/Fotoarchiv Hoffmann

7. Staged joy and genuine reverence during the first 'Führer's birthday' celebration after the seizure of power in 1933. This photo was first published in a cigarette card album. Children were part of the decor. At left, next to Hitler, head adjutant Wilhelm Brückner, dismissed in 1940.

© Bayerische Staatsbibliothek München/Fotoarchiv Hoffmann

8. Many petitioners and well-wishers turned to Hitler's half-sister Angela Raubal, who managed the household at Haus Wachenfeld and in Obersalzberg. She presented a few letters personally to Hitler. Thousands of others remained unread and were sent in bundles to the private chancellery in Berlin.

© Bayerische Staatsbibliothek München/Fotoarchiv Hoffmann

9. Hitler's birthday gift table in 1939. The piles of gifts were displayed in the Berlin Reich chancellery

© Bayerische Staatsbibliothek München/Fotoarchiv Hoffmann

10. In 1943, Hitler celebrated his birthday (20 April) in Obersalzberg. The gift table was still decorated with many flowers, but there were significantly fewer letters of congratulation and gifts from the people. At front left, Eva Braun; after Angela Raubal's wedding to a professor in Dresden, Braun became the hostess in Hitler's private home.

© Bayerische Staatsbibliothek München/Fotoarchiv Hoffmann

11. In 1930, Elsa Walter of Karlsruhe wrote an eighty-page Christmas letter to Hitler, the indisputable 'leader of the German freedom movement'. In it she described her political ideas and nationalistic sentiments. She deplored Jews, and connected unemployment with moral decline. Should he lack a woman in a 'place of action and care,' she offered her services. Elsa Walter became a high-ranking Nazi Party official, and from 1943 on she worked in occupied Poland. She later disappeared without a trace.

Courtesy of Henrik Eberle

12. This letter applying for employment was sent by the sixteen-year-old Anny M. from Frankfurt am Main in November 1933. 'Despite many efforts I have not yet succeeded in finding a position in an office or in sales, I would be very grateful to you, dear revered Herr Reich Chancellor, if you could employ me in a Party office, especially since my father is the sole support for five people. I can make available good recommendations.' On the next document we see Albert Bormann's typical red line, which meant: 'File away.'

Courtesy of Henrik Eberle

16. Gustav Jaindl of Vienna thanked Hitler for the integration of his homeland into what was now the 'Greater German Reich' with a poem. He wrote: 'His heart is like a flame that burns day and night, the world under its spell, the Wehrmacht keeps guard.'

Courtesy of Henrik Eberle

17/18. The Austrians in Argentina also voted. In a book bound in oxhide 3,679 fellow Germans from Austria declared their approval. According to the Nazi Party's Foreign Organization, 80 per cent of all Austrians living in Argentina signed the declaration. Emigrants of Jewish descent were presumably not asked to sign.

Courtesy of Henrik Eberle

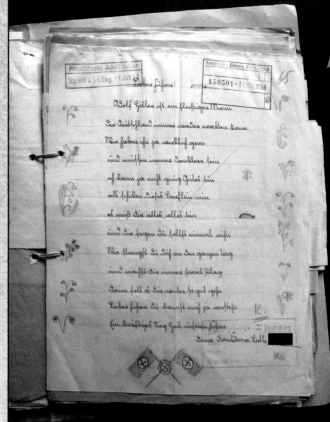

19. Many children were crazy about Hitler. Lotti H. from Berlin worried about her 'dear leader.' In her poem she cautioned him: 'You must rest now and then, how hard you work all day and always give yourself so much trouble.'

Courtesy of Henrik Eberle

20. On 8 October 1938 the twins Susi and Daisy J. from the Sudetenland thanked Hitler for having 'freed us and brought us into your beautiful Reich'.

Courtesy of Henrik Eberle

gewidmet:

Dank unsagbar großen Dank
dem seeligen Elternpaar
der
Mutter
die
„Unseren Führer"
gebar!

Lotte J. Kaiser

21. Like so many people, Lotte J. Kaiser tried to send Hitler 'valuable' good wishes. Thus she cobbled together a mother's day card made of thick, handmade paper to express her 'unutterably great thanks to the blessed parents, the mother who gave birth to "our Führer"'. Pulling the ribbons decorated with swastikas reveals portraits of Hitler's parents.

Courtesy of
Henrik Eberle

	Übertrag:	8414	Stück
Herrenunterhosen		18	"
Strampelhoserl		22	"
Krawatten		2	"
Windeln		159	"
Puppenstuben		5	"
Kindermäntel		16	"
Spielzeug		216	"
Handtücher		47	"
Taschentücher		110	"
Babyschuhe		30	Paare
Bettwäsche		20	Stück
Decken		22	"
Puppen		28	"
Handschuhe		31	Paare
Herrenhosen		2	Stück
2 fertig ausgestattete Kinderbetten		2	"
		9144	Stück

Gmunden, im Dezember 1938.

22. In this document, which was calligraphed on parchment, the leader of the Women's Association of the community of Gmunden in Upper Austria summed up the results of the Christmas donations for Adolf Hitler. The women had primarily knitted socks, but had also sewed clothing for little children. Giving was encouraged by 'the Party' in order to relieve need.

Courtesy of
Henrik Eberle

23. During the war, eulogies continued to flow into the various Hitler chancelleries; for example, the declaration made by the basalt works at Radebeule bei Melk in Austria, which produced paving stones for a ring road.

Courtesy of Henrik Eberle

24. Telegrams sent by important religious leaders in summer 1941 were typed on a 'Führer' typewriter – that is, in an especially large font – and presented to Hitler, who had in the meantime developed presbyopia. The writers express unanimous support for the campaign against 'godless' Bolshevism. At left, a letter from a Ukrainian archbishop, at right another from the German Evangelical Church.

Courtesy of Henrik Eberle

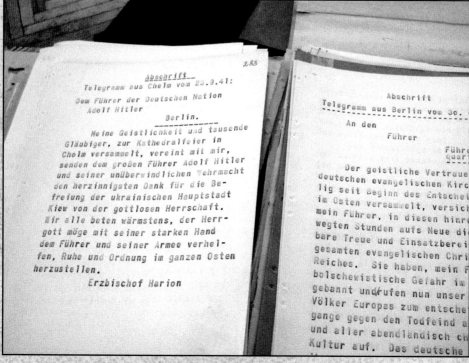

25/26. Erwin Walther composed the 'Heil Hitler, heil!' march (above). These notes were archived in Moscow along with the poems of Heinrich Ritter, a teacher from Markgröningen in Swabia (below). Ritter, a classical philologian, demanded the cleansing of the 'Augean stables,' referring to the extermination of the Jews. He sent his verses on the occasion of Hitler's birthday in 1941.

Courtesy of Henrik Eberle

27/28. The Red Army conquered Germany in difficult house-to-house fighting. Almost invisible in the photo is a Soviet war correspondent standing in the shadow of the façade of the Prussian masonry building, but the German corpses in the foreground are conspicuous (above). An anonymous Soviet photographer also took a picture of the body of a member of the SS, that is, of the group that served as bodyguards for Hitler and other Nazi officials. The corpse lies amid cardboard boxes meant to hold Iron Crosses and other decorations. His bare feet show that the body had already been looted (below).

RGAFKD (Krasnogorsk)

29/30. Russian soldiers, not tourists but victors, pose in 1945 in Hitler's study in the Reich chancellery, in front of his globe (above). Members of the NKGB's trophy commission, which preserved the files and prepared cases for the war crimes trials, also had their pictures taken – for instance, three soldiers in the forecourt of the Reich presidential palace. These military men, who were often historians or journalists in civilian life, collected the archival materials that have now been made available in the special archive.

RGAFKD (Krasnogorsk)

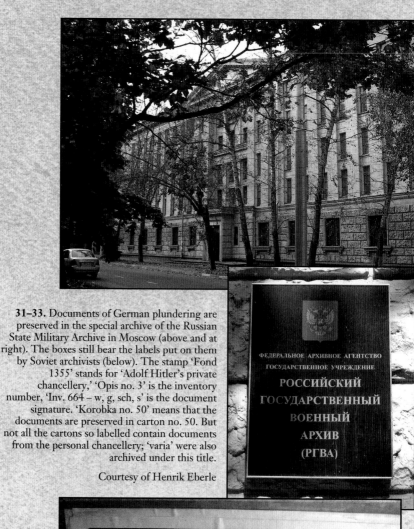

31–33. Documents of German plundering are preserved in the special archive of the Russian State Military Archive in Moscow (above and at right). The boxes still bear the labels put on them by Soviet archivists (below). The stamp 'Fond 1355' stands for 'Adolf Hitler's private chancellery,' 'Opis no. 3' is the inventory number, 'Inv. 664 – w, g, sch, s' is the document signature. 'Korobka no. 50' means that the documents are preserved in carton no. 50. But not all the cartons so labelled contain documents from the personal chancellery; 'varia' were also archived under this title.

Courtesy of Henrik Eberle

ФЕДЕРАЛЬНОЕ АРХИВНОЕ АГЕНТСТВО
ГОСУДАРСТВЕННОЕ УЧРЕЖДЕНИЕ

**РОССИЙСКИЙ
ГОСУДАРСТВЕННЫЙ
ВОЕННЫЙ
АРХИВ
(РГВА)**

Центральный Государственный архив
ГАУ при СМ СССР

ФОНД № 135

Опись № 3   Инв. №№ 664 – в,г,ш,з   Коробка № 50

344—15 000

self emphasized, a war veteran and a pensioner. He sent his birthday greetings on 7 April 1935 to Propaganda Minister Goebbels, with the request that he forward them to Hitler. They were dedicated to the 'beloved Leader' who had risked his life in the world war and had now erected a dam against the 'Red tide' of communism. He hoped 'the dear Lord' would therefore keep the Leader 'healthy and energetic in his difficult office for many years to come'. The poem could be sung to the melody of the old imperial hymn 'Hail to Thee in Victor's Crown', which was the unofficial national anthem of the German Reich from 1871 to 1918. Because it had previously been the Prussian anthem, and because its melody came from that of the British anthem God Save the Queen, it did not enjoy widespread popularity in Germany.

The poem itself is long and does not translate easily, particularly since it was not a lyrical masterpiece even in its original language. But Kahlke raises a number of interesting themes, which reveal his views on the Third Reich and on what Hitler had to offer for the future. He calls Hitler a 'prince of peace' and suggests that Hitler 'desires peace', but contradictorily: the population will follow you 'wherever and forever, to victory and death'. Hitler 'created the Labour Service' 'that serves our people'.

With pick and shovel
The young go along.
To work with song,
All down the street.

The young cheer you too,
Call out to you,
Hail to you, Leader.
It is a pleasure to see,
How erect they stand there.
It makes them all alike,
The Third Reich.

You've blasted the rats
The enemy hung on us,
Hail to you, Leader.

But you reach out to Jews
To those who sincerely want
Germany's prosperity
and Resurrection.

Providence, who gave you to us,
keep you with us many years.
Hail to you, Leader.
Because you live only for Germany,
And do not strive for honour,
We all follow here,
Hail Hitler to you.

It is clear that Nikolaus Kahlke had failed completely to understand Hitler's political programme. There could be no question of 'reaching out' to Jews. With the Civil Service Law and other regulations the Nazi Party had sooner or later driven everyone with Jewish ancestors out of state offices and key economic posts. Only people considered politically reliable were henceforth allowed to write for 'German' newspapers.

Kahlke's mix of devotion to Nazism with a relatively moderate view of Jews and a desire for peace had become the relative norm in letters to Hitler by the mid 1930s. In part this was probably because a far wider range of citizens were writing to Hitler, as opposed to the radical believers of the early years. However, the Stormtrooper E. Schwabe had maintained his fervent tone in his poem to celebrate the anniversary of Hitler's coming to power in 1936.

To my Leader on the 30th of January!

We don't just want to always name you by your name!
With our hearts we want to acknowledge you!
For you, we sacrifice the happiness of our homes!
And if it is necessary for Germany's freedom and happiness!
That we will storm the gates of Hell!
We'll storm them!
We'll break the necks of all our enemies!
And in 1930 we were not yet in your ranks!

Because we didn't understand your sacred will!
Today we fly your flags, so long as God wills it!
In every storm!
And it will not cease! Not even in a thousand generations!
So we look proudly to our elders!
And we look to them with pride!
For we shall hold the flag high!
The only way is forward!
But never, never backward!
You are our Leader!
We follow you!
Everything for Germany!
Hail to you, Leader!

E. Schwabe
Berlin

Dear Mr Schwabe!

The Leader has received your letter of 30 January 1936 and wishes to express his hearty thanks for it. He took great pleasure in the veneration expressed in it. Unfortunately, his exceptionally heavy commitments prevent him from replying personally.

With a German salute!
[unreadable]

That poems by men need not always be militant is shown by a poem that was received on 10 December 1936 by Angela Raubal at Obersalzberg:

As the sister of our Leader and Chancellor I beg you to forward the enclosed letter to your esteemed brother. You must have received hundreds of letters containing wishes. I, too, can do no other.

It seems my heart will explode,
When I hear people shout 'My Leader';
It seems a thousand voices

Sound at once from within,
When you, O Leader, are acclaimed.
Tears must spring forth –
But my heart lies in bondage,
Because it is not at your side, my Leader.
It would like to follow you everywhere
Early in the morning, late in the evening!
My tears flow –
I wish you could see it.
Would take me in your arms –
Draw strength, hourly go with you.
Sacred will would sprout forth:
Stand lithe and straight!

Horst Schrade

Not all those who sent letters and poems were naive about Hitler's future intentions. On 8 March 1936 two women from the Saarland thanked the Leader for his remilitarization of the Rhineland, an action that was a deliberate violation of international treaties.

Dear Leader,

We are all still under the spell of yesterday's events. The jubilation and enthusiasm that we people of Saarbrücken felt when German soldiers finally moved into our city again after seventeen years were indescribable. With overflowing hearts, we would like to thank you for having restored its honour and freedom to our beloved Fatherland. May Heaven bless you and your work, esteemed Leader, so that you can lead our German Fatherland to greater heights. We pledge you our unfailing loyalty in good times and hard times. So please come soon to Saarbrücken. We Saarlanders are longing to see you and would like to show you our veneration and loyalty.

Loyal German greetings from the Saar
two Party members from Saarbrücken
Klara and Elly Walterhöfer

The Reich Bank, Germany's central bank, was also satisfied with Hitler's policies. Its board of directors congratulated him on 20 April 1936 and enclosed a cheque.

My Leader!
Highly estimable Reich Chancellor!

In the absence of the Reich Bank Chairman Dr Schacht I have the honour of sending you, Mr Reich Chancellor, in connection with the letter of good wishes from the board of directors of the Reichsbank, instead of a bouquet of flowers a cheque for 5,000 marks (five thousand Reichsmarks), with the request that you use it for whatever purpose seems to you appropriate.

With the greatest deference
Your reverentially devoted
Dreyse
Vice-Chairman of the Reich Bank board of directors

Hitler's policies also received support from further afield. The summary translation of a letter written at the end of 1937 by Ali Ander of Ankara, Turkey, shows this particularly well:

Letter from Ali Ander, secretary of the Turkish finance ministry in Ankara to the Mr Reich Chancellor.
   The writer is a Circassian from the Caucasus and has had to see his relatives, who were seized by the Bolsheviks, exiled to Siberia and punished with forced labour. He declares that he is an irreconcilable enemy of the Soviets and that he knows that rage against the Soviet regime is widespread among the Russian people. Therefore if a small band of fighters were to invade Russia from Turkey, it would necessarily obtain significant results. He requests military support and leadership. He himself would not hesitate at anything and has already proven himself in the War of Turkish Independence.

Dedicated National Socialists continued to send Hitler good wishes during this period. One among many examples is the New

Year's greeting sent by the city of Frankfurt am Main in December 1937.

My Leader!

Along with the whole of the German people the city of German crafts commemorates with the deepest gratitude its head of state on the occasion of the New Year. I beg you to accept, from myself and the city of Frankfurt am Main,

HEARTIEST GOOD WISHES FOR A MERRY CHRISTMAS AND A HAPPY NEW YEAR.

Frankfurt am Main, 23 December 1937.
In unwavering loyalty and devotion

Friedrich Krebs
Lord Mayor and Prussian State Councillor

Lord Mayor Krebs was a respected jurist and at the same time a fanatical National Socialist. In 1924 he was already the local group leader of the National Socialist Freedom Party; in 1929 he joined the Nazi Party. In 1932 he became a delegate in the Prussian regional legislature, and in 1933 the Lord Mayor of Frankfurt, replacing the city's Jewish mayor Ludwig Landmann. A fervent anti-Semite, within several weeks of becoming mayor Krebs had fired all of the city's Jewish employees. He also dedicated his time to removing Jewish influences from the city's arts and culture scene. In 1944 he organized a rally under the motto 'We will never surrender!' Despite all this, in 1947 Krebs was classified as 'less incriminated' by the Allied occupiers and was given a lavish official pension. In the 1950s he was active on behalf of the extreme right-wing German Party. He died in 1961 without ever having been prosecuted.

Unrestrained and uncynical veneration of Hitler also affected Party members, however. An example is provided by the letter of a loyal SS-man from Halle.

My Leader,

I beg your pardon for taking a few minutes of your valuable time, but my heart forces me to write to you, my Leader, to ask you to take me with you when you travel to Italy. I know that this is not a pleasure trip, but I also know that as a . . . man of the general SS I would do my duty just as fully as the SS-men who are lucky enough to be at your side all the time. For me it would be the best opportunity to set eyes on you at least once in my life, my Leader, and maybe even to shake your hand. – Forgive me, my Leader, but I really can't think of anything more wonderful. – Please, my Leader, take me along.

> *Master Baker Oskar Jankowski,*
> *Halle*
> *born 21 April 1912 in Halle*
> *SS-Corporal in the 3rd Battalion Halle*

The answer from Hitler's private office dated from 22 January 1938.

Dear Party Comrade!

The receipt of your letter to the Leader dated as above was noted with great gratitude. I regret that I must inform you that the wish you have expressed cannot be granted.

> *With a German salute*
> *on behalf of Albert Bormann*

When the war started, Jankowski, who was a master baker and could have been deferred, volunteered for service. He died in 1943, presumably without ever having met Hitler. The bakery was then leased and in 1946 expropriated. Despite wishes from bewitched individuals such as Jankowski, by the mid 1930s, spontaneous outpourings of devotion were on the decline.

In 1937 there were again odes to National Socialism and to Hitler himself, but most of them consisted of propaganda slogans strung together

('Our Faith is Called Germany'). More common were congratulations from state employees and office holders, who felt it was expected of them to send good wishes on events such as Hitler's birthday.

One such example is a letter from the Colonel of the Marine Storm Battalion and mayor of Helgoland, a small group of islands in the North Sea.

Mr Reich Chancellor! My Leader!

For your birthday I send you, on behalf of the people of Helgoland and myself, our sincerest good wishes. May Providence long preserve you for the German people.

As its local leader I also permit myself to convey to you, my Leader, the best wishes for your birthday from the Marine SA 12 and 13/55.

As a birthday gift the people send you, as our honorary citizen, a picture offering an overview of the island as a symbol of love and veneration and as an expression of gratitude for all that you have achieved for Germany – and also for Helgoland.

> *With a German salute*
> *Bohm*
> *Colonel and Mayor*

For the framed photo Mayor Bohm received a pre-printed letter of thanks with Hitler's signature. One cannot help having the impression that the ritual of the Leader's birthday had petered out.

As in every totalitarian regime, propaganda needed real events to energize popular support. Mere satisfaction with already achieved political goals led to stagnation, as the philosopher Hannah Arendt noted in retrospect. And in 1937, stagnation seemed to have appeared, at least in domestic politics. Only in 1938, after the annexation of Austria, was it possible to energize the population again.

9

THE HIGHPOINT OF HITLER'S POPULARITY

By 1938, Germans had begun to connect the fortunes of Germany so closely with Hitler personally, that when a political crisis arose, people prayed for Hitler and his good health. 'God Almighty, help, oh help our Leader!', we read in one of these letters. When a situation calmed down, or Hitler made political progress, either domestically or internationally, the number of expressions of veneration increased accordingly.

This was particularly apparent during Germany's annexation of Austria on 12 March 1938. By 1934 Austria's Republic had disintegrated and the country had transformed into a quasi-fascist state, with power centralized to a Chancellor who ruled by decree. On 25 July the Nazis assassinated Chancellor Dollfuss in a failed coup d'etat, leading to a civil war, the second that the country had experienced that year. Most leading Austrian Nazis fled to Germany and continued to work towards a National Socialist takeover; many Nazis within Austria were imprisoned. Nonetheless the situation remained shaky, and by March 1938 Chancellor Schuschnigg organized a referendum for 9 March, in which the population would vote whether to remain independent or to join Germany. Only Austrians over the age of twenty-four were allowed to vote, as a way of disenfranchising Nazi supporters, who tended to be young.

Hitler refused to accept the plebiscite, and sent an ultimatum to the Chancellor, with the choice of either giving power to the Austrian National Socialist Party or being invaded by Germany. At the same time the Nazis began to disseminate false news reports that said that riots and disorder were breaking out across the country and that many Austrians were calling on Hitler to come and restore order. Neither Britain nor France offered any support, and so Chancellor Schuschnigg resigned. While Austrian Nazis took over Vienna, Hitler readied German troops, which marched into Austria on the morning of 12 March 1938. Hitler followed closely behind, and undertook a sort of victory parade, which ended in Vienna on 2 April. Hitler signed the law regarding the annexation of Austria on 13 March 1938; and to ratify it he ordered a plebiscite to be held on 10 April 1938, in which 99.73 per cent of voters supported the 'unification' (Anschluss) of Austria and Germany. Austria was now part of the German Reich.

The first poems sent from Austria to express good wishes had already been received in Berlin on 16 March. Typical is this one by Dr Erich Oberdorfer from Vienna.

Austria to the Leader.

Austria is free! Tyranny is over.
No sacrifice, no tears in vain,
all our sufferings are seen in the deepest sense:
only in that way is a new world born.

Shaken, we feel ourselves in the grip of destiny,
since the greatest son of our beautiful homeland,
in whom longing, hope, and will are united,
offers fulfilment, defying every enemy.

For you, my Leader, like a star
that rose radiantly from storm clouds,
you bring what was an unattainable dream,
the great age, you bring freedom, unity, victory!

At the same time the Tradition Association of the Forest Quarter in Vienna collected signatures, which were forwarded to Hitler before the end of March. Whether the Chancellor of what was now the Greater German Reich took pleasure in these greetings from his old homeland, is anybody's guess. In all, over a thousand signatures were sent. The chairman of the association, Karl Pollak, in a flyer bearing a swastika and an appeal to 'compatriots! People from the Forest Quarter!', called upon people to attend the first homeland evening 'after the enthusiastically received incorporation of Austria, and thus also our eternally green forest frontier, into the Greater German Reich'. On this occasion 'special thanks' were to be expressed to the Leader and Chancellor of the Reich Adolf Hitler, who, 'blood of our blood from land-owning farmers of the Forest Quarter, brought about this miracle'.

An elderly woman from Bregenz in Vorarlberg, the most western Austrian state, sent her thanks on 22 March 1938:

My Leader,

I write to you with tears of happiness in my eyes. Although it is most unlikely that you will personally read what I write, such a great miracle has taken place that anything is possible. I must write because my admiration for what you, my Leader, have enabled people to do through your example is too great! I thought of the coming upheaval only with fear, too many people were filled with thoughts of revenge, because what we have suffered up to now is unspeakable and the thought of revenge is just humanly justified. And now everything has gone so smoothly and this order, this discipline.

Nothing has yet happened of which the Party would have to be ashamed. Our opponents will be won over to our cause more by the behaviour of Party members than they could be by force – that can already be seen. We all contemplate the election with calm and we now have only one wish, to see our Leader in Bregenz as soon as possible.

One for all: Julie Oesterle

On 11 April 1938, the wife of Paul Irrgang, a Berlin wholesaler of glass, porcelain, and stone, wrote euphorically to Hitler. She wrote on her husband's letterhead stationery and did not use her own name, but instead signed as 'Mrs P. Irrgang'.

Our Leader Adolf Hitler!

There are no words to tell our Leader what we feel. Accept, our Leader, our thanks and eternal loyalty. It is to be regretted that some people still remain blind, but they are beyond help, unfortunately.

> *Until we draw our last breath*
> *our heart belongs to you.*
> *Hail Hitler!*
> *Mrs P. Irrgang*

According to Mrs Irrgang, those who expressed doubts and scepticism were to be counted among the 'blind'. In retrospect, we must see this differently. But the nationalistic enthusiasm quickly passed among some Austrians who felt themselves to be Germans when they became aware of the consequences of the annexation. Thus Franz Ippisch wrote to Hitler on 6 April 1938:

My Leader!

Excuse me, my Leader, for making a request of you during these days of extreme physical and mental effort. But the granting of my request is so important for me and especially for my family that in my desperation I can think of nothing to do but to appeal to your generosity.

I am a native Viennese, fifty-five years old and the son of an usher at the assize court. The documents I have been able to find so far show that I am of pure Aryan descent both on my father's side and my mother's side. When my father died in 1904 he left my mother nothing but unprovided-for children, of whom I, the youngest, was at that time about to finish my studies at the Vienna Conservatory. I would not have been able to complete these studies had the family of a Viennese Jewish businessman, which was itself not very wealthy, not made it possible for me to complete my musical studies. The only daughter of this family became my wife in 1906; we were first married in a civil ceremony and then, after my wife converted to the Catholic Church, married in the church. Since then my wife has been a faithful spouse and an excellent companion in all life's difficulties, and has always, despite her unfortunate Semitic descent, shown herself to be a dutiful German woman. She was an excellent mother to our child born in 1907, a son, and raised him to be a loyal and diligent man (he is a dispatcher for the Viennese Pharmaceutical firm of J. Voigt & Co.).

I myself was for almost thirty years a member of the Vienna People's Opera and a music teacher, and acquired a respected name as a composer (up to this point I have written two symphonies, about thirty chamber music works, about one hundred songs and smaller compositions) that appears in any modern musical lexicon. For my achievements as a composer and a music teacher, in 1933 I was awarded the title of Professor. After many problems at the Vienna People's Opera, in 1934 I was able to get a position as a military band leader in Salzburg. In this position I was able to raise the band entrusted to me to a high artistic level, a success that recently led my superiors to recommend me for a conspicuous honour.

Then came the great historical event of 11, 12, and 13 March of this year. We are all entranced by your great and brilliant act.

I was with my band, the first Austrian band to be in Berchtesgaden and in Munich after the changeover, and we were stunned by the hearty welcome we received.

But we were disturbed to see, once the first days of jubilation were over, that although I have the right to vote, my wife, branded as inferior because of her Jewish ancestry, must stand aside and in the great historical April is not allowed to express how much she supports the united Germany. When today I heard your speech in which you, my Leader, said that you wanted the vote of every individual who wants to help further develop the new Reich you have created, I decided to throw myself at your feet, my Leader, a generous and noble man, and ask you:

Set aside the disgrace of my wife's Jewish ancestry, which is not her fault, so that she can vote on 10 April. You would thereby gain in my wife and my descendants loyal and enthusiastic collaborators who would bless you all their lives for what you have done.

Please, my Leader, use your power and you will make the happiest man in the world your devotedly respectful

Franz Ippisch
Military Band Leader
Salzburg

Ippisch emigrated to Central America and was given a professorship in Guatemala. He never returned to Austria.

Austrians living outside the country also wanted to participate in April's plebiscite. In Argentina, public signature lists showed more than 80 per cent approval. The National Socialists who lived there bound the lists in a book that they then sent to Hitler. On the cover they wrote: 'One People, One Reich, One Leader.'

Hitler's visit to his parents' graves, which was staged for propagandistic effect, also aroused sympathy. On Mother's Day 1938, this act was mentioned in many letters. For example, on Mother's Day, 15 May 1938, Lotte J. Kaiser sent Hitler from Berlin a home-made card with the dedication: 'Thanks, inexpressibly great thanks to the holy parents, to the mother who bore our Leader!' In the accompanying letter we read:

My Leader, allow me to express my thanks for all the great and beautiful things that I have been allowed to experience with a token that is small and homely but comes from the soul.

Lotte J. Kaiser

In the paper greetings card, Kaiser had cut two windows in which she glued pictures of Hitler's parents. The 'shutters' could be opened using the red ribbons that had been glued to them. On the shutters a swastika was displayed.

This case really shows just one thing: Hitler's propagandists directed the cult of the mother purposefully and with intended effect. Carl Bauer, an office assistant in Dortmund, included along with his poem praising Hitler a newspaper clipping that showed precisely the picture also used by Lotte Kaiser. It was taken from the book *The Unknown*

Hitler, which had been put together by Hitler's personal photographer, Heinrich Hoffmann, and the leader of the Hitler Youth, Baldur von Schirach, a German-American who had joined the Nazi Party in 1925. Hundreds of thousands of copies of the book were sold.

This constantly repeated invocation of the cult of the mother also had a long-term effect. On 13 May 1938, Paula Ohland sent Hitler's office a poem she had written in January 1936, that is, after Hitler paid a visit to his parents' graves in Austria, with the photographs obviously appearing in all the newspapers shortly thereafter for maximum effect. In the accompanying card she said that the poem was 'dedicated with respect to the mother of the greatest of all architects, but to the son himself with gratitude'.

To Hitler's Mother

O mother, because you gave birth to this son,
You were destined to be queen.
What a gift you gave the world with this child,
So that your trace is not carried away by the wind!
It is granted him not only
To lead a people, no – oh – no!
A people is only part of the great realm
That God created for us, like a leaf on a tree.
A leaf that was limp but not dried up,
It yearns for the great throng of leaves;
With them it longs to gleam in the bright spring night:
'Through your son – O mother, this work will be
Completed!'

Three middle-aged women from Ludwigsfelde, south of Berlin, expressed their enthusiasm upon catching a glimpse of Hitler on 21 April 1938.

My Leader!

On election day we happened to be at the Ludwigsfelde railway station. When an express train came in (13:20) we saw a Party member in uniform on the locomotive. This immediately caused us to assume that our Leader must be in this train. Our assumption proved to be right.

Three women beaming with happiness were able to cheer their so joyful Leader and received a friendly wave as their reward.

Three exceedingly fortunate women thank their Leader with all their hearts and request, as a memento of this splendid and unforgettable moment an autograph for each of them.

> *Thanks!*
> *Victory and Hail*
> *our beloved Leader!*
> *Martha Imse*
> *Anna Loppien*
> *Elisabeth Pässler*

It's unclear whether the enthralled women received the autographs or not. However, because one of the women had an unusual family name, we are able to learn more about her. Born in Nordhausen in Thuringia in 1900, she trained to be a commercial clerk. In 1937 she joined the Nazi Party, (which was quite late really) and in 1945 she was still unmarried. Whether or not she survived the war we do not know. A request for information directed to her family met with the curt reply 'not interested'. To what extent the family, almost all of whose members belonged to the Nazi Party, was subject to reprisals after 1945 thus cannot be determined. However, it is clear that this woman came from a National Socialist background, which must have made her susceptible to Hitler's charisma. Her mother listed her profession as 'director' while her father was a master tailor; they joined the Nazi Party in 1932 and 1933 respectively. Several younger relatives joined during the war; on 20 April 1944 alone, three of them were admitted to the Nazi Party.

The reverence for Hitler during this time was limitless. An example is provided by the letter written by Elisabeth J., a girl from Schwarzburg in Thuringia, on 20 June 1938.

My dear Leader!

Please do not be angry that I have dared to address you so familiarly! I cannot write differently to the way my heart feels. On 23 May of this year I wrote to Field Marshal Göring with the request that he come to Schwarzburg! The whole time I waited for an answer, until finally it came on 18 June. The Field Marshal sent me a picture postcard with his own autograph!

Oh, how I rejoiced and wept. He answered me and little Schwarzburg! Can you, my beloved Leader, understand this joy? And how happy I would be if I could also receive a reply from you. Please, please, dear good-hearted Leader, answer me!!! I have one more request to make of you! In the autumn of this year I would like to make a great journey with the Schwarzburg League of German Girls group 9/218, a journey to Berlin! You will probably ask, why to Berlin, precisely?

You have not yet seen, my Leader, all my girls, and you cannot imagine how much each of them wants to see you just once. I would like to ask you with all my heart if it wouldn't be possible to write me a note certifying that we have permission to see you in the Chancellor's Office or at least expect to have no problems with the guards? Please, please dear Leader, have a heart for us girls, it needn't be more than five minutes. Please don't turn us down, ask what you will of us, if only we can see you! Oh, how glad we would be to see you in our own homeland! Is it completely impossible that you might come to Schwarzburg? I invite you, my Leader, to be for once a guest in the home of a worker, because my mother is an exceptional cook!

And now in conclusion, my beloved Leader:
Don't forget my request,
Let us see you once!

With love,
loyalty and gratitude,
your comrade
Elisabeth J.

Gertrud Juliane of Koblenz, western Germany, wrote several letters to Hitler in the summer of 1938, for example on 29 August. The letters were badly written, and the translation reflects this:

My dear Leader I send you a very pleasant Sunday. The days you devoted to your dear official visit must have been quite stressful. I witnessed everything.

Now my beloved Leader, yesterday I read your beloved work, and what I got out of it did not penetrate my little head, whether it is a joke or serious. I am beside myself with sheer joy.

Since you are after all the only man for whom I've always had great respect, it would be wonderful to have your great happiness.

And on 17 September:

My dear Leader, I send you the most heartfelt good wishes and good luck for your dear work. What was done at the Nuremberg Party rally was very ceremonial and uplifting. It gets better from year to year.

How are you otherwise, my dear Leader, I hope very well. Please take care not to catch cold. In Nuremberg it is cold and [there is] much rain this year.

Since the Reich Party rally is coming to an end, I wish my highly esteemed Reich Chancellor a very happy Sunday.

> *With a German salute*
> *a triple Hail Victory!*
> *Gertrud Juliane*

In five Sunday letters, Gertrud reported her feelings and described how beautiful it was on the Rhine. She received no reply. It was not possible to determine whether in this case Albert Bormann asked the Gestapo to put a stop to these letters or whether she stopped writing them herself.

Even more directly than Gertrud Juliane, an unemployed worker in Vienna, Austria paid homage to Hitler in a letter of 7 September 1938. But for just that reason his admiration soared to a still greater level of euphoria:

My Leader!

I am a hotel porter who has been out of work for seven years, because in the old regime it was impossible for me to get a job, despite five years' experience abroad and my knowledge of English and French, which meant that I already expected my future to be hopeless. But after the annexation [of Austria] to the old Reich I noticed how everything suddenly took a turn for the better and work and earnings became available everywhere, I regained belief and hope, and, although I am still unemployed today, I am convinced that within the foreseeable future I will be back at work and earning, and all because of our Leader.

Therefore I cannot resist expressing to you, our Leader, not only my own gratitude and admiration but also that of all Germans, in the form of a 'National Socialist' credo, and [ask you] to distribute and kindly approve it, since my conviction and, I assume, that of every true German, is that what Jesus Christ was for humanity in the religious sense, Adolf Hitler is for the German people in the worldly sense.

> *With the greatest esteem and respect*
> *and Hail Victory*
> *Karl Jorde*
> *Hotel porter*

My 'National Socialist' credo!

I believe in God the Father, the almighty creator of heaven and earth, and in Adolf Hitler, his chosen son, whom he has elected in order to deliver his German people from the vipers' brood (Jews, clerics and dynasties) and centuries-long disunity, downtroddenness, and increasing impoverishment, and on whom he has also conferred its leadership for the resurrection of unity, power, new creative energy and optimism to such an extent that it will continue, despite vilenesses and various animosities, from now unto all eternity. Amen.

Did Jorde really hope that his credo would be 'approved' and prescribed as a compulsory prayer in the churches? Certainly we can assume that this hope entered into the unemployed man's calculations, since a profession of faith printed in a million copies would have brought in significant royalties. But in retrospect, simply the idea of writing a new credo with Hitler as the 'chosen son' of God seems remarkable. While this shows the extent to which Germans idolized Hitler, it also reflects a basic misunderstanding of Nazism, which did not particularly approve of religion.

In addition to the letters celebrating Austria's integration into the German Reich, Hitler also received his yearly dose of birthday greetings.

The island of Helgoland sent, in addition to the official good wishes, a small, 'hand-made' lobster pot, along with a little card from Jan A. Jansen with 'Sincerest good congratulations to my Leader on his birthday.' Flowers were sent by workers in the tree nurseries and fruit orchards of Upper Silesia, along with a card that was received by Hitler's office on 23 April 1938. Their good wishes were addressed to the 'dear, good Leader', whom they asked to come to speak in Upper Silesia at least once. 'Oh, please come soon to Upper Silesia; we are all so much for you and have also voted for you. But we would all also like to see you some time, because up to this point we have only heard you on the radio. Please grant our wish soon! Hail Victory!' There was no reply to the letter.

Also 'filed away' were the 'best wishes for success and happiness' sent by two women from the 'Halle-Merseburg labour district'. On the occasion of Hitler's birthday they had written: 'May health and successful beginning further your work to give eternal Germany a timeless form! Hail Victory!' Someone wrote on the letter with a green coloured pencil: 'Kitsch'.

The members of the State Orchestra of Münster expressed their 'deepest gratitude, loyalty, love, and veneration' in a letter of 16 April 1938, and sent an oil painting that one of the group had painted. They received thanks, as did Margarthe Rathmann from Potsdam, near Berlin. She gave Hitler 8,000 marks that she had inherited. Hitler signed the letter on 21 May 1938.

Dear Mrs Rathmann!

Please accept my sincerest thanks for the donation that you have made on the occasion of my birthday.

You have thereby given me special pleasure.
The donation will be used to help needy fellow Germans.

> *With a German salute*
> *Adolf Hitler*

Great numbers of birthday poems were also received. For example, a
'Sonnet to the Leader' dedicated to him 'in great veneration and gratitude', combines joy at the annexation with Austria with birthday wishes:

> You are the one that God sent us
> In deepest need and highest distress,
> With a bold hand you ended Germany's disgrace,
> Now the bright dawn of the future shines forth!
>
> You are the sower of the German earth,
> And your sowing created a flourishing land,
> You said your homeland would grow greater,
> Now it reaches the coast of the North Sea!
>
> O name me a king who has achieved such a deed!
> You need no sceptre or diamond-studded crown,
> Your greatness has subjugated the whole world!
>
> Your throne stands higher than any emperor's:
> You have won a place in the hearts of your people,
> Now the gratitude of Greater Germany will be your reward!

> *E. Jurima, Vienna, 20 April 38*

Bertha Over from Bonn wished Hitler a happy birthday and asked for
his autograph as a birthday present. Her wish was granted. On 15 April
1938 she had written:

My Leader!

I humbly take the liberty of telling my Leader that my birthday is also
20 April.

Therefore it would be my fervent wish to receive this year as a birth-day gift a picture of my Leader, and it would give me great joy if my wish could be dealt with favourably.

My husband is a 50 per cent handicapped war veteran; his left arm is completely crippled and since 1932 he has been a member of the National Socialist War Victim's Care Organization [a welfare associa-tion for severely injured war veterans].

Hail Hitler!
Mrs Bertha Over

[P.S.] In 1933 my parents celebrated their Golden Anniversary in Pforzheim and are still alive thank God.

For the regime, however, the mobilization of reserves of all kinds was as important as such veneration. A letter accompanying good wishes on the stationery of the Hans Oldag firm, 'Uniforms, Clothing', Berlin, is set out below.

To our Leader and Reich Chancellor

ADOLF HITLER

on his 49th birthday
the female staff
of the Hans Oldag firm, Berlin S.O. 16
gives

1 children's dress
1 baby jacket and bonnet
8 pairs of baby sleeve holders
10 pairs of wool stockings

that were made during their evenings at home.

Shop Steward   Women's Stewardess
Bauer   Herubke

Hitler's private office thanked the senders on 29 May 1938.

The Leader sends you his sincerest thanks for the thoughtfulness you have shown on the occasion of his birthday. The clothing sent will be forwarded to the Office of People's Welfare.

With a German salute
Albert Bormann

The regime also was pleased by a letter from Vienna.

To the Leader and Reich Chancellor!

The staff of the Austrian Wood Products Council has collected 110 shillings to buy flowers for your birthday.

However, by common agreement this amount will not be used for flowers but rather donated for the support of a fellow German in Vienna who has many children.

We ask you to accept this decision regarding the intended gift of flowers.

In irrevocable loyalty
and deeply felt gratitude
the staff of the Austrian Wood Products Council

The Leader's private office replied on 5 May 1938.

The Leader wishes to express his sincere thanks for your good wishes on his birthday and for the notice that the funds you collected will be used for the support of a needy fellow German. The Leader took great pleasure in the willingness to sacrifice thereby expressed by all involved.

With a German salute
on behalf of [unreadable]

Soon, the German people would be asked to make another type of sacrifice. But the war that would begin within a year was not yet visible on the horizon. By autumn 1938, doubt, fear and concern had disappeared from the people's letters to Hitler. The dictator had reached the highpoint of his popularity. Hitler's critics had fallen silent, not because they agreed with him, but because they realized that it was pointless to write to him.

Part III

Crisis and War: 1938–1945

10

JUBILATION AND CONCERN

The model suggested by the letters of good wishes, that of increasing 'trust in the Leader' up to 1938 followed by a decline in popularity, cannot be explained solely by the intensity of the Hitler-cult, whose highpoints were certainly reached in early 1934 and in 1938. The politics of the day, its successes and failures, played an important role. In 1938 Hitler was politically triumphant.

Only the regime's insistence on further revisions of the borders caused some people to have doubts. As we have seen, many of the letters to Hitler during the 1930s praised Hitler for bringing peace to Germany. Although Germans supported Hitler's plans to make Germany the global giant, at the same time, most of them did not want to risk the stability they were now enjoying. As Hitler's military plans became clearer, and as it became clearer that war was not a distant and vague idea, but was actually approaching, the letters received by Hitler's private office suggested a change in the public mood.

The German Army had prepared to invade Czechoslovakia in the summer of 1938. Hitler sold his plans to his people by suggesting that Germany needed to invade to rescue the German minority within Czechoslovakia, a population called Sudeten Germans because of their proximity to the mountain range near the border. Supposedly this minority population was being persecuted by the Czech government.

But, in reality, this was an excuse. If the Sudeten Germans were of value it was because they would inevitably support Hitler's plans and then fight for him. The Sudeten Crisis made headlines throughout the rest of the summer. Unexpectedly, the British Prime Minister, Neville Chamberlain, flew out to Munich and met with Hitler on 15 September 1938. Hitler demanded the territory inhabited by the Sudeten Germans, and was shocked when Chamberlain not only agreed, but also succeeded in gaining approval from the French and the Czechs. When Hitler then tried to raise new demands, the British and French prepared for war, causing Hitler reluctantly to back down. It was clear that the German public did not want war; neither did Germany's key ally, Italy. At Mussolini's request Hitler conceded to the acquisition of the Sudetenland at the Munich conference of 29 September.

Germans continued to correspond with Hitler throughout the crisis. The content reflects the population's preoccupation with and fear of war. Elsa Opel of Kulmbach in Bavaria asked for the establishment of a world police and, in case this proved impossible, recommended single-seater airplanes in the form of arrows, since these would be needed in the future war. In addition she claimed to be 'clairvoyant, with a knowledge of the future – and it is no use for me not to believe in this, because everything turns out to be true anyway'.

On 9 September 1938, a diviner styling himself an 'experimenter in psychic sciences and radiaesthetics' wrote to Hitler. He addressed 'His Excellency and Leader of the German Reich Adolf Hitler, strictly personal', which meant that the letter landed on Albert Bormann's desk.

Excellency,

Since I foresee good things for the future of Germany, I do not want to fail to inform Your Excellency of certain things that I have learned through the power of clairvoyance:

– The League of Nations will be finally dissolved in the course of the month of April 1939.

– In May 1939 world war will break out.

– In the battle between France and Germany, Germany will be the ultimate victor. Take care with regard to Italy.

– It is necessary for Germany to achieve good relationships with the Orthodox countries, that is, the Balkans.

– In the war Germany will also conquer Turkey, which will cease to exist as a country.

– All the Balkan countries, along with Czechoslovakia, will be united in a single state structure under Germany's leadership.

If these predictions prove correct, I hope your Excellency will kindly remember me.

I recommend myself to Your Excellency with the expression of deepest respect and esteem,

Devotedly,
Fori S. Terpini

P.S. Through Radiaesthetics I have determined that major petroleum deposits are to be found at a depth of 1,100 metres in the Hüttenberg-Landsberg-Klagenfurt triangle. [This refers to the region of Carinthia, in southern Austria.]

Austria's petroleum deposits were, in fact, not in Carinthia but rather in the eastern part of the country, and had already been tapped in 1935. With regard to Turkey and Italy, the seer Terpini's predictions probably reflected the wishful thinking of an Albanian patriot. An economic community in southeast Europe under German leadership was not particularly difficult to predict, since it had already emerged in outline. Hitler should have heeded the warning about being careful in handling the Orthodox countries. But since the dictator put no stock in the predictions of clairvoyants, this letter also ended up being ignored.

Many writers were relieved at the peaceful solution to the Sudeten Crisis. The declaration made jointly by the British premier Neville Chamberlain and Hitler – that their two countries would never wage war against one another – seemed even more popular. Young Helga J. from Wandsbek, Hamburg, who wrote to thank Hitler for maintaining peace on 30 September.

My dear Leader,

I had my birthday on 29 September, so I am nine years old. Now I thank you for having given me such a wonderful birthday gift by bringing the Sudetenland back into Germany, since now daddy does not need to go to war, because daddy is still young.

Now I wish you good luck and a long life.

Warm greetings from your Helga J.

Adults were also grateful for what they considered to be the preservation of peace in Europe. For example, a couple from Berlin wrote:

Leader and Chancellor of the Reich!

From the depths of our hearts we thank you, our Leader, for all your efforts.

It makes us happy and glad to know that peace exists and will remain. With all our hearts we wish you, our esteemed Leader, good health, a long happy life, [and] may a favourable fate continue to stand at your side, our Leader.

This is our wish from grateful hearts
with Hail Hitler
Josef and Elli Jablonski

An elderly Party member from Eisenach in Thuringia, central Germany, who wrote on 1 October 1938 was more belligerent:

To our dearly beloved Leader Adolf Hitler!

Accept the gratitude of a worker from Thuringia for your efforts and actions to maintain the peace.

I have already read a great deal about miracles, but the ones you have achieved and will achieve, my Leader, will go down in German history as a unique, eternal, unforgettable document.

My Leader, be assured that we Thuringians are still just as loyal as we were during the period of struggle [the time from 1919 until the Nazis came to power in 1933]. When on 26 September 1938 you said: I marched at the head of my people as the first soldier, a feeling from the time of that time of struggle was awakened in me.

I would have gladly obeyed my Leader's command in battle against Jewish Bolshevism. Today every German knows why and for whom he is fighting. Anyone who really loves his people also bears within himself the greatness to hate the mortal enemy of his people. Namely: the Jewish people.

May the Almighty bless you once again with good health, my Leader, so that you will reach old age and continue to protect us against the danger of Jewish Bolshevism.

Hail my Leader
Party Member Walter Orthmann
Eisenach

A farmer's wife from a village near Straubing in lower Bavaria felt quite differently. She described her feelings on 2 October:

Dear Leader!

Today, on the occasion of the harvest festival, we are eager to express our heartfelt thanks to you, our Leader, for your efforts to preserve peace. In recognition of this averted great danger we also thank the Creator for the blessing of a good harvest.

The memorable day in Munich kept us glued to the radio, the first communicator of all events. With anxious concern we put ourselves mentally in your position, fearing that you would be forced to make still further concessions in the interest of your people that is now about to flourish. Our joy was all the greater when the agreement of the great statesman and thus the splendid victory was announced.

We can indeed say that Germany's fate lies in good hands, and that our great trust in the Leader will never be disappointed.

A Hail Victory to our Leader!
Maria Obermeier and children,
our Father is called up for an Army exercise

In early October the first letters of thanks from the Sudeten Germans began to come in, including those from two young girls who had fled into the German Reich during the unrest. They enclosed a photograph of themselves and on the reverse side wrote 'To our beloved Leader in memory of the twins Susi & Daisy J., Komorau bei Troppau [in the modern-day Czech Republic]':

Our beloved Leader!

Today we saw you at the railway station in Patschkau [today Paczków, Poland]. We thank you for having freed us and having taken us into your beautiful Reich.

We send you many warm greetings from our dear parents, our brother.

Your two Sudeten German refugees
Susi & Daisy J.
Komorau bei Troppau

The apparent solution of the conflict of nationalities and Czechoslovakia provided by the Munich agreement consolidated Hitler's prestige on the international level as well, as is shown by a letter from Mary Albrecht of Brussels written on 10 October 1938.

My Leader!

Permit me to express my deeply felt gratitude to you. The consequences of what you have achieved still cannot be measured! But the day will come when all humanity will thank you and recognize your greatness! Today the whole German people both inside and outside its borders thanks you once again!

My dear Leader, now those of us who live abroad can prove to all enemies, in black and white, that you only seek peace and always only wanted to have peace, so long as this peace is compatible with our conceptions of honour.

I have had the text of your agreement with Mr Chamberlain framed, and it hangs in my parlour, and I always carry another copy in my handbag, it will be my best argument for your desire for peace, but at the same time my best weapon, because here we are fighting a running battle every day. We are fighting for you, my Leader, with enthusiasm, with patience, with persistence: we are grateful that we are able to fight for you at all, each according to his strengths. My life and that of my family belong to you, my Leader and Germany!

When as a foreigner (Armenian) I married a German man twenty-six years ago, I was well aware of the obligations I had to Germany! My children are true German children and as they were the first to be allowed to join the Hitler Youth, they were neither unprepared nor was there anything really foreign to them in the ideas of National Socialism and its goals.

Dear Leader, how wonderful it is to be able to live and fight for the most splendid country in the world, for Germany, but I cannot say how much more wonderful it is for Germany to fight under your leadership!

In eternal loyalty, gratitude and admiration
Mary Albrecht
née Parséghian

The level of praise from Baroness Else Hagen von Kilvein, who wrote from Alexandria in Egypt on 21 November 1938 seems rather absurd:

Mr Hitler,

I am not sure how I should begin this letter. Long, long years of hard experience, moral torment and cares, the lack of self-knowledge, the striving for something new – all that is suddenly over, in an instant, in which I understood that I have you, Mr Hitler.

I know that you are a great, powerful figure, and that I am only an insignificant woman who lives in a distant foreign land, out of which we may perhaps not be able to travel, but you should understand me. What happiness/bliss that I have suddenly found my life's goal and have lived to see a shaft of light suddenly piercing the dark clouds and growing in brightness!

So it is in me – everything has been illuminated by such a great love, the love for my Leader, my teacher, that I sometimes would like to die, while I have your picture in front of me, so that I might no longer see what is not you.

I write to you, but not as the chancellor of a powerful Reich – perhaps I have no right to do that – I write to you simply as a person who is dear to me and will remain so until the end of my life.

I do not know whether you believe in mysticism, in something higher that surrounds us and remains invisible and that one can only feel. I believe in it, have always believed in it, and will always believe in it. I know that there is something in the world that binds my life to yours.

My God, whether I shall never be able to sacrifice my life for you, even though it would be the greatest happiness for me to die for you, for your teaching, your idea: my Leader, my knight in shining armour, my God!

It is very possible that these lines will never reach you, Mr Hitler, but I am not sorry that I am writing this letter. In these moments I am experiencing such wonderful joy, such a security and such a respite from my moral battle, that I even find my happiness in it.

I have no God but you and no Gospel but your teaching.

Yours unto death
Baroness Else Hagen von Kilvein

The young man who wrote from Upper Egypt on 10 December 1938 expressed his enthusiasm less emotionally.

Your Excellency,

I have the honour to inform you that I am an Egyption [sic] of 17 years. I had obtained the secondary education serteficata [sic. He means certificate] this year 1938. From my boyhood I have wanted to be an officer in the German army because of what I had knew of its power.

Sir,

Kindly allow me to herewith present my application for being a student under your superintendence. I am well acquainted with English, French and of course my own language, Arabic. I was tought [sic] how to fire a gun and a pistol. Many times I went for hunting birds and sometimes I hunted animals such as foxes and deers.

If my application is not well accepted, I will be sorry till my death.

I remain your,
obedient servant
Adolphe Malaty

One wonders whether Adolphe was really the young Egyptian's first name. Both letters went into the files without reply.

A letter from Maria Oberhummer of Vienna dated 1 November 1938 also reports her boundless reverence and was not answered. Her letter, written one month after the Munich conference, shows that worries about a possible war had been forgotten. She invoked God – but only in order to thank Hitler.

Much esteemed, beloved Leader!

On 18 April 1938 I gave birth to our second son. Unfortunately it was not possible for me to delay his arrival until the 20th. During the great liberation celebrations I had to avoid all crowds, and I never had a chance to see you even from afar! Also, unfortunately, too rarely have I had an opportunity to hear your voice, because for the time being we must still forego a radio in our house. But we have your picture – and I often speak to it.

Beloved Leader! You hear so many jubilant and grateful voices, only mine was not among them – I am pinned down by housework and my infant – and that never ceases to bother me.

My debt of gratitude grows steadily larger. I wish I had the power of a thousand trumpets to make myself noticeable so that a little of my voice might reach your ear! Now I want to take advantage of the written words in order to express somehow our love and our unlimited trust.

In times of the greatest affliction, thinking of the danger of war and my imperilled children, there was one idea that could always fight back my tears: our Leader! His love deserves the most courageous trust, he knows what for, why, how, and when – I must accept whatever comes.

Your great deeds, your infinite efforts for the welfare of all of us give us strength for the present and hope for the future!

To your so inexpressibly heroic heart, which beats for us all and indefatigably watches over us, we feel deeply indebted.

I speak as a woman and a mother – and as a child of the city of Vienna.

May God always preserve you in his very special care and bless you a thousand times!

With the most respectful love and loyal obedience
your sincere
Maria Oberhummer

11

THE CALM BEFORE THE STORM

With the threat of war seemingly passed, things returned to much the same pattern of the previous few years, with a steady stream of letters – a veneration of requests. The birthday wishes also continued. In 1939 Hitler's birthday, his fiftieth, was celebrated as an official holiday for the first time. Hitler also received many good wishes and gifts; for example, a valuable silver platter, an antique leather chest, and a watercolour of a street scene in Munich. Particularly striking was a model of Wachenfeld House (later known as the Berghof) made by a handicapped war veteran. After reading the cover letter Albert Bormann arranged for him to be given 200 marks in support.

But something had undoubtedly shifted. It was now less the people than institutions that sent congratulations and often valuable gifts. Thus, for instance, the Reich Veterans' Association sent a model of the Barbarossa monument (also known as the Kaiser Wilhelm Monument) sculpted in amber. The monument is on the top of the Kyffhäuser Mountain, which is near Bad Frankenhausen in Thuringia, central Germany. The monument was built between 1890 and 1896 by the German War Veterans' Federation, and showcases the Holy Roman Emperor Frederick I von Hohenstaufen, more famously known as Barbarossa (The Red Bearded), just awoken from sleep. Legend had it that Barbarossa had been asleep beneath the mountain and would awaken if Germany needed him. A bronze statue of Kaiser Wilhelm I, the first emperor of the second German Reich, sits on horseback above him. Here Wilhelm had succeeded in unifying Germany in the way that Barbarossa would have wanted. The mythology had clear appeal for Nazi supporters, given that Hitler had succeeded in creating the Third Reich, and was intent on unifying all Germans within his empire.

It is possible that the gigantic expenditures for the celebration of Hitler's fiftieth birthday also contributed to the drop in birthday greetings from individual Germans. There were countless state visitors, and an ostentatious decoration of the capital suited for filming made the often-used term 'People's Chancellor' look absurd. A spectacular military parade was the focus of the day; clearly Hitler was now to be perceived as a great military leader, ahead of the planned-for war. As such, the Party had been busy trying to redirect the population's enthusiasm into a willingness to sacrifice. This also contributed to the decline of birthday letters to Hitler. The people were no longer supposed to write letters, but rather to collect money that Hitler could use at his own discretion for welfare, or for projects such as the Hitler Youth.

A close look at the level of birthday donations for 1939 is very informative. Altogether, the amount collected was almost three million, or more precisely 2,764,307.99 marks. One group (the files do not record which) made a gift of a million marks. A further million had been collected by the German Medical Association. Five hundred thousand marks were given by Walter Darré, the Reich Peasant Leader, who had received the money from prosperous landlords. A certain Mrs von Brauchitsch gave 61,600 marks. From the total 141,762.99 marks were sent to Hitler's private office for use in specific projects. As the adjutant's office noted, the other donors gave only 60,945 marks. Part of it was contributed by smaller banks such as the German Agricultural and Industrial Bank of Trübau in Moravia (6,800 marks).

Few of these donations came from 'the people'. On the list of donors, only thirty-three women and fifty-four men appear as individuals with their names. Their donations range from small amounts (one Reichsmark) to 25,000 marks. But several factory workers' groups and school classes had taken up collections: for example, workers at the construction site of the Luftwaffe's military hospital in Greifswald in northeastern Germany sent 260 marks, and the National Socialist Women's Association of Asch in the German Sudetenland sent 1,000 marks. Even if we assume that all two hundred and sixty construction workers each gave one Mark and that behind the 1,000 marks there were a thousand individual donors, the group of people who donated money for Hitler's birthday is not impressively large.

In 1939, the language of the birthday greetings was also different, as a letter from the board of the Rheinmetall-Borsig works in Berlin shows.

My Leader!

Tomorrow you will celebrate your fiftieth birthday and all Greater Germany will celebrate it with you. What you mean to us and to what extent the German people venerate you will be expressed by this celebration in a more unique and convincing way than can be formulated in words. What you have achieved for Germany, and thus for all of us, over the past years is part of history, and only later generations will be in a position to gauge fully and wholly the greatness of your work.

Therefore we should like to limit ourselves to words and believe that we can best express our veneration for you personally by assuring you that we are always prepared to dedicate all our strength to your work and to fulfil with complete devotion the tasks assigned to us. As an external sign of this commitment and at the same time as a birthday congratulation from our whole workforce, we take the liberty of sending you the model of an anti-aircraft gun produced in our workshops.

Hail my Leader!
Rheinmetall-Borsig, Ltd.
The Board of Directors
H. Roehnert
Breuniger

The manager of a stocking factory in Auerbach in the Erzgebirge Ore Mountains] sent brief congratulations on behalf of this workers. The firm's patriarch had a worker produce a gift for Hitler.

My Leader!

On behalf of the ARWA Factory Association I take the liberty of sending you, my Leader, my sincerest wishes for happiness and success.

Unalterable loyalty and tireless work in your spirit, my Leader, are pledged you by the ARWA Factory Association.

At my request, a member of our workforce, Hermann Haase, has carved your parent's home in Leonding in the Erzgebirge style.

The ARWA Factory Association hopes thereby to give you pleasure, my Leader, and asks you to accept the birthday gift.

Hail, my Leader!
ARWA Factory Association
Factory Manager
Wieland

The letter of thanks was addressed to the wood-carver Hermann Haase and the ARWA Factory Association.

Please accept my sincere thanks for the pleasure that you have given me with your thoughtfulness on the occasion of my birthday.

Adolf Hitler

Hitler was not to be deterred from his plans to annex all of Czechoslovakia for long. He had regretted signing the Munich agreement almost immediately. He felt cheated out of war. Knowing that the population did not want one, he set about organizing a propaganda campaign in which the necessity of immediate war would be explained. At the same time the regime intensified its persecution of its Jewish citizens. On 8 November 1938 the seventeen-year-old Herschel Grynszpan, whose Jewish family had experienced discrimination in Germany, shot Ernst vom Rath at the German embassy in Paris.

On 9 November 1938 vom Rath died. Hitler and his inner circle quickly organized a pogrom; Joseph Goebbels, the propaganda minister, told Nazi officials assembled in Munich for the anniversary of

WIR·DEUTSCHE
IN·DER·SLOWA·
KEI·GRUESSEN
UNSEREN·FÜH·
RER ADOLF
HITLER
PREßBURG
20·APRIL·1940

In 1940 supporters of the 'German Party' [Deutsche Partei] and the 'Slovakian People's Party' [Slowakischen Volkspartei] collected signatures for Hitler's birthday. The lists, containing more than twenty thousand names, were bound in a book and sent to the Reich chancellery (see the following page).

Source: RGWA (Moscow)

the Beer Hall Putsch that while no planned demonstrations had been organized, spontaneous acts of retribution would not be stopped. That night a series of attacks against Jewish Germans, their homes, and their businesses took place across Germany, events known collectively as the Night of Broken Glass. Ninety-one people were killed and 30,000 Jewish men were arrested and sent to concentration camps.

The Night of Broken Glass provoked outrage internationally. But Hitler no longer cared. In his mind he was soon to defeat his international opponents and was busy organizing the subordination of Hungary and Lithuania to Germany. Poland refused to give up its independence and so Hitler decided to undertake war against Poland before his planned hostilities against Britain and France began. In the meantime, in March 1939 Hitler annexed the remainder of Czechoslovakia, creating Bohemia and Moravia and the client state of Slovakia.

Letters of good wishes and approval continued to arrive and were now answered by State Minister Otto Meissner. As head of the President's Office he also decided which letters were to be forwarded to other ministries and who would receive a reply.

For example there was no reaction to the thanks of the girls engaged in Labour Service to the Reich from the recently inaugurated Reich Labour Service camp of Cämmerswalde in the Ore Mountains. The Reich Labour Service had been formed in 1934 to help combat the widespread unemployment caused by the Great Depression. Members took part in civic, military and agricultural projects.

Nor did Mathilde von der Schulenburg, who swore an oath of loyalty to Hitler on the occasion of her marriage on 28 July 1939, receive a reply. However, Meissner did thank, in Hitler's name, the participants in an international wine-making conference, a paradentosis conference, a gathering of Germans living abroad, and a meeting of the Evangelical Association in Vienna. In all, the notation 'the Leader's thanks' is found on fifteen letters, and the notation 'thanks not necessary' on eight letters. The authors of poems usually received thanks from Meissner. In the six weeks before war broke out ninety-eight letters were received that could be interpreted as approval of Hitler's policies.

On 21 July 1939, Louis Kessler from Mülheim an der Ruhr in western Germany sent Hitler a poem:

To my Leader!

  Throughout the country there is jubilation;
  A new Germany is emerging!
  We are no longer a land without defence!
  We are no longer a people without honour!
  The Leader created with a strong hand
  A people of iron persistence

A people that never perishes
Because the new spirit blows through it.

Refrain:

And if the Leader calls us to battle,
We stand ready to fight!
The heroic spirit of the dead goes with us,
Encouraging us step by step.
Thus we keep our borders intact
From the Belt to the Rhine!

Millions who were in great need
Got work again, bread again.
But the work-song rings through the land.
The farmers are also concerned,
The hammer strikes, the motor wheezes,
It whistles and groans, glows and roars!
And the workman laughs with joy,
Because now he can work again.

Refrain:

And if the Leader calls us to battle, etc.

Now despotism does not stall everything,
No more harassment, no more strikes!
Now the people's best defence is growing.
The aroma of meals floats upward,
Every German heart beats fast!
We are becoming by the Leader's hand
A single people! A Fatherland!

Refrain:

And if the Leader calls us to battle, etc.

We are always inclined to peace.
But if an enemy bears his teeth,
Then the wheels stop turning in the land,
A people stands up with arms in hand!
And if from West, East or South,
A people, burning with Hitler's spirit,
Rises up like a face,
To arms and to the Last Judgement!!!

Refrain:

And if the Leader calls us to battle, etc.

With a German salute
Louis Kessler
Mülheim-Ruhr

On 28 July 1939, Meissner sent the usual letter: 'the Leader and Reich Chancellor thanks you very much for kindly sending him your poem. Hail Hitler, Dr Meissner.'

No poem sent to Hitler in the summer of 1939 shows the influence of National Socialist propaganda more clearly than that of Louis Kessler. He obviously still believed in Hitler's constantly declared desire for peace, but thought that enemies stood on all sides, only waiting to attack Germany. The reverse was true. Because of their internal political problems, the Soviet Union and France were absolutely not in a position to threaten Germany.

An unbroken stream of telegrams expressing loyalty and support came into the Chancellor's Office. The director of the state school of architecture in Höxter in western Germany, Dr Eng. Krieger, wrote on 24 July 1939.

My Leader!

As the state architecture school at Höxter, the first architecture school founded in Prussia, hereby delivers to you by my hand the commemorative book produced for its 75th anniversary celebration, we ask you to accept this very insignificant gift as it is intended: as an expression of the highest, everlasting loyalty to you, my Leader, and to your work.

On 29 July about 800 architects and engineers from all districts of the Greater German Reich will meet here in our small city on the Weser. The thoughts of all these men will then turn to you, and our hearts will be united in a single ardent commitment to you, my Leader, come what will.

With boundless respect,
Dr Eng. Krieger

The reply is dated 1 August 1939.

Dear Mr Director!

The Leader has asked me to send the participants in the 75th anniversary celebration of the state architecture school at Höxter his thanks for the greetings sent him.

Hail Hitler!
Dr Meissner

On 28 July 1939, the following telegram was received from Gerbstedt in the Mansfelder See district, eastern Germany:

TO THE LEADER, CHANCELLOR'S OFFICE, BERLIN.

IN THE WEDDING HOUSE OF THE GERBSTEDT OFFICE WE COMMEMORATE OUR LEADER IN GRATEFUL LOYALTY.

MATHILDE VON DER SCHULENBURG
FRITZ MARKUS AND BRIGITTE V. STEPSKI,
DOLIWA

In view of the later events, this expression of loyalty shows that even within families there were both supporters and opponents of Hitler.

Several members of the central German noble family of the von der Schulenbergs were executed by the Nazis for 'high treason' in 1944.

A telegram of thanks received by the President's Office on 29 July 1939 can be classified under the heading of insignificant approval:

CANOEISTS FROM ALL GERMAN DISTRICTS MEETING IN VIENNA FOR THE NIBELUNGEN TRIP GREET THEIR LEADER IN INALTERABLE LOYALTY

Meissner's undersecretary Hinrichs assigned Reich Sports Leader Hans von Tschammer und Osten to 'communicate to the senders of the telegram the Leader's thanks for their greetings, which he warmly returns'.

Clearly in Berlin normality was to be celebrated. There is no other way to explain the attention paid a telegram from Dingelstädt im Eichsfeld in Thuringia, central Germany, that was received by the President's Office on 29 July 1939.

MY LEADER!

THE MANY THOUSAND PEOPLE FROM EICHSFELD FROM THE HOMELAND AND FROM THE WHOLE REICH SEND YOU THEIR MOST DEVOTED GREET-INGS FROM THE HOMELAND FESTIVAL IN DINGELSTÄDT. THE EICHSFELD HOMELAND FESTIVAL IS AN EXPRESSION OF LOYALTY TO YOU, MY LEADER, AND TO THE GERMAN FATHERLAND. BECAUSE OF THE LACK OF APPROPRI-ATE INDUSTRIES WE PEOPLE OF THIS AREA HAVE BEEN AND ARE FORCED TO EARN OUR LIVINGS FAR AWAY FROM OUR ANCESTRAL HOMELAND IN EICHSFELD AND FROM OUR FAMILIES. OUR MOST HEARTFELT REQUEST ON THE OCCASION OF OUR HOMELAND FESTIVAL IS THAT IN YOUR GREAT DEVELOPMENT OF THE REICH YOU, MY LEADER, ALSO CONSIDER GIVING EICHFELD INDUSTRY SO THAT WE CAN LIVE IN OUR FAMILIES ON OUR NATIVE SOIL ALL THE TIME.

HAIL HITLER!
HILLMANN, SECRETARY OF THE EICHSFELDER
TERRITORIAL ASSOCIATION,
HUTZLER, LOCAL GROUP LEADER OF THE NAZI PARTY AND
BÜRGERMEISTER OF DINGELSTÄDT

The reply telegram was sent to the correspondence in Dingelstädt at 5:30 p.m. It was written in the President's Office, and signed by Minister Meissner. He was authorized to reply in Hitler's name.

MR SECRETARY HILLMANN, DINGELSTÄDT, EICHSFELD.

I THANK THE PEOPLE OF EICHSFELD WHO HAVE GATHERED AT THE HOMELAND FESTIVAL IN DINGELSTÄDT FOR THE GREETINGS SENT ME BY TELEGRAPH, WHICH I WARMLY RETURN.

ADOLF HITLER

Even holiday greetings were answered. For example, the telegram sent on 18 August 1939 by a tour guide from Rochlitz an der Iser in the Sudetenland. The German hikers had taken great pleasure in the 'splendid view' in the Giant Mountains (the phrase occurs in Baedeker's Auto Touring Guide to Greater Germany).

TO OUR LEADER ADOLF HITLER, BERLIN,

250 PEOPLE FROM THE MARK BRANDENBURG DISTRICT VACATIONING IN ROCHLITZ IN THE GIANT MOUNTAINS THANK YOU FOR BRINGING HOME THE SPLENDID SUDETENLAND. WE WERE ALLOWED TO SPEND OUR HOLI-DAYS ON THIS SPLENDID PIECE OF LAND. OUR HEARTS AND THOUGHTS ARE CONSTANTLY WITH YOU. WHEREVER YOU MIGHT LEAD US, WE WILL FOLLOW.

HAIL VICTORY!
FOR THE THANKFUL VACATIONERS,
KURÖDE
TOUR GUIDE

Conversely, Sudeten Germans now also took vacations in the old Reich organized by the 'Strength through Joy' Organization (KdF), the Nazis' official leisure organization. It was part of the German Labour Front, and was established as a means of stimulating the tourism industry, as well as a propaganda organ which delivered its message by making holidays and other cultural activities such as concerts, plays, and day trips, available to the lower classes. Workers' leisure time was thus not of their own making, but instead organized by the state so that it could serve the interests of the national community.

A telegram of thanks from 'Rügenwalde on the beautiful Baltic seacoast', was sent to Hitler's office on 11 August 1939. Tour guide Josef Roelling from Böhmisch-Leipa thanked the Leader and Reich Chancellor in the name of the tourists of the KdF group 9/39 'with all his heart'. Meissner replied on 14 August.

The Leader has asked me to communicate to the vacationers of the first KdF group his thanks for their greetings from the Baltic, which he warmly returns.

Hail Hitler!
Dr Meissner

Meissner replied just as noncommittally to letters and poems that clearly reflected the writers' expectations of an impending war. A few of these correspondents not only expected war but hoped for it, while others were moved by a naive longing for peace. There was also uncritical, unreflective admiration for the glamour of the Army. In each case the head of the President's Office expressed thanks on behalf of Hitler and found words of acknowledgement. It is interesting that the letters do not all consist of trivial homage. For instance, on 9 August 1939 Horst, a young man from Poland, expressed his fears and hopes:

Dear Leader!

I would like to send you two poems that I wrote during my vacation in Poland. I am a Polish refugee and am now so happy to be able to stay in your Reich. Unfortunately, not all my fellow Germans in Poland have been as lucky as I am. After I completed Middle School in Kattowitz [today Katowice, southern Poland] this year and, as a German, had no future in Poland, since my father had already been unemployed for nine years and we had to live without an apartment or any support, I decided to cross the border. I was lucky. Now I am employed as a farm labourer. I am very happy here. My parents also succeeded in reaching German soil. That is what gives me the greatest joy.

To comrades in rank and file,
We sing today the liberation song.
To comrades, let us sing,
Let our land resound throughout the world.
We are fighting for the Leader,
We are fighting for his country,
We are fighting for honour,
We give him hearts and hands.
Whether death or victory,
Whether peace or war,
We Germans in Poland sing the movement song.
We thank the Leader for all his deeds,
But we ethnic Germans also await him with longing.
We hope soon to be freed from our difficult lot,
We are helping the Leader with the victorious thrust.
And now it is ended,
Please read it with care.
I speak in the name of all Germans in Poland:
'Oh, dear Leader, come to get us!'

To our dear Leader!

Dear Leader! Come to us,
Deliver us!
Many Germans are without bread,
The German minority suffers need.
We had to endure such a long time,
Now they make it impossible for us.
We are mocked and beaten,
Do what we will,
Dear Leader, shut their traps!
The press invents many things about you,
But we Germans will not abandon you!

We sing your songs, we wear your garb,
We hope East Upper Silesia becomes German
–Overnight!
We shall still have to put up with much,
But soon we will raise your flag!

Greetings to our beloved Leader from:
Horst T. (14-½ years old)
Currently living with Mr Fritz Kappenberg
Hanover

On 16 August 1939, Lotte-Renate Pfeiffer wrote to Hitler from Wittenberg in eastern Germany:

My beloved Leader!

Yesterday and the day before I rode my bicycle 100 km and more through the military manoeuvre grounds in the Elbaue area. In the following poem I was able to express my enthusiasm and gratitude, which I felt as a result of what I saw and experienced, for you and for the splendid German Wehrmacht.

If it gave you, my Leader, a little pleasure, that would extraordinarily please

Your Lotte-Renate Pfeiffer

Manoeuvre

Stubblefields and ripened fruits,
Drone of motors endless marching columns.
In the sky planes trace bold ribbons
Until tomorrow, when the battle will be won!
The struggle already reaches the broad stream.
And now, sappers, tackle it with a hard hand!
Far away the proud artillery sees to it
That your bridge comes surely and quickly to land.
Hard is battle, virility is harder.

Courage and military duty are joyfully tested.
And German swords are stronger than ever,
Where the enemy's cunning rages most insolently!

Lotte-Renate Pfeiffer

State Secretary Meissner replied on 18 August.

The Leader has asked me to send you his warmest thanks for your amiable letter of 14 August 1939.

Hail Hitler
Dr Meissner

A poem by Elisabeth Korb was received on 18 August 1939 by the President's Office. The notation reads: 'thanks from the state secretary and head of the President's Office'.

Germany

A treasure lies upon this earth,
a high wall protects its worth.
The treasure sheds its light from hidden ground
over cities, lands, the sea's abyss.
It is mightily desired by the enemy,
Envied and silently revered.
Mixed races and foreign peoples murmur
About stealing it when darkness falls.
But Germany won't let itself be torn apart,
The Leader will weld its parts together.
Foreign hearts bleed from their wounds,
Their mouths testify to greedy longing.
Avid and brutal are their faces,
But we retain the pure German possession.
They stand ready with poison bombs and spears,
We fear them not, we take up our weapons.
With strong arms and hard fists,

We strike the foreign race.
The sense of truth, the virile strength
Show them the German nature.
Our light illuminates the foreign world,
There weeds and fire rampage in the fields.
We ward off the source of fire,
And eradicate weeds from the soil.
We trust the Leader, the German guide,
The God-sent, the noble thinker.
Hail Victory! to you, beautiful German state.
Greater Germany puts its trust
in its own seed.

Elisabeth Korb (widow)
Neustadt
Hail Victory! My Leader

Not a poem but rather a declaration of loyalty was sent by an association of Czech combat veterans on 25 August 1939. The letter was certainly not shown to Hitler but it was used on several occasions.

To His Excellency
Reich Chancellor Adolf Hitler
in Berlin.

On the basis of the tense situation on the Polish border, the Association of Czech combat veterans in Prague takes the liberty of making the following declaration.

We Czech combat veterans have fought with honour alongside German comrades on all fronts. We have shed our blood together and conquered together.

Today we solemnly declare that in the event of a war we are willing to fight shoulder to shoulder with our German combat veterans until the final victory is won, just as we did twenty-five years ago.

We ask that note be taken of this and sign with comradely greetings,

12

AT WAR

On 23 August 1939 the Germans agreed to divide Poland with the Soviets in a secret agreement. This time Hitler made certain that there would be no possibility of a peaceful resolution to his demands for more territory. Although he pretended to be on holiday, Hitler was in fact working on military plans. On 1 September 1939 Hitler declared war on Poland; Britain and France responded with their own declaration of war two days later, on 3 September. The Second World War had begun.

In the seven weeks after the invasion of Poland Hitler received only eighteen letters. None of the excitement that followed the annexation of Austria or the peaceful resolution of the Sudeten Crisis was to be seen. While Hitler wanted war, his population clearly did not.

On 8 November 1939, the anniversary of the 1923 Beer Hall Putsch, Georg Elser, a craftsman who was a virulent anti-Nazi and sometime communist, tried to assassinate Hitler when he gave a speech in the Munich Beer Hall cellar. Elser left a bomb in the cellar that was supposed to detonate during Hitler's speech. When the bomb did go off, it killed seven people and injured a further sixty-three. But Hitler, who had finished his speech early and left, was unharmed. Elser, who was quickly arrested, was imprisoned and then executed in 1945, just before the end of the war.

The actor Eugen Rex and his wife Helene, from Berlin, wrote to thank God that Hitler had survived the assassination attempt. Rex, whom his former colleagues in exile described as a 'sycophant', played secondary roles in anti-Jewish hate films. He died in 1943; what happened to his wife Helene is not known.

My Leader!

Together with the entire German people I would like to express my most sincere good wishes on the occasion of your miraculous salvation.

We thank God and beg him to keep you in good health and strength for us for a long time.

With a German salute
your Party comrades
Eugen Rex & wife

Hitler's private office replied on 22 November 1939.

Dear Mr Rex!

The Leader wants to express his sincere thanks to you and your spouse for your concern and for the good wishes that you have communicated to him on the occasion of the Munich attack.

With a German salute
Albert Bormann

Other dedicated Nazi supporters continued to write. Good wishes for the new year were received from the writer Hanns Johst, who on 29 December 1939 sent his congratulations.

My Leader!

The enormous gravity of this time obligates me to thank you for the determination that you have put into every heart devoted to you. Our love for you makes every task easy and makes everything done for you a song of praise. The truth is that for all of us you have become Germany, and so this is our wish and prayer at this turn of the new year: may heaven bless your creative power, so that in 1940 you may achieve your work: the Great Reich!

I would not be your poet and visionary, my Leader, if I did not already see this.

But veneration puts the courage of prophecy before the humility of the earnest inner wish!

All the best from your obedient
Stormtrooper
Hanns Johst

The notation on the letter reads 'Thank with facsimile stamp'. To what extent Hitler was aware of such tributes cannot be determined.

Hitler did read the letter from his former orderly Max Wünsche. Wünsche, who had in the meantime become a company leader in Hitler's personal bodyguard regiment, wrote on 31 March 1939 to the then Head Adjutant Brückner to report on the real facts of the preparation for the war against France. Brückner had the letter retyped on the 'Leader's typewriter' – a typewriter with oversize letters to counter Hitler's extreme far-sightedness. Brückner then presented it to Hitler.

Esteemed: Lieutenant General [of the SS]!

Since I assumed that at Easter you would in any case be very busy dealing with the mail, I have waited until today to send you my Easter greetings. They are no less sincere on that account, and even though they are belated, I ask that you communicate them to all the gentlemen and ladies in the Adjutant's office.

For me, Easter coincided with my recovery from a terrific cold. In the past weeks we have often travelled over and also in the Ems river, and in doing so have gotten somewhat damp, and so I also caught cold. But after Easter we merrily continued and even had to submit to several inspections. In such matters Wünsche is always the leader of the advance party (15th motorcycle company, armoured reconnaissance unit, infantry artillery unit, anti-tank unit and sapper unit, and also a mobile radio), that's the make-up of this bunch. It is an incredible pleasure to work with such a group, and also with our young men, who are all simply splendid fellows. So we have not been asleep, but rather have been preparing everything for the attack, and we now believe we are ready for any assignment. Although we are very comfortable in our present quarters, and the local population, while very Catholic, are exceptionally helpful to us, we are neverthe-less waiting with great excitement for the day when the attack will finally begin. I am particularly impatient, I never imagined it would be so long. But now I hope that the Leader gives me enough time to prove myself.

How is the Leader? I would have liked to write to him, but I know that he has so much to read every day that I did not want to burden him with my letters as well. But I may ask you to tell the Leader that I am well and that I will try, as the leader of a company of his regiment, to do my best; and therefore I ask for as much time as is necessary for the mis-sion. We are all very confident, whether officers, non-coms, or privates, and the Leader can be sure that his regiment will never disappoint him. In the same vein I ask that you too, Lieutenant General, accept my belated Easter greetings, and remain

Your Max Wünsche
SS-First Lieutenant

Wünsche rose in the armed wing of the SS, the Waffen-SS, to become commander of the Hitler Youth tank division. When he married, Hitler gave him a cheque for over 10,000 marks.

Brückner sent his reply on 5 April 1940 to the military postal number 33752.

Dear Wünsche!

Unfortunately, I received your letter of 31 March belatedly, also as a result of sickness. I, too, lay doubled up in bed for two weeks with a stupid case of phlebitis (a sign of old age!). Now I am hobbling about in the Chancellor's Office part-time again, to the annoyance of others and with no great joy to me! But I also hope that I will get over this sad episode of 'springtime' pneumonia.

I was very happy to hear that you and your young men are well.

The Leader read your letter. He often asks about you, and that is why I ask you to report on your experiences from time to time.

Schaub had to undergo a goiter operation that was exceptionally painful. But now he is doing better, and he will show up in a fortnight.

With all good wishes for you and your comrades and

Hail Hitler!
Your Brückner
Head of the Leader's Personal Adjutants' Office

When Hitler turned fifty-one in 1940, German troops were fighting north of Oslo, and the war at sea was in full swing. There was no public celebration. The commanders in chief of the various branches of the Wehrmacht sent their congratulations, and Hitler awarded a few medals. Hermann Göring, who was the head not only of the Luftwaffe but also of the four-year plan office responsible for armaments, called for an increased use of labour. Good wishes from the German people were rare. Instead, the supporters of the German Party in Slovakia and the fascistic Slovakian People's Party in Bratislava (Pressburg) collected signatures. In the Party offices bureaucrats set out sheets of paper that Hitler-admirers could sign. The lists, bearing more than twenty thousand names, were bound in a book and sent to the Chancellor's Office. This homage was highly official, and the first pages of the book were filled with organizations' stamps. Only much further on were the lists of signatures finally found.

A large-format 'certificate', sumptuously produced and decorated with swastikas and oak leaves, was received from Melk in lower Austria. However, the text was more a prayer than a homage.

For our Leader and supreme master builder's fifty-first birthday we ask the Almighty's eternal blessing!

May his noble life goal fully succeed to the benefit of the whole
German people!

> *For the plant manager & the workforce*
> *of the*
> *[stamp] Radebeule Basalt Works*
> *Enterprise for concrete construction and road repair, successor*
> *Anton Kosta, Vienna*

On his next birthday, 20 April 1941, Hitler was travelling in his special
train, his personal locomotive that he used to travel between his various
headquarters and that was a mobile headquarters in its own right. Once
again Hitler received only a few birthday greetings, but they include
a very interesting poem of homage, though the cover letter has been
lost. The unknown author sent congratulations on the occasion of 'Our
beloved Leader's birthday! War year 1941', and drew a large swastika
in the upper corner.

If every country had such a leader,
as Providence has given us,
How nice it would be in this world,
how happy and content all would be!

Wars would no longer need to rage,
everyone would protect his land from them.
And trade and change ever gloriously bloom:
for every leader would seek that goal:
They would sit peacefully at green tables,
and with pure zeal rack their brains
to quickly solve problems, even the hardest,
not with weapons, no, with good, not evil;
and pointless blood need then no longer flow,
here everyone could enjoy his bit of life
For this life is short, comes only once, and lies
in God's hand!
Must it be taken before its time and by force
by the enemy's hand?

Yes, even the most pious cannot live in peace,
When it does not please the evil neighbour.
So it has always been, and so it still is today
in this otherwise so beautiful world.

But if every country had such a leader
as Providence has given us,
then there'd be no more war in this world,
we would have only the finest peace!!!

But this wish, I have to admit, seems even to me a dream,
for its fulfilment would be too beautiful, I think I could hardly
    imagine it
But still I must think of the beautiful word
and hope that Providence will yet guide us

THAT THE WHOLE WORLD WILL STILL
BE HEALED BY GERMAN NATURE!!!

We thank our LORD GOD that he has given us the Leader,
stands ever at his side and guides his step himself!
Some may have already considered in a quiet moment
How the Leader might have also made his life easy!
Some would have already bent down after a short battle
and thrown in the towel, would have preferred
perhaps to work as a writer in some nice quiet place
wholly undisturbed
and lead his life there as comfortably as possible,
but our Leader set himself a higher goal, the
very highest goal,
and chose a path that was very hard and demanded
much from him:
He fought, suffered and struggled and struggles still today for
    our nation!!!
For that the dear LORD himself gave him his well-deserved
    reward!

Has it ever already occurred in history,
has it ever been already heard or read anywhere,
that a soldier, once nameless, almost unknown,
was named leader of a *great empire?*

Thus GOD *crowned* his fighting and his struggling
and also *helps* subdue the enemy today!
For dear GOD likes to help whoever helps himself:
protects, preserves, shelters him, keeps not far from him!

In fighting for us the Leader often made his life *very hard,*
And for that today the whole people stands behind him like a
    wall:

Millions of hearts reaffirm once again today their loyalty in great
    love and gratitude to the Leader!
Millions of hearts are prepared to make any sacrifice for the
    Leader!
The bravest soldiers with the best leadership of all stand at his
    side.
Millions of hearts hail today their beloved Leader and wish
    with all their hearts that he might soon have his well-deserved
    rest
after this war forced upon us by the enemy
with a victory granted us by the dear LORD!!!

So at the centre of this day today stands our great request:
May GOD protect our beloved Leader here in our midst!
Grant the brilliant general constant health,
that highest earthly good,
continue to give him
strong willpower,
decisiveness,
endurance, and *courage,*

fulfil his wishes for *the future of Germany*
for *peace with nations* here in this world

and help prevent the one who rejected the hand of peace, who always wanted war, from resisting too much longer!

The unknown author assumed that victory would come, though neither the war at sea nor the war on land had been decided. The Air Force sent its 'greetings' with an attack on London, whose 'terrible effect' was emphasized in the Wehrmacht's report, but Great Britain was not considering capitulation. Hitler himself celebrated his birthday by drawing new borders in the Balkans.

A few, rather formulaic, telegrams were received from Nazi Party leaders, including this one:

Sincerest wishes for happiness and success in the New Year.

Georg Joel, deputy Regional Leader

On 21 April 1941 Joel received the standard answer:

For the good wishes you sent me on the occasion of my birthday, I offer you my sincerest thanks.

Adolf Hitler

Among the good wishes sent by artists and writers that of Hanns Johst once again stands out. He sent his greetings from Starnberg in Bavaria to the Leader's headquarters.

With my heartfelt personal wishes for your well-being I send you, my Leader, a birthday homage from all those working on the German book. Never in the course of our history were poets and scientists, publishers, booksellers, and printers more united in loyal sentiments than they are today.

Hail Hitler,
ever your obedient and devoted
Hanns Johst

Hitler answered the state councillor and SS Group Leader on 21 April:

For the good wishes that you sent me on the occasion of my birthday, on your own behalf and on that of all those working on the German book, I offer you my sincerest thanks.

Hitler did still continue to receive some letters from individuals. One was Dagmar Dassel, a woman living in Berlin. There are no letters of reply from Hitler's private office. It is more than probable that Dassel never received any mail from the centre of power. She sent enthusiastic, long, and verbose letters to Hitler, amounting to more than 250 pages in all.

It began with the seven-page letter of 25 February 1940, on the occasion of the twentieth anniversary of the founding of the Nazi Party. Dassel described her feelings on hearing Hitler's speech broadcast on the radio ('it rang throughout the ether...') and went on, 'chosen and blessed is the people – to whom God Almighty has sent such a noble-brilliant-industrious-envied and religious Saviour and leader in its misery'. She had been glued to the radio, full of 'joyful expectation', and was not disappointed, because 'the Leader is with us'.

On 30 January 1941, she sent an eleven-page letter full of 'gratitude, happiness, and pride' to 'this unique, splendid, deeply loved Leader – the prayed-for and God-sent – the anointed chosen by God – crowned and beloved child – who with a stronger, firmer, surer hand [will raise] his people to never before seen heights and greatness – to the most splendid triumphal total final victory – to peace – to world peace – and thereby all people the freedom of national popular and cultural development in creative and productive work and prosperity to the profit and benefit of all humanity – that is your world domination.'

On Sunday, 11 May 1941, she added to her letter a complementary report entitled 'My path to the culminating splendour to the divine realm of a high and noble humanity.' This letter is informative and is cited here in full, not because it expresses an exceptional veneration, but rather because it refers to Hitler's speech in the Berlin Sports Palace, where he spoke to 6,000 officer candidates. On 4 May 1941,

Dassel could write only 'with an overflowing grateful, happy, and proud heart':

My Leader – today I can only once again emphasize my steadfast – unchanging – inalterable loyalty and love: my whole life – thoughts and feelings belongs to you – my Leader – my most beloved – best – noblest – greatest – most splendid – unique most brilliant man – the prayed for and divinely sent – only to you – my Leader – only to your splendid work of salvation and peace – only to you, the chosen – anointed – crowned and beloved child of God – God's emissary of peace – the executor of God's will on earth – to your greater German people and Reich – now in particular to your splendid heroic Army – to you – my Leader – the first soldier and the supreme commander of this splendid Army – to the most brilliant and greatest general and strategist of all times – to the most brilliant statesman – to the greatest German – only to you – my Leader – the most sublime hero – the greatest victor in time and eternity – only to you – my Leader – to the pure and inner man – do I ceaselessly work, watch and pray in silence – with a pure heart – joyful in love for you and your great German people and Reich for God's protection and blessing – my soul surrounds you and thanks your splendid heroes – the Army on all your victorious campaigns with the armour of divine love – and also your loyal allies until the final victory – my soul rejoices without cease.

My Leader!
Mrs Dagmar Dassel

Dassel, who was obviously seriously ill, died in April 1941. She sent her farewell letter to Hitler, telling him that she believed in him 'in unchanging fidelity and love of the sacred future'.

In the meantime, the Party office was dealing with requests for support that came in simultaneously, for example, one from a father with eight children who had lost his apartment because he was behind on his rent payments. Such letters did not reach Hitler any more than did the requests for apartments made by victims of the bombing war, for which the Reich Housing Commissioner and Hitler's chief architect, Albert Speer, was responsible. But Hitler was made aware of a letter of thanks from Garmisch-Partenkirchen in Bavaria dated 19 March 1941.

My Leader!

I ask you to forgive me for only now thanking you for the wonderful jardinière you gave us for the birth of our third child, little Klaus. You have given me and my husband great pleasure.

If I am only now thanking you, that is because it took me a little longer to recover from the third Caesarian than the earlier ones.

I am also eager to report the competence and importance of the consultants who treated me. Professor Wagner, who also regularly treats Mrs Speer, Mrs Morell and Countess von der Goltz, can claim the rare fame of being especially active in population policy. Numerous women become mothers through his brilliant operations!

I write this to you, my Leader, because I would like you to know what competent gynaecologists you have in Germany. Professor Wagner is the only physician whom I would trust with confidence for a fourth Caesarean.

Hail my Leader!
Your
Annelies Reinhardt

Annelies was referring to Georg August Wagner, the retired head physician of the obstetrics clinic of the Berlin Charité hospital. The family's close relationship of trust with Hitler is also expressed in a letter written on 31 December 1941 by her husband Fritz. Fritz Reinhardt had previously been a Regional Leader and was now a state secretary in the finance ministry, where he was responsible for the financing of rearmament and for reprocessing the dental gold taken from Jewish prisoners in the death camps. Reinhardt didn't want to talk about that, but rather about the state's financial situation.

My Leader!

My wife and I send you our best wishes for the year 1942, especially for health and for the full success of all your enterprises, and for victory after victory for the German Army. Even if the war should still go on a long time, the Reich's finances will prove to be unshakeable.

In the current financial year the Reich's regular revenues will in fact reach 45 billion marks and in the following year may even reach 50 billion marks. The remaining financial needs will be covered by means of credit.

The Reich's debt at the end of the war will be more than balanced by the economic values and opportunities that have been won by the German sword.

Hail Victory, my Leader!
Your Fritz Reinhardt

At the end of the war, the debts were not covered. At the end of 1932 the Reich's debt was 8.5 billion marks, and in 1939 it was 47.3 billion. By 1945, it had grown to 387 billion marks, a sum that could in fact have been covered only by the permanent conquest of other states. In 1950 Reinhardt was 'de-Nazified' and finally died, without ever having been put on trial, in Regensburg in 1969.

Hitler also continued to receive requests, including some from the nobility. Prince Friedrich, the head of the house of Hohenzollern-Sigmaringer, which was related to the former ruling house of Prussia, wrote to Hitler's office on laid paper decorated with a stamped and gilded crown in keeping with his status. The disempowered prince sent his letter on Christmas Eve 1941 to Otto Meissner, the head of the President's Office, probably because of some old connection. Meissner seemed to be the right man to fulfil a private wish.

Dear State Secretary!

I request that the enclosed sealed letter to the Leader be forwarded to the highest level.

On the occasion of the new year, I ask you to accept my most sincere and heartfelt good wishes.

May the new year be a good and happy one for you and your family, and also for your position, which involves great responsibility.

At the conclusion of the old year, I wish to express my very special gratitude for the many favours and counsels that you have been so kind as to give me.

With the assurance of my particular esteem, I remain as always, with Hail Hitler,

> *Your devoted*
> *Friedrich*
> *Prince zu Hohenzollern*

Meissner forwarded the enclosure, the letter so expressly characterized as 'sealed', to Hitler. The latter dealt with it with surprising speed and had the notoriously underemployed Meissner answer it. His letter, with the letterhead 'State Secretary and Head of the President's Office of the Leader and Reich Chancellor', is dated 29 December 1941 and clearly reflects the spiritual ancestry of this bureaucrat, who had already held office under the Republic:

Your Royal Highness!

I am honoured to confirm the reception of your letter of the 24th December as well as the letter to the Leader dated the same day. The Leader has asked me to express his sincere thanks for best wishes you sent him for the new year.

With regard to your request that your son-in-law, Count Heinrich zu Waldburg-Wolfegg, be promoted to Reserve Officer, I have forwarded, as ordered, your letter to the Leader to the army personnel office, Berlin, for the relevant examination and processing.

For the good wishes for the new year you have addressed to me personally, I most respectfully thank your Royal Highness; I reply with my best wishes for a good and happy new year.

> *Hail Hitler*
> *Your Royal Highness's*
> *most respectfully devoted*
> *Dr Meissner*

Bodewin Keitel, General of the Infantry and Head of the Army's Personnel Office, examined the case of the very aristocratic officer and noted: 'No doubts regarding political attitude'. As a result Heinrich

Maria Willibald Benedikt Albrecht Philipp Ulrich von Waldburg-Wolfegg became a Reserve Lieutenant.

In the summer of 1941 several congratulatory telegrams from high ecclesiastical officials were presented to Hitler. On 28 June, 1941, one week after the attack on the Soviet Union was launched, the bishop of Jaroslaw in occupied Poland sent the following telegram to the Leader's headquarters.

PLEASE INFORM THE LEADER OF THE GERMAN PEOPLE OF THE FOLLOWING EVENT:

THE UKRAINIAN GREEK CATHOLIC CLERGY IN THE GENERAL GOVERNMENT COMMUNICATES TO THE LEADER ITS FEELING OF GRATITUDE FOR THE BATTLE AGAINST THE ENEMY OF CHRISTIANITY AND CHRISTIAN CULTURE AND ASKS ALMIGHTY GOD'S HEAVENLY BLESSING ON HIM IN THIS BATTLE.

THE CATHOLIC BISHOP IN JAROSLAW

Representatives from the German Evangelical Church wrote to Hitler on 30 June 1941:

To the Leader, Leader Headquarters

The ecclesiastical executive council of the German Evangelical Church, which has assembled for the first time since the beginning of the decisive battle in the East, once again assures you, my Leader, of the inalterable loyalty and devotion of the whole of evangelical Christianity in the Reich in these breathtakingly eventful times. You have, my Leader, averted the Bolshevist peril in our own land and now call upon our people and the peoples of Europe to wage the decisive battle against the mortal enemy of all order and all Western Christian culture. The German people, and with it all its Christian members, thank you for this act of yours. The fact that British policy now also openly serves Bolshevism as its accomplice finally makes it clear that it is concerned not with Christianity, but solely with the destruction of the German people.

May Almighty God stand by you and by our people, so that we can succeed against the twofold enemy with the eventual victory to

which we must devote all our will and action. At this time the German
Evangelical Church recalls the Baltic Evangelical martyrs of 1918.
It recalls the unspeakable suffering that Bolshevism has inflicted on
the people of its own sphere of power and seeks to inflict on all other
nations, and, with all its prayers, it stands by you and by our incom-
parable soldiers, who are now engaged in eliminating the heart of the
plague through such powerful blows, so that a new order might emerge
under your leader[ship] throughout Europe and so that all internal subversion, all defilement of the most holy, all desecration of freedom of
religion might be put to an end.

> *The Ecclesiastical Executive Council*
> *of the German Evangelical Church*
> *Maharens, Schultz, Hymmen*

The Evangelical Free Church declared its approval on 12 July 1941.

To the Leader and Reich Chancellor in the Leader's Headquarters

The union of Evangelical free Churches sends you, my Leader, its
heartiest congratulations on the magnificent victory in the East, in the
certainty that you, as God's instrument, are thereby finally breaking the
power of Bolshevism, which is hostile to God and to Christianity, and
so ensuring not only the future of our beloved German Fatherland, but
also a new order in Europe. We assure you once again of our intercession and unreserved devotion.

> *Director Paul Schmidt*
> *Bishop Melle*

The telegram from the Holy Ascension monastery in Pochaev (Ukraine)
arrived in the Chancellor's Office on 25 August 1941.

The bishops assembled on Mt Pochaev, in the Temple of the Ukrainian
people in Volhynia, congratulate Adolf Hitler and his victorious Army
on the occasion of the liberation from a world deprived of God by the
Bolsheviks.

The ecclesiastical assembly of Ukraine, with its faithful population, asks in belief and love the great God to grant the creator of the great German Reich, Adolf Hitler, who has the divine gift of directing the future of peoples along good paths, a long and happy life.

We bishops once again thank our liberator Adolf Hitler and his victorious Wehrmacht.

Simon, Archbishop of Ostrog
Panteleimen, Bishop of Lemberg
Benjamin, Bishop of Vladimir in Volhynia

And on 23 September 1941 a telegram came from Chelm (Ukrainian Cholm) in the General Government that was addressed to:

The Leader of the German nation, Adolf Hitler, Berlin

My clergy and thousands of believers, assembled for the Cathedral celebration in Chelm, unite with me in sending the great Leader Adolf Hitler and his unconquerable Wehrmacht the most heartfelt thanks for the liberation of the Ukrainian capital Kiev from godless domination. We all pray most warmly that the Lord God might with his strong hand help the Leader and his army to establish peace and order all over the East.

Archbishop Herion

Hitler may have noted approval of his 'crusade' against 'godless Bolshevism' from Christian dignitaries, but politically it had no impact. Ukrainian farmers had often welcomed the armed forces with bread and salt, but they waited in vain for the reversal of collectivization. German rule ultimately took the form of an occupation regime that plundered and terrorized the country. The repressive apparatus had to be developed even in the German Reich itself. Resistance increased as well as the number of those who refused military service. The number of death sentences imposed increased dramatically. Before the war civilian courts handed down 664 death sentences. Between 1939 and 1945 they handed down 15,896. Military courts imposed capital punishment in at least 20,000 cases. As head of state, Hitler had the right to remit any sentence. But he had no interest in clemency; he had, after all, blamed the defeat in the First World War on an inadequate crackdown.

How 'clemency matters' were dealt with is shown by the case of Maria Sölkner. The Gestapo had put her brother-in-law in a concentration camp, even though he had completed his regular prison sentence. On 28 July 1942 an assistant secretary put the following notation on her petition sent to the Chancellor's Office:

Mrs Maria Sölkner, of Berlin Wilmersdorf, requests a consultation in the Chancellor's Office. Her brother-in-law Josef Neuhauser is said to have spent two years in preventive detention because he had listened to a foreign radio station; but he had been sentenced to only sixteen months' imprisonment. His wife was apparently told that he would have to serve his sentence only after the end of the war. The wife and her two-year-old child are said to be in severe financial difficulty.

The original of the letter was forwarded to the Ministry of Justice. Sölkner received this reply: 'Your petition of 24 July 1942 was sent to the Reich Minister of Justice for further investigation. I ask that you desist from requesting a meeting in the Chancellor's Office.' The letter was returned by the Ministry of Justice on the ground of 'lack of jurisdiction'. Thereupon Reich Minister Lammers, the head of the Chancellor's Office, concerned himself personally with the case, and on 6 August 1942 he had the letter sent to 'SS National Leader and Head of the German Police in the Reich Ministry of the Interior', that is, to Heinrich Himmler. Thus the office that was responsible for the arbitrary imprisonment of Sölkner's brother-in-law was now supposed to deal with the request for clemency . . .

Practically all the petitions and letters of request received from the people were dealt with in this way, no matter whether they concerned divorces or alimony and child support (Reich Justice Minister), housing issues (Reich Housing Commissioner), or arbitrary arrests (SS National Leader). Only when officials in the Chancellor's Office had the impression that it was a matter of a bad decision made by a department or a court did they examine the decision itself, as is shown by a case dating from 15 July 1942.

On this day the Chancellor's Office received a denunciation. Hermann Pfeiffer, from Frankfurt am Main, titled his letter 'Application for Review' and also gave the file number of the district court (6NS36/42). Without a formal salutation, he came immediately to the point:

According to court judgment v. 6.7.42 in matters regarding the married couple Leo and Elfriede Stellbaum, who were living in Frankfurt am Main, because of the forging of documents and fraud the accused were sentenced to pay a fine of 1,000 marks. Since this judgment may be an especially serious miscarriage of justice against all sound sense of law, as the informer who reported the accused I ask that the case be reviewed.

The facts of the case: Since the beginning of the war, all goods not important for the war effort may be shipped only temporarily in limited quantities, and for that reason every dispatch must first be approved by the consignment note pre-examination office. This was known to the accused. Nonetheless, from the beginning of the war up to the present, the accused had illegally taken enormous freight space for themselves by means of cleverly forged consignment notes. In this way, they greatly hindered or significantly endangered supplies to our armed forces in ten to fifteen instances. The last case occurred during the fur collection in January 1942, when every metre of freight space was urgently needed. I immediately informed the Reich Railway investigation office. At that time the accused had obtained permission to ship eight (empty) crates. After the consignment note had been approved, the number of crates was increased from eight to ninety-eight (by altering the consignment note). The investigative office intervened and put a stop to the Stellbaum couple's criminal activity in violation of the war laws. During the court proceeding it turned out that the accused had been committing these forgeries or frauds against the people, the state, and the Wehrmacht continuously since the beginning of the war. Nonetheless, the accused managed to prevent these matters from coming before a special court. The sentence was three months in prison. The audience (fellow Germans), and I as the *informer*, were disappointed by this sentence. The accused even had the insolence to appeal this sentence, and when the case was heard again the judgment was reduced to a fine of 1,000 marks. That such an offence against the war laws can be expiated by paying a fine is incomprehensible; especially since the accused are wealthy and the fine amounts precisely to the cost of one of Mrs Stellbaum's fur coats. Everyone was outraged by this judgment and rightly so. In addition, we must consider the many hundreds of German soldiers who may have sacrificed their lives because of these dirty tricks. We should also note that in court it was acknowledged that the accused had not been straight in other things; for example, altering med[ical] prescriptions and profiteering on scarce commodities, which the accused admitted to the district court judge Mr Haas during the proceeding. It is also incomprehensible that such a blatant case, which should be of interest to the entire German people, was kept out of the daily newspapers and even treated as trivial. If there were more of these war criminals, the whole German victory would be imperiled.

I therefore request a review of the imposed judgment, which ought to be, in accord with general sense of law, considered a clear miscarriage of justice, especially since the saying is 'Wheels must turn for victory!'

Hail Hitler!
Hermann Pfeiffer

N.B. For comparison! A newspaper clipping on a judgment against a miner who was not able to expiate his punishment with money.

The newspaper clipping concerned a judgment issued in Neurode, in Hesse. A miner was ill with influenza and the medical officer declared that he was incapable of working for a few days. In order to get more time off, he altered the certificate, changing the date of the end of his inability to work. The falsification was noticed and reported to the authorities. The miner was sentenced to six months in prison. The employee at the Chancellor's Office who was responsible for entering correspondence forwarded the letter to the minister of justice, 'most respectfully, with the request that it be returned with a response'. Pfeiffer was told that he would hear back.

Assistant secretary Ernst Schäfer in the ministry of justice had the files of the criminal proceeding sent to him and examined Pfeiffer's petition. On 21 August 1942 he sent his opinion to the Chancellor's Office:

Enclosed I am forwarding, along with the petition of the informer and filer of the complaint, the files of the criminal proceeding you requested.

The legal judgment of the act issued by the criminal chamber in Frankfurt a. M. seems to me tenable, especially since securing a capital advantage was not found to be the goal of the act.

The offenders did not in fact seek any economic advantage by returning the empty crates.

Although the criminal chamber's judgment is not severe, I do not consider special measures against the judgment necessary, since the offenders have no previous record and are very elderly.

Dr Schäfer

Assistant secretary Ficker acknowledged this letter, but decided to examine the files once again. In doing so he came across a notation that Pfeiffer had apparently been employed by the Stellbaums as a warehouse worker, and that his denunciation could be interpreted as an act of personal revenge for his dismissal. On 7 September, Ficker wrote the reply to Pfeiffer and had it signed by Minister Lammers:

In accordance with your petition of 13 July 1942 the criminal proceeding against the Stellbaum couple was examined in the Chancellor's Office. I have found no basis for taking any sort of action.

Lammers

The Stellbaums were lucky; they could also have been simply sent to a concentration camp as 'saboteurs'. Schäfer, whose judgment was exceptionally lenient in this case, left the justice ministry in 1943, after it was reorganized. He was replaced by a convinced National Socialist and member of the SS.

Petition no. 2159 was processed on 30 December 1942 in the Chancellor's Office. Hilde Städele from Zizenhausen bei Stockach on Lake Constance received the following answer:

I have forwarded your petition to the Leader dated 19 December 1942 to the SS National Leader and the head of the German police for examination. You will hear further from that office.

On behalf of
Ficker

Her letter was filed away with the notation 'Release of her husband from the concentration camp'. A letter from Rudolf Peick from Heydekrug in the Memel Territory was dealt with in the same way. His petition for the 'Release of his son from the concentration camp', dated 23 December 1942 (Petition no. 1795) was forwarded to SS head Heinrich Himmler.

On 9 April 1943, assistant secretary Dr Wolfgang Laue processed a petition from Paula Lewin from Berlin-Wilmersdorf and summarized the facts of the case in the following manner:

Re: The petitioner says that the non-Aryan Rudi S. (fourteen years old) was deported to the East (Oświęcim Camp) [Oświęcim is the Polish name for Auschwitz] on 12 March 1943. She asks that he be released with a pardon because he is not Jewish but mixed race. His mother is supposed to be the divorced Jewess Margot S. His father, who has co-signed the petition and is described in the petition as being of German blood, is a certain Kurt Winkler, Berlin. Because of unfortunate family relationships a clarification of his descent is apparently still lacking.

Laue forwarded the letter to Heinrich Himmler and notified Lewin that he had done so.

On the instructions of the Reich minister and Head of the Chancellor's Office your letter of 28 March this year has been forwarded for further consideration to the SS National Leader and head of the German Police in the Reich Ministry of the Interior in Berlin as the competent authority.

I leave it to you to advise Mr Winkler regarding this matter.

Dr Laue

Since Winkler was not satisfied with this reply, he wrote to Hitler again. Laue also forwarded this letter to Himmler and informed the father of what he had done.

In the matter of your son, Heinz Rudi S., following the petition you co-signed with Mrs Paula Lewin dated 28 March of this year, I have forwarded your petition to the Leader from 27 May of this year, which pertains to the same case, to the SS National Leader and Head of the German Police in the Reich Ministry of the Interior in Berlin for further examination. Given the multitude of tasks burdening him in connection with the direction of the war and the state, the Leader cannot concern himself personally with your case.

> *On behalf of*
> *Dr Laue*
> *Assistant Secretary*

It is unlikely that the young man survived deportation to Auschwitz.

Despite the deportation of Jews, the growing terrorism, and military defeats on all fronts, letters of thanks and homage were still coming in.

On Hitler's birthday in 1942 the deputy Regional Leader of Oldenburg, in northwest Germany, sent his greetings by telegram:

To the Leader Adolf Hitler, Berlin

On your third wartime birthday I send best wishes, particularly for your strength and health for the great tasks of this decisive year.

> *Joel, deputy Regional Leader*

Although Hitler celebrated his birthday in 1942 with a large congratulatory reception, Regional Leaders and other Nazi officials were not invited. Hitler shunned most of his National Socialist colleagues, including only his innermost circle. German officers and politicians from subjugated or allied states were, however, invited to the Leader's headquarters in the Wolf's Lair, Hitler's eastern front military headquarters. It was built during the planning stages of the German invasion of the Soviet Union in 1941. Hitler left for the last time in autumn 1944. His choice of guests reflects Hitler's focus during these war years.

In the files of Hitler's private office there was also a Leitz file box with the title 'The Twelve Labours of Hercules – Dedicated to his Excellency Mr Reich Chancellor Adolf Hitler on 20 April 1942'. An architect, Heinrich Ritter from Markgröningen in Baden-Württemberg, southern Germany, had written the poem of homage to Hitler in the 'war year 1941'. This repulsive concoction takes the form of a classical dialogue and shows that Ritter was a convinced National Socialist who was educated in classics. The original classic poem describes a series of penitential acts undertaken by Hercules, the greatest Greek hero. He had killed his own children after being driven mad by his step-mother Hera. Hercules was compelled to perform exacting tasks, including slaying the Nemean Lion and the nine-headed Lernaean Hydra, both vicious monsters, as well as capturing the Golden Hind of Artemis, a deer so quick it could outrun an arrow.

Ritter's re-telling takes the form of a fictitious conversation between a teacher and a pupil, condensed into a 'heroic poem in twelve cantos'. Each of Hercules's twelve great labours was described in turn from the teacher's and the pupil's perspectives, and each demonstrated the superiority of the National Socialist cause against a host of enemies. And who played Hercules? 'There our Leader' appeared the obvious choice to Franz, the eager German pupil. 'That is what a hero is, he is a man who can carry out such labours.' Franz casts England in the role of the Nemean Lion, whose neck Hitler 'wrings' and who he 'strikes' so that its 'fur flies'. England would eventually 'grovel and writhe in blood' at a time which only 'the Leader can determine'. The teacher applauds Franz's interpretation, responding that 'If Hitler attacks England, He no longer needs to ask us. Count us in, we're ready for the trial. We have our Hercules!'

The poem carried on in this fashion through the other eleven labours, with Soviet Russia playing the part of the giant serpent Hydra, who spews 'poison, venom, gall, hellfire'. Hercules 'with a quick blow' 'struck off their heads'. Where two regrew 'from the wound' 'Hercules was not afraid. He struck twice as hard and fought until he'd done it in!' In Ritter's imagination 'Soviet Russia was completely annihilated!' Poland appeared as the Golden Hind, while Yugoslavia was a Boar, and international Jewry the Augean Stables. Augeas' famous stables housed more cattle than any other except in Greece. The stables had never been cleaned out, until Hercules was charged with the task of doing so.

Ritter's epic poem concluded with the following lines. Although the original rhyming scheme was impossible to preserve in translation, they encapsulate both Ritter's views on Hitler and Germany, as well as how well Ritter copied the classical lyric style of writing:

So this ancient Greek myth
Has become a mirror-image of our time.
To be the leader of this new age of heroes
Hitler is predestined and prepared!

His whole self, the spirit, his work, his life,
He has given us, the German people!
What he is to us will never fade and be forgotten,
But his greatness will be measured by his work!

It is a heroic saga, a heroic song,
A heroic battle, from which a will radiates:
To be equal to the heroes, to this heroic time,
With heart and mind ever ready for battle!

And Adolf Hitler stands, a paragon among heroes,
High and sublime over all spirits of the world!
Grant him, who fights and creates for Germany's peace,
O Lord in heaven: superhuman power!

Markgröningen, 20 April 1942
Heinrich Ritter

Ritter's dream of Soviet annihilation was not to be. Between August 1942 and February 1943 National Socialist forces became embroiled in a battle with Soviet forces for control of Stalingrad, a city in southwest Russia. Stalingrad was a crucial point along the transportation route along the Volga River connecting northern Russia and the Caspian Sea. If the Germans held Stalingrad, the Russians would no longer be able to move people and resources through Russia. Given its name, winning the city would also serve an important propagandistic function.

Brutal and bloody, over two million were killed during the fighting, with neither side distinguishing between militants and civilians. Things started off promisingly for the German side. The Air Force quickly destroyed much of the city, and at one point German forces held about 90 per cent of the city. But they were unable to totally remove the Soviet forces, who had seemingly endless numbers of replacement fighters. By November 1942 Germany's Sixth Army had become surrounded within the city, and was cut off from reinforcements. Any calls for retreat by Germany's military leaders had been ignored by Hitler. By the end of January 1943, almost exactly ten years after Hitler had come to power, the Soviets had totally destroyed the Sixth Army.

At the same time that the Sixth Army was about to capitulate in Stalingrad, a Viennese woman thanked Hitler for an increase in her pension. She wrote on 4 January 1943.

My Leader!

As a war widow from the 1914 war, I received at Christmas an increase in my pension. For this generous decision I ask you, my Leader, to accept my most heartfelt thanks.

I add to my thanks a prayer to the Almighty that for the welfare of the German people he might keep you mentally and physically vital for many years.

Hail Victory, my Leader!
Pessek, Karolin

A file in the Chancellor's Office also contains various word puzzles that one of Hitler's admirers had sent him. To solve the riddle, one had to construct Hitler's sayings out of various syllables. One of the sayings was: 'Economic growth is inseparable from political freedom.' The invocation of freedom was absolutely not intended as an affront to Hitler, that is, as an unmasking quotation or something to be taken in a liberal economic sense. Like Hitler, the author of the puzzle, who signed 'Sy', meant by 'freedom' the state's ability to act, freedom from the 'fetters' of the Versailles treaty. Freedom of action for the German nation meant a lack of freedom for the enslaved workers of other European countries. That did not bother 'Sy'. Instead, he intensified this attitude even further in his fanatical belief in Hitler.

Another was 'Precisely our German people needs the suggestive power that resides only in self-confidence.' German self-confidence was being systematically shattered by Allied bombing squadrons. From February 1942 onwards, the British had been systematically bombing German cities, both to destroy crucial industrial works and also to break the morale of the German population. These bombing raids increasingly brought heavy civilian casualties.

Despite the increasingly difficult military situation, many Germans remained totally dedicated to Hitler. One such individual was the wife of a Stormtrooper, whose family and property were seriously harmed by the bombing raids. Rudolf Brandt, Himmler's personal adviser, communicated her story to Major Friedrich Rauch, Lieutenant Colonel of the SS and Reich Minister Lammers' adjutant. Rauch, who was also in charge of Hitler's safety at the Chancellor's Office starting in 1942 is thought to have participated in hiding gold, which the Nazis had looted from their victims in 1945. It is unclear what happened to the gold.

Dear Fritz!

In the attempted attack made by British aircraft on the Skoda works [where some of the Third Reich's 'Panzer' tanks were produced] during the night of 16–17 April 1943, the small town of Wiesengrund [on the German–Polish border] in the SS Senior District Main was partly destroyed. Twenty SS families were hard hit. The property of the wife of the Second Lieutenant of the general SS and Sergeant of the Armed branch, Kosak, was completely destroyed. Martha Kosak's parents were killed in the attack. Mrs Kosak is currently in the municipal hospital in Pilsen. When asked how the SS Senior District Main could help her, she requested that she be sent a picture of the Leader and an earthenware candlestick. She had lost both of hers in the air attack.

Perhaps in this case it would be possible for you to get a signed picture of the Leader. I will see to it that the candle is sent from here. If you send the picture not to me but rather directly to the leader of the SS Senior-District Main in Nuremberg, please send me a short note to let me know.

> *Warm Greetings and Hail Hitler*
> *Your Rudi*
> *SS-Lieutenant Colonel*

Rauch gave the letter to Lammers, who presented it to Hitler and told Rauch:

To the Adjutant.

The Leader has signed the enclosed picture.

I would like to recommend that it be placed in a wooden frame (if possible, with silvered mouldings).

> *FQ, 19 May 43*
> *L.*

The worsening military situation brought with it the need to improve the public's mood. As a result, it was seen as important to insist on large-scale celebrations for Hitler's birthday in 1943. In view of the psychological consequences the Battle of Stalingrad had had on the public mood, it seemed necessary to insist on the German people's steadfastness and determination. On the eve of Hitler's birthday, the Berlin Philharmonic produced a celebratory programme on the radio, in which Goebbels described the seriousness of the situation and foresaw additional burdens and suffering. A commitment to National Socialism and its Leader followed; only he could guarantee the 'security' of the Reich. The speech did not fail to produce the desired effect, and the number of congratulatory telegrams again rose into the hundreds. Hitler received all kinds of gifts.

The city of Braunau organized a dinner for five hundred survivors of the Battle of Stalingrad to celebrate Hitler's birthday. There is some irony in this – shellshocked survivors were compelled to celebrate the good health of the man who had stubbornly insisted that troops must not retreat even when the battle was clearly hopeless, thus causing the deaths of many of their comrades.

SS Lieutenant Colonel Karl Wolff, who was at that time in the Hohenlychen military hospital north of Berlin, had a box of candy sent to Hitler and attached a visiting card: 'With best wishes for your New Year! Most obediently! Karl Wolff.' Another SS leader sent sardines in oil to Obersalzberg, Hitler's Bavarian retreat, while Hitler's former manservant, SS-Sergeant Ernst Krause gave him an oil painting titled 'Famous Armed-SS'.

Naturally, all the Regional Leaders and Reich ministers congratulated Hitler by telegram or in person. For the most part they gave him books; from the Regional Leader of Saxony, Martin Muschmann, there was a vase from Meissen, a town near Dresden in Saxony, eastern Germany, which is famous for its porcelain. It was the first good quality porcelain to come from outside Asia. It arrived with the wish 'that the Almighty continue to give you, my Leader, health and strength for the absolute security of our people's Living Space and the achievement of your life goal' [i.e. controlling Eastern Europe].

The longest of the Regional Leaders' telegrams came from Fritz Wächtler of Bayreuth in northern Bavaria:

MY LEADER

IN REVERENCE AND PROFOUND GRATITUDE AND FAITHFUL TRUST IN YOUR UNIQUE HISTORICAL MISSION OF LEADING TO VICTORY THE GERMAN PEOPLE'S BATTLE FOR FREEDOM THE BAYREUTH DISTRICT OF THE NAZI PARTY BEGS ON THIS DAY TO BE PERMITTED TO CONVEY ITS SINCEREST WISHES FOR YOUR PERSONAL PROSPERITY WITH THE RENEWED PLEDGE OF THE TIRELESS DEDICATION OF ALL HEARTS AND HANDS TO OUR PEOPLE'S FATEFUL BATTLE

HAIL MY LEADER
FRITZ WAECHTLER
REGIONAL LEADER

Wächtler's 'faithful trust' did not last until the very end of the war: on 19 April 1945 he was shot for 'desertion'.

A hand-written greeting card also arrived from the sewing room of the Schill local group, whose twenty members were led by Anneliese Schmundt, the wife of Hitler's adjutant:

Our Leader!

As we did last year, we women of the Women's League and the German Red Cross, who work together in the sewing room of the Schill local group at Mrs Schmundt's home, wish to send you, my Leader, our most loyal good wishes! In choosing our birthday gift we have this time directed our attention to those who have suffered from bombing damage.

New and useful things have been made out of scraps of wool and fabric with the intention of providing relief from need and giving pleasure.

For the new year we wish for you with all our hearts, my Leader, sound health, much joy, and military good fortune and success on all levels! Then victory will be ours!

> *Hail our beloved Leader,*
> *Anneliese Schmundt*
> *[Signed by nineteen other women.]*

Good wishes for sound health and military good fortune immediately after the defeat at Stalingrad, and in addition the reference to bombing damage: one wonders whether Hitler was pleased. The women of the Leader's headquarters, among them several wives of the highest officers, knew what the state of Hitler's health was. The twenty women of the Schill sewing room were the only ones who alluded directly to the turning point in the war. They were thanked in a letter from Albert Bormann.

Hitler himself signed a letter to an old Munich acquaintance who had congratulated him on 19 April 1943.

Dear Leader!

For your birthday we continue to wish the fullest blessing of Providence for your deeds and intentions. It is, after all, for the benefit of the German people.

We believe and trust in everything that happens. May the Lord God grant you health to carry out your great work.

In loyalty
Your Family July

Hitler replied on 5 May 1943.

Dear July Family!

Please accept my sincere thanks for your good wishes on my birthday.

I always take pleasure in greetings from old acquaintances from the time of struggle.

With a German salute
your
Adolf Hitler

Enormous bouquets of flowers were sent, for example by the Adlon Hotel, together 'with sincere good wishes and greatest veneration', and also by the sculptor Robert Ullmann, who owed his 'discovery' to Albert Speer, and by the employees of the bicycle factory in Solingen, which was now making hand grenades and mines. Artists like Ullmann, who were protected by the regime, did not forget to whom they owed their rise, fame and financial success.

Like the good wishes sent by former comrades in battle, artists' congratulations formulated in the spirit of true German subservience must have pleased Hitler. Many prominent artists sent Hitler 'sincere, heart-felt good wishes', combined with a belief in 'him and in the final German victory', as actor Otto Falckenberg, a German theatre director, manager and writer, put it. The children's choir of the Regensburg cathedral in Bavaria wrote that they were 'inspired by ardent love for the Fatherland'. And his favourite composer Franz Lehár, who wrote to Hitler that he was 'deeply indebted for' Hitler's 'whole-hearted support for art'. Lehár had an interesting relationship with National Socialism. His wife Sophie was Jewish, and he often used Jewish librettists in his operas. Despite his dedication to Hitler, and his birthday gifts, he could not prevent the murder of his librettist Fritz Löhner-Beda in Auschwitz, although he tried personally to guarantee his safety.

Typical formulations were used by the singer Eugen Fuchs (Munich), the sculptor Robert Ullmann (Vienna), who was known for his nudes, and Heinrich George, the director of the Schiller Theatre in Berlin.

My Leader!

On your birthday I ask you, my Leader, to accept my sincere wishes for happiness and success. May the Almighty continue to protect you, my Leader, to the benefit of all humanity.

> *Hail, my Leader*
> *Your truly devoted*
> *Eugen Fuchs*

My Leader!

Allow me, my Leader, to give you on your birthday my sincerest good wishes, which arise out of feelings of deepest veneration.

I am also eager to convey to you my lasting gratitude for your wise direction of German art, which through you, my Leader, has taken such a powerful upswing.

> *Hail, my Leader*
> *Robert Ullmann, sculptor*

My Leader!

On your fifty-fourth birthday we pay you homage with the truly devoted wish and confidence that all the wise plans that you have for the prosperity of our country will be victoriously achieved in the course of your next year.

We ask you, beloved Leader, to accept, as a humble birthday gift ten etchings by Bernhard Witschel – commemorating the achievements of our incomparably brave air force and submarine men – as a wall decoration for the crew rooms and soldiers' homes of our military.

> *In loyalty and devotion*
> *Heinrich George*
> *and the Schiller Theatre*
> *of the Reich capital city*

Heinrich George paid with his life for his closeness to Hitler; he died in 1946 in a Soviet prison camp that had been set up in the former concentration camp of Sachsenhausen in August 1945. Robert Ullmann and Eugen Fuchs remained sought-after artists: Fuchs continued to sing at the Bayreuth Festival and Ullmann continued to sculpt statues of nudes, only now they bore titles such as 'Peace for Africa'.

Another well-wisher had to accept changes in his career. All his life, the Munich sculptor Fritz Koelle had made statues of workers, for example steel workers or miners. In 1934 he was arrested by the Gestapo because of his 'Bolshevist cultural views'. But Koelle was able to convince people that he had absolutely no Communist sympathies, and henceforth his sculptures were somewhat more heroic and in tune with the times. After Hitler bought one of his statues, Koelle regularly sent him good wishes. In 1943 he gave Hitler the original of a letter written by the Prussian Field Marshal Helmuth von Moltke, the chief of staff of the Prussian Army and brilliant strategist of the Franco-Prussian war of 1870–1.

Dear Leader!

May I this year once again congratulate you most sincerely on your birthday, with the sole wish that you remain with us in full creative power! Spend the day in contentedness and peace. You have achieved superhuman things. This winter you have overcome the greatest danger, but without danger no globally historic upheavals can take place! A wise decision will always be made by a single man, just like Frederick the Great, who had himself briefed in the morning, and Field Marshal Helmuth von Moltke, with whose original letter I honour you on your great day!

Once again with the sincerest good wishes, good luck for the future and a German salute!

Your always loyally devoted and thankful sculptor
Fritz Koelle

In 1945 Koelle was heavily criticized for his opportunism. But since his friend Fritz Cremer, the later creator of the memorial at the Buchenwald concentration camp just outside Weimar, vouched for him, he received a professorship in Dresden and in 1948 moved to East Berlin. He died in 1953 in a train travelling from Berlin to Munich.

In 1943, letters were received from only a few well-wishers in other countries. However, one of Hitler's admirers was the Spanish circus clown Charlie Rivel. Rivel's telegram makes it clear how badly it was possible to misunderstand Hitler's political and military goals. On 20 April 1943 he sent this telegram to the Leader's headquarters:

I COMMEMORATE YOUR EXCELLENCY AGAIN THIS YEAR WITH MY SINCEREST GOOD WISHES ON YOUR BIRTHDAY, MAY GOD ALSO CONTINUE TO GRANT YOU HEALTH POWER AND STRENGTH AND UNDER YOUR LEADERSHIP BRING ABOUT FINAL VICTORY AND A NEW HAPPY EUROPE FOR THE PEOPLES OF EUROPE

CHARLIE RIVEL
MUNICH
HOTEL SONNEHOF

During the war, poems of homage were still being put into the Chancellor's Office's files. A very elderly woman named Luise Sellwig, from Wolfenbüttel in central Germany, repeatedly tried to console her Leader. She sent poems on the occasion of the death of arms minister Todt, on the turning point in the war at Stalingrad, and this one, on 1 May 1943:

O Adolf Hitler, great, wise
Sublime, be Europe's Emperor!
Soon all peoples will trust you,

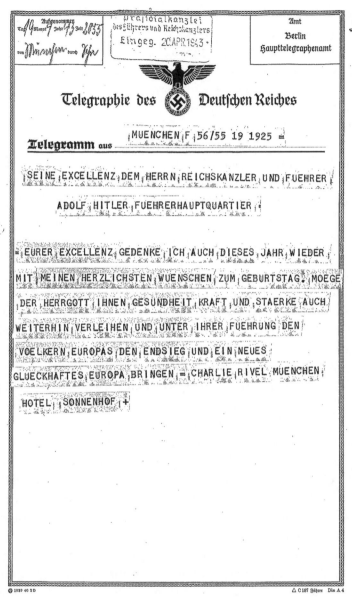

The famous French clown Charlie Rivel ('bee-you-ti-full acrobat!') completely misunderstood what Hitler was up to: in a birthday telegram sent in 1943 he still expressed his belief that Hitler's rule would produce a 'new, happy Europe' for people.

Source: RGWA (Moscow)

And will incessantly build on you.
Receive their gift in your hands,
and give them rest and benediction.
May you be victorious over the enemy,
And may Europe be fed by your work.
Then they will know happiness,
There will be eternal peace!

Adjutant Rauch thanked her.

The letter from Marie Schicklgruber, dated 24 August 1943, reflected a mother's daily concerns in the fifth year of war.

My Leader!

Our family tree shows that my husband is very closely related to you, my Leader. Your grandfather Georg Hiedler married [my husband's] great-aunt Anna Marie Schicklgruber in Döllersheim [Austria] on 5 October 1842. Only on this basis do I dare to burden you with a few lines, and I would like to ask you, my Leader, for your help. Our oldest son Anton Schicklgruber, an apprentice roofer, had to enlist in the Reich Labour Service on 1 November 1943. He was born on 6 July 1925. Because he was big and strong, after only a fortnight he was transferred to the SS. Following a short training period in Prague he went to the East. There he underwent further training. On 7 July, already eighteen years old, he was deployed under the field post number 05452C. On 10 July he died a hero's death from a head wound suffered during a night attack on the Belenichino rail line. He was buried in Lutschki, 50 km north of Belgorod [in western Russia]. We would like to return him to the homeland.

Therefore we ask you, my Leader, to help us convince the duty station 05452C of the SS to grant permission for the repatriation of his body. The Ravelsbach Nazi Party would also consider it the highest honour to have buried a hero from the bloodline of our beloved Leader in the Ravelsbach cemetery [Austria].

The father of the fallen hero, Anton Schicklgruber sen., born 23 March 1899, a veteran of the World War, has been enlisted since 29 April 43. He is serving at the great Air Force training field at Gorno

107/17 Post Reichshof, Cracow district, General Government. There are many partisan resistance groups there. I have written to the Znaim district army headquarters to request a deferment of military service. I have been told that if the son is killed, the father is deferred.

And since I am also now sick, I am not able to do the work by myself. I am supposed to handle the apartment and the horse and cart about 100 days [a year], and in the summer to boot, because in the winter our landlord doesn't need anyone. I also have two children of school age, and I also have work at home. My request was denied in Znaim, because the Local Peasant Leader did not endorse it. And so many strong young men are at home who have not even seen the inside of a barracks. Whole active age groups are even deferred. But a worker may not be deferred because then young people are afraid that they might have to enlist, if a worker is given an extended deferment. And how much I need my husband. I cannot pay the wages either, because for myself and three children I get only 51 marks family support and 12 marks housing aid. But my husband earned 1,350 marks in the preceding year. In the summer he did farm work, and in the winter he worked in a saw-mill. Moreover, we have worked by deputation 28 acres owned by the Ravelsbach estate administration. And this year I have to live with only this support and pay all the wages. During the summer, we were supported by our eldest son, who made weekly contributions of 30 marks. Therefore I ask you, my Leader, to help us with our son's repatriation to our homeland. And with my husband's deferment.

I thank you in advance for your help.

With a German salute
Marie Schicklgruber

The letter was processed by Lammers' personal assistant. Assistant secretary Laue had a photocopy of the letter made and sent the original to the Supreme Command of the Armed Forces (OKW). This was part of the command structure of Germany's armed forces. It was formed in February 1938 and replaced the Reich War Ministry. The reorganiza-tion occurred in part because Hitler wished to assert his authority as Leader and reduce the influence of Germany's military leaders, who traditionally had enjoyed a large amount of power. Laue forwarded a copy of Marie Schicklgruber's letter to the Office of the Leader's personal adjutant. The decision was left to the Chancellor's Office. On 2 September 1943 Schicklgruber received an answer:

The Reich Minister and Head of the Chancellor's Office expresses his sincere sympathy for the heavy loss that you have suffered through the heroic death of your eldest son. You may be consoled by the certainty that this sacrifice made for the Leader, the people, and the Reich will not be in vain. Because of the requested deferment of your husband from military service, the Reich Minister has forwarded your letter to the Supreme Command of the Armed Forces in Berlin for further examination. The Reich minister cannot take further steps because he lacks jurisdiction in what is an exclusively military matter. Further notification will be sent you from the military department.

The repatriation of fallen soldiers to the homeland is not possible. The sons who have fallen for Germany find their last rest and a worthy burial place among their fallen comrades. Since no exceptions can be made, your wish can unfortunately not be granted. Because of the relationship to the Leader you mentioned, the original copy of your petition was forwarded to the office of the Leader's personal adjutant.

Hail Hitler!
Dr Laue
Assistant Secretary

It's unclear whether Anton Schicklgruber senior was deferred from military service and survived the war.

A remarkable proof of expressions of loyalty during the crisis was the declaration made by the general field marshals of the Army who were in command on the fronts, dated 19 March 1944. These commanders were inspired by General Walther von Seydlitz-Kurzbach's defection to the Soviet side. Kurzbach had commanded the 12th Infantry Division and fought at Stalingrad. After being arrested and imprisoned by the Soviets, he formed a group called the League of German Officers, an anti-Nazi group. For this betrayal, he was sentenced to death in his absence, and his family were arrested. The Soviets later condemned him to imprisonment for twenty-five years for war crimes. He was released to West Germany in 1955 and lived for another twenty years. Gerd von Rundstedt read the general field marshals' declaration out loud in the Leader's headquarters.

My Leader!

We field marshals of the army have now determined, with the greatest concern and vexation, that the General of the Artillery Walther von Seydlitz-Kurzbach is committing a despicable betrayal of the holy cause.

He has, therefore, stabbed in the back the troops on the battlefront that we have the honour of commanding on your behalf. Through his disgraceful behaviour this general has forfeited the right to wear the uniform in which almost 50,000 army officers have sacrificed their lives in this war for you, your idea, and the German people united under you.

We are all deeply disturbed that someone from our ranks has broken our oath of loyalty to you, my Leader, who bears the enormous burden of responsibility for this fateful battle.

We know, my Leader, that you stand by the officers and soldiers of your army and are also yourself convinced that this is an isolated case to be vehemently condemned.

Nonetheless, as the leaders of the German army you have appointed and assigned, we feel the need at this time to appear before you and assure you, individually and in the name of all officers, that we have severed the bond of solidarity between us and this cowardly traitor.

He has trampled on the sacred tradition of German heroism. He has sullied the memory of those who have fallen in this war.

He is for all time covered with disgrace and opprobrium.

At this time we promise you, my Leader, to stand by you and your cause with renewed, innermost solidarity and unwavering loyalty.

More than ever it will be our task to instil your highly idealistic ideas, so that every soldier in the army becomes an all the more fanatical fighter for the National Socialist future of our people.

We know that only an army trained in National Socialism will withstand the severe tests that still stand between us and victory.

Please accept, my Leader, this declaration made by your field marshals of the army as a testimony to our inalterable loyalty.

von Rundstedt
Rommel
von Kluge
von Manstein
von Kleist
Frhr. von Weichs
Busch
Model

Despite this declaration of loyalty, a few months later the majority of its signatories were no longer among the 'leaders of the German army'. On 2 July 1944 Gerd von Rundstedt was replaced as the supreme commander on the western front. He was later captured by the Allies. Although he was charged with war crimes, his health was bad and so he never faced trial.

Erwin Rommel had connections with the plot to kill Hitler on 20 July 1944. Lieutenant Colonel Claus Schenk Graf von Stauffenberg, a right-wing Catholic nationalist, became convinced after the disaster at Stalingrad that assassinating Hitler was a lesser moral evil than allowing the war to continue. In Operation Valkyrie he, together with several other military and political leaders, arranged to plant a bomb in Hitler's Wolf Lair headquarters, which would kill him together with Heinrich Himmler and Hermann Göring. Stauffenberg himself planted the bomb; but a table deflected the blast and saved Hitler's life. Unaware that Hitler was still alive, Stauffenberg and his co-conspirators attempted to take over Berlin and disarm the SS. But by 7 p.m. Hitler contacted Berlin and troops retook the city. Stauffenberg and three others were shot that night. Rommel's support of the plot was soon discovered and, in order to spare his family, he agreed to commit suicide on 14 October.

On 19 August Günther von Kluge took potassium cyanide after he was dismissed. In his suicide note he once again assured Hitler of his loyalty and urged him to end the war. Erich von Manstein knew, like Rommel and von Kluge, about the conspiracy to kill Hitler, but he refused to participate in it because 'Prussian field marshals do not mutiny.' Hitler replaced him in 1944 because of differences over military strategy. After the war Manstein served four years in prison for war crimes.

Hitler also replaced Ewald von Kleist, who was arrested by the Gestapo after the assassination attempt of 20 July 1944. He died in a Soviet prison after the war. Maximilian von Weichs held on as commander in the southeast, although he undertook, against Hitler's instructions, the evacuation of Greece. After the war he was accused of war crimes during the Nuremberg Trials. Hitler blamed the breakdown of the eastern front in the summer of 1944 on Ernst Busch, who was consequently dismissed, but brought back in 1945 in an attempt to prevent British Field Marshal Bernard Montgomery from invading Germany. Busch later died in a Prisoner of War Camp in the United Kingdom.

In April 1945, Walter Model, the most loyal of the field marshals, deserted. He was known for his defensive strategy during the later stages of the war. He fell out with Hitler after his defeat at the Battle of the Bulge, during which he ordered his group to dissolve. The oldest and youngest were discharged and the rest could decide for themselves whether to surrender or attempt to break out. Model then committed suicide, after learning that the Soviets intended to try him for war crimes. He told his generals that the hopeless situation was to be attributed to the contamination of large segments of the population and the troops by 'the Jewish and democratic poison of materialistic modes of thinking'.

How did the Supreme Commander of the Wehrmacht react to the field marshals' declaration of loyalty? Hitler dictated to his adjutant, Rudolf Schmundt, the head of the Army's personnel office, a letter to the commanders of the Armed Forces. The letter was printed in two hundred copies, but was to be communicated to the subordinate ranks only orally and in extracts.

Re: Subversion of the Wehrmacht

1. Enemy propaganda has in recent months been particularly geared towards undermining confidence in the German leadership and claims

that there are conflicts between the Leader and his political or military leaders. Bolshevism has subjected German soldiers of all ranks who have fallen into its hands to a dialectic that is truly Jewish in its slyness, in order to break the loyalty of German officers who are being held prisoner.

[There follows here a description of the case of Seydlitz-Kurzbach]

The general field marshals of the army, who are in command on the fronts, have personally sent the Leader the enclosed solemn declaration, in which they condemn Seydlitz's treachery, assure the Leader of the inalterable loyalty of the officer corps, and emphasize the crucial importance of strengthening all soldiers' commitment to the [National Socialist] worldview.

In addition, the Reich war court has sentenced von Seydlitz in absentia to death and declared him unworthy to bear arms. This judgment has been confirmed by the Leader and is therefore legally in force.

The conduct of all other accused soldiers is currently being examined. The necessary repercussions will be decided without mercy.

This betrayal by a few officers demonstrates very clearly that National Socialist training and political education are of crucial importance. Only a soldier who is fanaticized and educated to fight will never forget his oath of loyalty even when taken prisoner and will resist all corrosive influences.

2. For the officer corps, the betrayal by the former general of the artillery von Seydlitz and a few officers is an unambiguous, disturbing fact. However, the public is to be informed that all officers who appear in Soviet propaganda in opposition to National Socialist Germany are acting under a kind of hypnosis produced by the relevant means. [. . .]

On behalf of the Leader
Schmundt

The assassination attempt carried out on 20 July 1944 shows that there were more than a 'few officers' who were engaging in 'treason'. Many petitions and requests for pardon were probably sent to Hitler after the failed attack. They were presumably forwarded to the 'office responsible'. One such letter was forwarded to Heinrich Himmler, who, as the head of the German police, had responsibility for dealing with resisters. He also oversaw the growing network of concentration camps. Only because this appeal for clemency was, intentionally or not, wrongly filed, was it preserved.

The widow of the deceased Air Force adjutant Curt Mantius wrote to Hitler from Berchtesgaden on 26 August 1944. She was apparently quite close to Hitler, because her address is on the list of persons to whom Hitler had genuine coffee sent for Christmas 1944. Curt Mantius had been killed during a flight in 1937.

The widow was interceding on behalf of one of the conspirators in the 20 July 1944 attack who would have been appointed military plenipotentiary for religious and ecclesiastical matters, that is, as the de facto minister of religion in the new regime of the German Reich. Mrs Mantius sent the letter to her husband's successor, Nicolaus von Below, who was an officer in the German Air Force. Hitler reportedly told von Below in the winter of 1944 that he knew the war was lost, blaming Germany's failures on the plot to assassinate him. Hitler also made it clear that he would never surrender. Von Below witnessed Hitler's will before leaving Berlin on 30 April 1945. Von Below forwarded Mrs Mantius' letter directly to Julius Schaub, the head of the office of Hitler's adjutant. At the end of the war Schaub burned everything of Hitler's from the Chancellor's Office and in the Bunker, before flying to Munich and doing the same at Hitler's apartment there. He also destroyed Hitler's special train, before being arrested by the Americans on 8 May 1945 and labelled a 'fellow traveller'.

On 10 September 1944 Below wrote from Nienhagen on the Baltic Sea:

Dear Mr Schaub!

The enclosed letter was sent to me by Mrs Mantius. I asked my wife to tell her that I was not acquainted with the details, but in any case believed that a request for clemency would be successful. I ask you to deal with this letter as you see fit.

As for myself, things are unfortunately not going so well. I still feel every little activity in my head. But I hope that with peace and bed-rest I will gradually 'unjam' it.

My present situation involves having to be on the sidelines a great deal and focusing on myself. But, conversely, I have to say that out there in the Wolf's Lair I wouldn't be able to be of much help.

I hope, however, that in October I will be more or less back to normal.

With warm greetings and Hail Hitler
Your Claus Below

Here is the text of the enclosed letter:

My Leader!

The sympathy you have repeatedly shown me, my Leader, since the death of my husband, gives me the courage to make the following request. It concerns the husband of my cousin, Doctor of Theology Eugen Gerstenmaier, who was arrested by the Gestapo when he returned from an International Office course for teachers held in Carinthia. Apparently an accumulation of coincidences led to his incrimination. In the firm belief that this man cannot have had any-thing to do with the criminal attack on you, my Leader, I ask you to accept Mrs Gerstenmaier's petition.

Hail my Leader!
Your thankfully devoted
Edith Mantius

In January 1945 a people's court sentenced Gerstenmaier to only seven years in prison; it is not known whether this written intercession had any effect on his fate, however. He survived and later in 1945 entered politics. At first he led an all-German evangelical aid society, and repre-sented the Backnang-Schwäbish Hall electoral district in the Bundestag national Parliament. In the 1950s he was the deputy representative of the Christian Democratic Union, and from 1954 to 1969 the president of the Bundestag.

13

THE END

In the last months and weeks of the war some letters and cards were still coming into the Chancellor's Office. But fewer than thirty New Year's congratulations were forwarded from the Chancellor's Office to Hitler's private office. In the special archive in Moscow there are only a few items relating to Hitler's birthday in 1944. And the number of requests for autographs and declarations of support fell to zero. Instead, there were many prayers for the German people – not for Hitler himself. The number of those who recommended inventions that would make it possible to win the war after all rapidly increased. Suggestions for improving radios, crampons, or funnels for Tiger tanks were forwarded and implemented. The letters contained ideas that now seem modern, for example an actually functioning methane motor that drew its power from a fuel cell in the tank itself.

The engineer Wilhelm Evers, an employee of the Reich Patent Office, developed a machine for sorting and recognizing punch cards that could have freed up thousands of workers in the area of data processing. Engineer Rudolf Rohrböck, the owner of a steel and iron firm in Vienna, constructed an anti-aircraft projectile that developed an independent trajectory and thus allegedly increased eightfold the probability of hitting a target. On 29 March Rohrböck received an interim notice that his suggestion would be tested. But it must have been clear to him and to the developers of the suggestion for improvement that such a change in the production of anti-aircraft shells was no longer possible.

The futile suggestions for effective weapons made by the people were indirect reproaches about the inefficacy of the German arms industry. It was repeatedly suggested that rockets be constructed to launch nets or parachutes: no doubt enemy bombers would be caught in the tangle of steel cables hanging in the sky. Such suggestions were filed away. But a suggestion made by Franz Perl of Vienna was examined. In October 1944 he sent to Berlin his application for a patent on the design for a shock-cord explosive device. The weapon was to combine the crossbow anti-tank weapon with the hand grenade. What is more interesting about the letter, though, is the mindset of the sender, who obviously still wanted, shortly before the end of the war, to take advantage of the desperate situation. On 7 November 1944 he received a reply from the section of the Nazi Party Technical Office for inventors.

Re: Shock-cord explosive device W/G

The same and similar suggestions have already been often made, but have not led to any result. The device you suggest is not capable of a usable range. Moreover, weapons are available that fully meet our requirements.

Suggesting a catapult device combined with a firearm is wrong-headed and backward. To judge by the information you give, you have no idea of the current state of weapons technology.

Nonetheless, thank you for your efforts to contribute to the perfection of our weaponry.

Hail Hitler!
On behalf of Müller

In the following suggestion made by a non-commissioned officer to develop the 'net rockets' mentioned above, not only the request in itself but also the addressees are noteworthy. The non-com sent his letter on 20 February 1945 to the Reich Minister for Weapons and Munitions, Albert Speer, with carbon copies to 'The Leader Adolf Hitler, Reich

Marshal Hermann Göring, Reich Defence Minister Dr Goebbels'. He dispensed with a formal salutation.

Re: (a) Net rockets, (b) short-range rockets, (c) parachute rockets
(a) Net rockets
1. Purpose:
Net rockets are intended to combat and destroy enemy bombers, fighters, and fighter-bombers flying in formation.

2. Use and mode of action:

Net rockets are shot in salvos. When the outer shell of the projectile (made of thin sheet metal, aluminium, or another substitute material) explodes, the internal parts form a web-like net about 200 metres in diameter. With a salvo of only 20 rockets in front of, in, and around the enemy formation a net or wire tangle 2 km in breadth is formed (air-wire barrier). The tail assemblies, propellers, or other sensitive parts of aircraft, even heavy ones, become entangled in the wires and crash, and the rest are dealt with by means of individual explosive devices. The destruction of the greater part of the formation should be inevitable. Correct and not too sparing use would make it possible to neutralize enemy air forces over the whole Reich.

3. Construction:

The enclosed sketches should provide an approximate representation of the way the net rockets are conceived. The form, assembly, and driving mechanism as well as the distributing mechanism are to be determined by weapons engineers.

It is to have the form of a rocket, but one that consists of a large number of individual explosive devices (Sketch A) or of individual rockets (Sketch B). These, connected by a spool of 100 metres of wire to the middle axis, are projected outward by an explosive charge (in A) or a spring-loaded device and their own power (in B) to form a web-like net. In the event of failure or other cases, impact and timer detonators on the individual elements ensure that the latter will explode before falling to earth.

(b) Short-range rockets

1. Purpose:
This is a means of defence against low-flying aircraft and fighter-bombers, to be used by infantry, convoys, tanks, and especially railway trains. Like the bazooka, it is to be available for all units and delivered in ready-to-use sets. It should be kept small and easy to handle, and only a few individual elements connected by about 10 metres of wire are necessary. The detonation must be adjustable from 50 to about 200 metres and the explosives connected with each other by wire should spread out in a funnel shape in the direction they are shot. Here too the result is a wire barrier in which the aircraft are caught and brought down.

They are to be constructed on the principle of the net rocket. It is crucial that the net form spreads out.

(c) Parachute rockets

1. Purpose:
Protection of our own aircraft against pursuing enemy fighters.
2. Use and effect:
It will also be delivered in ready-to-use sets and must be widely distributed. Mounted over or under the tail assembly, it is triggered from the pilot's seat of the pursued aircraft as the pursuing fighter approaches. Instead of explosive charges the capsules contain the wire ends of small invisible cellophane parachutes that cause the net to hang in the air for a longer time. Because of the arrangement and coverage in sets, here too a wire barrier is formed and, being invisible to the pursuer, cannot be avoided and therefore causes the latter to crash.

I have tried to express my ideas as clearly and concisely as it is possible to do on paper.

I am not an engineer or technician, and therefore ask you to consider the inadequate sketches as merely illustrative.

The desire to give my country and those close to me respite from the enemy's airborne terrorism and to provide a basis for the final battle by putting a stop to this terrorism occupies my thoughts day and night, and I hope to have hereby provided a fruitful incentive.

Successful use would be the greatest reward.

The outcomes resulting from the successful use of the three R[ocket]-types are the following:

Internal: the bringing down of the enemy air force, and as a result, undisturbed work, an increase in production, the safeguarding and reorganizing of the transportation system, which has also suffered greatly, and the safeguarding of supplies to the front.

Regarding the front and enemy territory: Safeguarding supply to our own bases (Atlantic), disruption of the supplies to enemy bases (Eastern area), undisturbed replenishing of the front areas with reserves, materials, and also the deployment of attack armies that are no longer detectable by reconnaissance aircraft.

The German manufacturers who have been able to create the V-weapons will surely succeed in constructing this weapon, which is certainly much simpler but may nonetheless, if used in sufficient numbers, be decisive for the war.

> *Hail Hitler*
> *H. Schilling*

The sketches showed the connected individual rockets and a heavy bomber formation being entangled in wire.

Staff Sergeant Kurt Raum, a member of the schoolboy company in Bug auf Rügen, Germany's largest island, located in the North Sea, also sent a letter. Raum, who was actually from Fürth in Bavaria, also wanted to shoot wire cables into the sky. He also thought low-flying planes could be brought down in this way. He recommended that cables be attached to the locomotive of a refugee train in such a way that they could be shot up by the driver: 'I am convinced that the result would at first consist in the destruction of the attackers. When the defence measure becomes known to the enemy, in future he will beware of making air attacks with the same aggressiveness.'

Another method was suggested by a corporal from Hanau, who sent his letter to the Leader's headquarters on 22 February 1945, after he had received no reply from the Armament Ministry. On the envelope he had written: 'To be forwarded preferentially!, the sender.'

Re: 'Flam' method of destroying motors

To the Leader's headquarters

From the enclosed copy it can be seen that this is my fourth letter regarding the above method.

Since I have had no response to my letters of 5, 6, and enc.[losed] 11 February, but am nonetheless convinced of the importance of my suggestion, to be on the safe side, I am sending the enclosed copy once again as a 4th petition with a request for a return and confirmation by telegram that it has been received.

The letter was received by the Leader's Adjutant Office on 5 March. On 8 March 1945 it was forwarded to the Nazi Party's head office for technology. On 22 March the Reich leadership forwarded the letter to the Technical Office in the Armaments Ministry with the request that Leading Airman Willy Emmrich 'be given a brief response to his suggestions as soon as possible'. Whether Emmrich actually received a response cannot be determined.

Re. Flying sand method of destroying internal combustion motors of all kinds (especially the flying sand air terrorism defence method, called 'Flam' for short)

To the Reich minister for Armaments and War Production, Berlin

On 5 and 6 February I sent through office Fp. no. 12000 the suggestion that the above method be used.

I repeat the gist of the above letter and enclose the latter in full.
Presupposition: It is presupposed that we know that in desert areas after a sandstorm (on land and in the air) internal combustion motors (of all kinds) are always made unusable by the fine airborne sand (which stops up carburettors and finally ruins pistons).
Assertion: The idea of producing an artificial sandstorm by suspending flying sand (in the air) or flying sand zones (on land) is therefore natural and (as will be seen) technically feasible.

I. Flying sand–air terrorism-defence–method, called 'Flam' for short, using a special aircraft

(1) flies above the enemy bomber formations and
(2) by laying a barrier curtain in the approach area,
   (a) spreading flying sand from compartments,
   (b) using blowers (compressed air or exhaust gases)
II. As additional armaments on fighters for use against enemy fighters
III. as additional armaments for low-flying aircraft used against tanks and other motorized vehicles
IV. as additional night warfare weapons for the infantry (using a discharge mechanism similar to or combined with a flamethrower against foreign motorized vehicles)
V. possible use of flying sand as filling for anti-aircraft shells.

For both defence and attack, all-inclusive, as simple as it is brilliant, the use of flying sand as a weapon against the motor is a revolutionary idea in air and land warfare!

Proof: This follows automatically (after the intellectual conception of the idea, which means almost everything) from the aforementioned presupposition.

I only point out urgently that a simple thing that proves to be revolutionary – and that has strangely remained hidden from millions of brains for half a century – may easily be falsely viewed as impossible, fantastic, etc. The more educated the head and the more elevated the social status, the more unconscious the rejection of the simple solution, which promises to solve in such an unimaginative and even banal way problems that escape even the most complicated thinker and educated eyes – here lies the danger that also imperils the flying sand method!

I must request and beg you, Mr Reich minister, to boldly envisage the project's technical realization from the testing bench on.

I myself make no claim to any benefit for myself. I am concerned only to retaliate and conquer for the future beautiful Germany.

With Hitler Hail!
W. W., Corporal

The belief in the often-invoked 'final victory' had been lost by most people, as even these apparently erroneous suggestions for 'wonder weapons' show. Although propaganda continued to promise that this next generation of super-advanced weapons would win the war, Germans wanted peace and an end to the bombing attacks. Most of the population sank into apathy and thought mainly about sheer survival, not about new inventions that could turn what was quickly becoming an obviously hopeless situation around.

An exception is constituted by two soldiers from East Holstein. Wilhelm Zimmer and Joachim Schwenn wrote to Reich Minister Lammers on 12 February 1945. Only the cover letter of their communication has been preserved, but it shows the writers' intent.

Dear Reich Minister!

We humbly ask, since we are not otherwise able to contact our Leader, that the enclosed letter to the Leader that you see here be forwarded as quickly as possible to headquarters. It concerns plans that will lead Germany and Japan to a rapid victory. We ask you again to forward the letter as quickly as possible to the Leader, since it will determine the outcome of the war.

Hail Hitler!
Joachim Schwenn & Wilhelm Zimmer

Lammers dutifully forwarded the letter. Schwenn and Zimmer did not receive a notice that it had been sent on. The outcome of the war had already been decided, and trust in the Leader was exhausted. Very few people wrote to Hitler any more. Nonetheless, deserters were still being hanged, concentration camp prisoners were driven on death marches and murdered. The killing machinery that Hitler had set up continued to operate and had to be overpowered by Allied troops.

And some Germans still sent Hitler their birthday wishes to his mountain retreat in Obersalzberg. It seems unlikely that any birthday greetings reached Berlin that year. On Hitler's birthday, the Americans had just taken Leipzig in Saxony, and the Soviet Army was in the Baruth glacial valley in Brandenburg, only 53 km south of Berlin. Nonetheless Hitler had a celebration, a rather spooky event that was described by several contemporary witnesses. Only three international guests signed their names in the Chancellor's Office's guest book: the Afghan envoy, Thailand's ambassador, and a Japanese sea captain. At the fiftieth birthday celebration in 1939 sixty-seven foreign diplomats were among those present.

Elisabeth Fürstin Fugger zu Wellenburg sent her congratulations by telegram.

MAY GOD PROTECT AND BLESS YOU, MY LEADER, AND OUR BELOVED FATHERLAND

ELISABETH FÜRSTIN FUGGER-WELLENBURG BEI AUGSBURG

On 27 February 1945 Friede Nögler of Düsseldorf had already written to Hitler, who was not, however, in Berchtesgaden, as she had expected, but rather in Berlin.

Motto: Through human suffering to the greatest happiness!

My Leader!

First of all my sincere good wishes on your birthday. May the new year bring you everything good and spare you the suffering you had to bear in the past year. Now the bad and yet also so good old year is over, thank God. I am so thankful to destiny that the chalice of suffering has not been even bitterer for you. How happy I was when on 30 January I was able to hear again in your good voice the old energy and freshness. Then I knew that the old had been overcome and the new achieved, and on the ground of your vitality I take the liberty of joining the well-wishers on 20 April.

Last year I already harboured the wish to be able to thank you at last for the great happiness that you gave me with your dictum 'Whoever has belief has the greatest power in the world!', but I still hesitated, at such a time, to approach you with such matters. But today, after precisely one long year, my wish has grown to such titanic proportions that I simply can do no other. [This phrasing might be a reference to Martin Luther, who is quoted as having said 'Here I stand. I can do no other', when ordered to stand before the Diet of Worms to answer questions over his banned 95 Theses.] I must express my joyful thanks to you, to be able to thereby give you a little joy, because the joy that we give comes back to our own hearts. Years went by before I was finally able to understand what you meant by this idea, for only slowly and with great difficulty did I manage to understand this conviction of yours. But now – after I have completely wrapped myself in this mantle of belief, I am permitted to recognize its true value. 'Belief' – what a great inexpressible happiness this word conceals in itself, and this happiness I receive at a time when almost everyone is struggling with suffering, and I owe this happiness to you. Together with this belief of mine, my strength has also grown to almost superhuman proportions, and I want to use this excess of strength for the benefit of my hard-pressed fellow Germans, so long as I am able.

Everywhere where I encounter weak people, I give them some of my power of belief, in order to make them also strong and confident. The successes are still small, but I know that I shall still find such souls weak in belief here, and these I shall help raise and strengthen in your sense of confident belief in the final victory, which is closer to us than we ourselves suspect, and may God help me in this!

In the hope that these lines might give you a little joy, I remain in sincere gratitude

Friede Nögler

On 8 April 1945 congratulations were sent to Hitler by an attorney who had defended him in a few trials between 1920 and 1923. He wrote from Mittenwald in Bavaria and in an aside he informed Hitler's private office that 'on 7 January 45 I myself was completely bombed out of my apartment and office in Munich (fire and explosive bombs) and am continuing to practise my profession from here'.

My Leader!

As I am about to enter my 79th year of life, that is, already at an advanced age, I may perhaps once again offer you, on the occasion of the approaching celebration of your 56th birthday, in most grateful memory of our common battle more than twenty-three years ago, from my heart, and indeed from all my heart, and at the same time also on behalf of my wife and our whole large family, our sincere wishes for happiness and success.

This year 20 April falls in a time in which your willpower, so often tested and proven in this battle, demands of us fellow Germans the utmost vigour.

But may it be granted to your prudent, temporizing leadership, as we all confidently hope it will, at the right moment, with fullest health, to put a compelling halt to the enemy who has penetrated so far into German lands in the East and West. To protect our so hard-pressed people from the defeat the enemy intends to inflict on it. To destroy the enemy's will to fight. And, thus, to shape the future of a Greater Germany that is, together with the rest of Europe, converted National Socialistically. And do so very differently than is imagined in the insolent madness of the still so presumptuous arrogance of world Jewry.

In so doing you fulfil, my Leader, a further divine work to achieve your great goals!

> *Hail Victory! Hail Victory!*
> *Yours in gratitude and loyalty devoted*
> *Party member Justizrat W. von Zezschwitz*

There was little 'prudent, temporizing Leadership' taking place at this late stage. Hitler was at that point temporizing only with respect to his own end. His war was now on the verge of being lost; his allies were largely gone. Even the dedicated Heinrich Himmler offered on 21 April 1945 to surrender Germany if it would enable him to escape prosecution. Adolf Hitler, together with his wife Eva Braun, committed suicide on 30 April 1945 in the Leader Bunker in Berlin. Many other National Socialist leaders and supporters followed suit over the coming days and weeks, including, most famously, Joseph Goebbels and his wife Magda, who poisoned their six children before killing themselves. Himmler committed suicide after being arrested by British troops on 23 May 1945. The dream of a German-dominated Europe was over.

FURTHER READING

A number of excellent books discuss in more detail the events mentioned in this collection:

For an informative and accessible introduction to Germany's modern history, see Mary Fullbrook, *Twentieth Century Germany: Politics, Culture and Society, 1918–1990* (2001).

For a more detailed look at the Weimar Republic, your first port of call should be Anthony McGelligott (ed.), *Weimar Germany, Short Oxford History of Germany* (2009).

Likewise, for the Third Reich, the best compact introduction is to be found in Jane Caplan (ed.) *Nazi Germany, Short Oxford History of Germany* (2008). It comes complete with a fantastic, and comprehensive, timeline of important events, glossary, and further reading.

A more fulsome discussion is to be found in Richard Evans' magisterial trilogy of the Third Reich: *The Coming of the Third Reich* (2004), *The Third Reich in Power* (2006), and *The Third Reich at War* (2009). These books cover all the crucial political issues while also paying attention to the experiences of ordinary people.

Sir Ian Kershaw gives Adolf Hitler the same complete treatment in his fascinating biography of Germany's dictator: *Hitler, 1889–1936: Hubris* (1998) and *Hitler, 1936–1945: Nemesis* (2000).

For a closer look at why the ordinary Germans in this volume felt able to write to Hitler in the way they did, look at Kershaw's *The Hitler Myth: Image and Reality in the Third Reich* (1987).

For an account of how so many people were swayed by Hitler's appeal, see Peter Fritzsche, *Germans into Nazis* (1999). For a discussion of those who weren't, read Joachim Fest, *Plotting Hitler's Death: The German Resistance to Hitler, 1933–1945* (1996).

An excellent account of how the Nazi regime maintained its control over the German population is to be found in Robert Gellately, *Backing Hitler: Consent and Coercion in Nazi Germany* (2002).

If you are looking for a discussion of when and how the Nazis extended their control over Europe, check out Mark Mazower's outstanding book, *Hitler's Empire: Nazi Rule in Occupied Europe* (2008).

Finally, two great books on the Second World War more generally are: Gerhard d L. Weinberg, *A World at Arms, A Global History of World War II* (2nd edn, 2005) and Max Hastings, *All Hell Let Loose: The World at War, 1939–1945* (2011).

There is a lot of misinformation on the web about the Third Reich. Three good, and very reputable, websites are that of the German Historical Institute (*www.germanhistorydocs.ghi-dc.org/*); Calvin College's collection of German propaganda (*www.calvin.edu/academic/cas/gpa/ww2era.htm*); and Yale University's collection of Nuremberg Trial documents (*http://avalon.law.yale.edu/subject_menus/imt.asp*).